3rd Edition Extra

with business skills lessons and self-assessment

Upper Intermediate

MARKET LEADER

Business English Course Book

David Cotton David Falvey Simon Kent

Contents

Introduction

What is *Market Leader*, and who is it for?

Market Leader is a multi-level business English course for businesspeople and students of business English. It has been developed in association with the *Financial Times*, one of the leading sources of business information in the world. It consists of 12 units based on topics of great interest to everyone involved in international business.

This third edition of the Upper Intermediate level features completely updated content and a significantly enhanced range of authentic resource material, reflecting the latest trends in the business world. If you are in business, the course will greatly improve your ability to communicate in English in a wide range of business situations. If you are a student of business, the course will develop the communication skills you need to succeed in business and will enlarge your knowledge of the business world. Everybody studying this course will become more fluent and confident in using the language of business and should increase their career prospects.

The authors

David Falvey (left) has over 25 years' teaching and managerial experience in the UK, Japan and Hong Kong. He has also worked as a teacher trainer at the British Council in Tokyo, and was Head of the English Language Centre and Principal Lecturer at London Metropolitan University.

David Cotton (centre) has over 45 years' experience teaching and training in EFL, ESP and English for Business, and is the author of numerous business English titles, including *Agenda*, *World of Business*, *International Business Topics* and *Keys to Management*. He is also one of the authors of the best-selling *Business Class*. He was previously a Senior Lecturer at London Metropolitan University.

Simon Kent (right) has over 25 years' teaching experience, including three years as an in-company trainer in Berlin at the time of German reunification. He has spent the majority of his career to date in higher education in the UK where he has taught on and directed programmes of business, general and academic English.

What is in the units?

STARTING UP

You are offered a variety of interesting activities in which you discuss the topic of the unit and exchange ideas about it.

VOCABULARY

You will learn important new words and phrases which you can use when you carry out the tasks in the unit. You can find definitions and examples, and listen to the pronunciation of new vocabulary in the i-Glossary feature on the DVD-ROM. The DVD-ROM also contains further practice exercises. A good business dictionary, such as the *Longman Business English Dictionary*, will also help you to increase your business vocabulary.

READING

You will read authentic articles on a variety of topics from the *Financial Times* and other newspapers and books on business. You will develop your reading skills and learn essential business vocabulary. You will also be able to discuss the ideas and issues in the articles.

LISTENING

You will hear authentic interviews with businesspeople and a variety of scripted recordings. You will develop listening skills such as listening for information and note-taking. You can also watch the interviews and find further practice exercises on the DVD-ROM.

LANGUAGE REVIEW

This section focuses on common problem areas at Upper Intermediate level. You will become more accurate in your use of language. Each unit contains a Language review box which provides a review of key grammar items. A Grammar reference section can be found at the back of the book and on the DVD-ROM. The DVD-ROM also provides extra grammar practice.

SKILLS

You will develop essential business communication skills, such as making presentations, networking, negotiating, cold-calling and dealing with communication breakdown. Each Skills section contains a Useful language box, which provides you with the language you need to carry out the realistic business tasks in the book. The DVD-ROM supplements the Course Book with additional activities.

CASE STUDY

The Case studies are linked to the business topics of each unit. They are based on realistic business problems or situations and allow you to use the language and communication skills you have developed while working through the unit. They give you the opportunity to practise your speaking skills in realistic business situations. Each Case study ends with a writing task. After you've finished the Case study, you can watch a consultant discussing the issues it raises on the DVD-ROM.

WORKING ACROSS CULTURES

These four units focus on different aspects of international communication. They help to raise your awareness of potential problems or misunderstandings that may arise when doing business with people from different cultures.

REVISION UNITS

Market Leader Upper Intermediate third edition also contains four revision units, each based on material covered in the preceding three Course Book units. Each revision unit is designed so that it can be completed in one session or on a unit-by-unit basis.

EXTRA BUSINESS SKILLS

The new Business Skills lessons offer the learner a task-based, integrated skills approach to the development of core business skills such as Presentations, Negotiations, Meetings, and Small Talk. These lessons appear at the end of every three units and incorporate performance review, suggestions for professional development and goal setting. They are based on the Global Scale of English Learning Objectives for Professional English. These objectives are signposted at the top of each new lesson in the Student's book and the carefully scaffolded activities are crafted around each objective, creating a clear sense of direction and progression in a learning environment where learners can reflect on their achievement at the end of the lesson.

UNIT 1

Communication

'When people talk, listen completely. Most people never listen.'
Ernest Hemingway (1899–1961), American writer

OVERVIEW

STARTING UP

A **Think of a good communicator you know. Explain why he/she is good at communicating.**

B **What makes a good communicator? Choose the three most important factors from this list.**

- fluency in the language
- grammatical accuracy
- an awareness of body language
- an extensive vocabulary
- being a good listener
- not being afraid of making mistakes
- a sense of humour
- physical appearance
- no strong accent

C **What other factors are important for communication?**

D **Discuss these questions.**

1 What forms of written and spoken communication do you like using? Why?

2 What problems can people have with the different forms of communication?

3 How do you think those problems can be solved?

VOCABULARY
Good communicators

A **Which of these words apply to good communicators and which apply to bad communicators? Add two adjectives of your own to the list.**

articulate	coherent	eloquent	extrovert	fluent
focused	hesitant	inhibited	persuasive	rambling
reserved	responsive	sensitive	succinct	vague

B **Which of the words in Exercise A have these meanings?**

1 concise
2 reluctant to speak
3 talking in a confused way
4 able to express ideas well
5 clear and easy to understand
6 good at influencing people
7 outgoing
8 eager to react and communicate

C **Complete the extract below from a talk by a communication expert with the verbs from the box.**

clarify confuse digress engage explain interrupt ~~listen~~ ramble

'Good communicators really ..listen..[1] to people and take in what is said. They maintain eye contact and have a relaxed body language, but they seldom ....[2] and stop people talking. If they don't understand and want to ....[3] something, they wait for a suitable opportunity.

When speaking, effective communicators are good at giving information. They do not ....[4] their listener. They make their points clearly. They will avoid technical terms, abbreviations or jargon. If they do need to use unfamiliar terminology, they ....[5] by giving an easy-to-understand example. Furthermore, although they may ....[6] in order to elaborate a point and give additional information and details where appropriate, they will not ....[7] and lose sight of their main message. Really effective communicators who have the ability to ....[8] with colleagues, employees, customers and suppliers are a valuable asset for any business.'

D CD1.1 **Listen to the talk and check your answers.**

*See the **DVD-ROM** for the i-Glossary.*
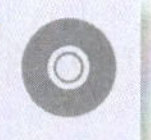

E **Think of a poor or bad communicator you know. How could they improve their skills? What advice would you give them?**

LISTENING
Improving communications

A CD1.2 **Listen to the first part of an interview with Alastair Dryburgh, an expert on communication. Does he think technology makes good communication easier?**

B CD1.2 **Listen again. What four key points does Alastair make about communication?**

Alastair Dryburgh

C CD1.3 **Listen to the second part of the interview. Alastair gives an example of a company which has used technology to change the way it communicates with customers. Give reasons why it communicates well.**

D CD1.4 **Listen to the final part, where Alastair is describing a bad customer experience. What mistakes did the company make, and how could they have improved the customer experience?**

*Watch the interview on the **DVD-ROM**.*

E **Discuss an example you know of a company which communicates well with its customers or a company which communicates badly. What advice would you give to the bad communicator?**

READING

E-mail: for and against

A **What irritates you most about these forms of communication?**

e-mail

mobile phone

conference calling

voicemail

BlackBerry

web presentation

B **What are the advantages and disadvantages of using e-mail?**

C **Read the article on the opposite page quickly and choose the best title.**

1 Time to switch your BlackBerry off

2 How to deal with your inbox

3 A quiet word beats sending e-mail

D **Read the article again and list the advantages and disadvantages of using e-mail. Does the writer mention any that you listed in Exercise B?**

E **Find expressions in the article which mean the following.**

1 looking at another person (paragraph 2)

2 upsetting or embarrassing someone by being rude or tactless (paragraph 2)

3 not be caught or punished when you have done something wrong (paragraph 4)

4 pretend something is true in order to deceive people (paragraph 4)

5 keeping writing or talking to someone, even though you do not see them often (paragraph 8)

6 aiming an idea or product at someone (paragraph 8)

F **Complete this text with the expressions in Exercise E in the correct form.**

I don't have a problem with him ....[1] his family whilst he's posted overseas and sending e-mails in office time. That's not the main issue. However, if he thinks he can ....[2] sending such abusive e-mails to colleagues, he is sadly mistaken and he'll have to face the consequences of his actions later. He is clearly ....[3] about his colleagues and spreading nasty rumours. He'd be better off speaking to colleagues ....[4] if he has problems with them. He's slightly better when speaking with customers, but he needs to think about who he's speaking to when he's ....[5] our products to them. And he just doesn't know how to say no to people without ....[6].

G **Discuss these questions.**

1 'Business is best done face to face.' Do you agree?

2 How could communication be improved in your organisation?

3 How will communication change in the office of the future?

4 What do you do when you receive a nasty e-mail?

5 Is communication better these days with all the new technology?

FT

by Luke Johnson

E-mail might just be responsible for the productivity increases that economists tell us are the key to rising prosperity. But it could also be sending us all mad.

The truth is that business is generally best done face to face, and if that is impossible, then speaking via the phone. But too many of us now hide behind silent, typed communications. The trouble is that the recipient of an e-mail does not hear a tone of voice or see a facial expression; nor can the sender modify their message halfway through, sensing that it is causing offence. When you read an e-mail, you cannot tell the mood of the e-mailer.

A permanent written form is deadly if you are feeling impetuous and emotional. Too often I have made the mistake of sending an irritable response, which will have festered and angered the other end much more than a difficult telephone exchange. Spoken words fade, but e-mail is forever.

It is so much easier to be tough via e-mail, or to get away with weak excuses, or to make things up, or to say no. Almost invariably, it is more human and serious to have a real discussion rather than a bizarre online conversation. I know employees who have been fired for sending abusive e-mails, or who have faced severe legal consequences for writing something they should have just said verbally.

Everyone in business finds their inbox is almost swamped every day with spam. I notice I spend longer and longer sorting out the e-mails that matter from all the junk. It has become, I'm afraid, a dangerously corrupted medium. Large companies suffer chronic overuse of 'reply to all'.

Moreover, e-mail can be a terrible distraction, especially if you use a BlackBerry. I was recently reprimanded for peeking at mine during a board meeting – a gross form of hypocrisy on my part, because I once threatened to sling out of the window any PDA-type devices being used in meetings I chaired. I have now vowed to switch off both BlackBerry and mobile in all meetings – anything less is uncivil.

It must be admitted that e-mail is hard to beat as a transmitter of documents and data. It forces the sender to carefully think through their arguments and express themselves logically. It allows you to reply swiftly to a host of different questions when time is short. You don't have to worry about journey times or travel costs, unreliable postage or engaged phones or voicemail.

E-mail is a marvellously economical tool for keeping in touch with far-flung commercial contacts; you can send them a note at your leisure, 24 hours a day. It is also a terrific method of discreetly and directly pitching to someone powerful. It certainly beats trying to get a meeting or even reach them on the phone.

Like it or not, I could not do my job without e-mail. Meanwhile, I know a senior financier, an ex-chair of a FTSE company, who still has his secretary print out his e-mails for him to read so he can then dictate replies for her to e-mail back. Now that really is mad.

LANGUAGE REVIEW
Idioms

A **Complete the idioms below with the words from the box.**

bush grapevine loop mouth nutshell picture point purposes stick tail wall wavelength

a) to put it in a ....

b) to get straight to the ....

c) to hear it on the ....

d) to put someone in the ....

e) to get the wrong end of the ....

f) to be on the same ....

g) can't make head nor .... of it

h) to talk at cross-...........

i) to beat about the ....

j) to get it straight from the horse's ....

k) to be like talking to a brick ....

l) to keep someone in the ....

to keep someone in the loop

to be on the same wavelength

B Match the idioms in Exercise A to these definitions.

1 to fail to understand anything 9
2 to share similar opinions and ideas
3 to give the main facts in a short, clear way
4 to not understand something
5 to delay talking about something
6 to give the latest information
7 to talk about the most important thing
8 to hear about something because the information has been passed from one person to another in conversation
9 to be told something by someone who has direct knowledge of it
10 to try to communicate with an unresponsive person
11 to include someone in group communication
12 to not understand someone

C Complete these sentences with the idioms from Exercise A in the correct form.

1 OK, I'll .... I'm afraid it's the last time we're going to miss a deadline.
2 Paola and I and agree on most things. We seem to be ....
3 A lot happened while you were on holiday. Let me ....
4 I think we are .... I mean next week, not this week.
5 He never gives you a straight answer. He's always ....
6 I .... that he's been fired. Is it true?
7 The new organogram is very complicated, but to .... , we still report to the same manager.
8 I'm afraid that isn't right. If you think our biggest problem is communication, then you have ....
9 This document from our subsidiary makes no sense at all. I ....
10 I've tried to get my supplier to give us a discount several times, but they just won't. It's like ....
11 The company is going bankrupt. The CEO told me himself. I heard it ....
12 I'll need regular updates about the progress of the project. I'll also need to know what's going on when I'm away. Please ....

D Ask your partner these questions.

1 What have you heard on the grapevine recently?
2 When is it necessary to put someone in the picture?
3 In what situations is it good to get straight to the point?
4 Is there anything you can't make head nor tail of?
5 Who are you on the same wavelength as? Why?
6 Have you ever felt you were talking to a brick wall?
7 When have you been kept either in or out of the loop? How did you feel?

SKILLS

Dealing with communication breakdown

A **What expressions can you use in these phone situations?**

a) the person speaks too fast or too quietly

b) you want someone to stop talking while you do something

c) you don't understand a word/expression the other person uses

d) you want to make sure of the spelling of something

e) you want more information about a subject

f) the connection is not good and you can't continue the conversation

g) you want to confirm some information

B CD1.5 **Listen to a telephone conversation between Bernard Klebermann and Koichi Sato. Which of the problems mentioned in Exercise A do the speakers have when communicating?**

C CD1.6 **Listen to the same two speakers in a similar conversation. Explain why the second conversation is better. Give as many reasons as you can.**

D CD1.6 **Listen to the conversation again and complete these extracts with words or expressions from it.**

1 That's good. Could you .... while I get a pen?

2 Sorry, Bernard, I .... Could you .... a little, please? I need to take some notes.

3 Let me .... that: 200 posters, pens and pencils and 50 bags. .... it.

4 Seel- ... sorry, could you .... me, please, Bernard? I don't think I know the company.

5 'They've placed an order for 518 of the new lasers ...'
'Sorry, ... 580 lasers?'

6 Sorry, I don't follow you. What .... 'roll-out' .... ?

7 But I need details about the company ... Sorry, it's .... Could you ...., please? I can't hear you very well.

8 Sorry, I still can't hear you. I'll ...., maybe the line will be better.

E **Match each extract in Exercise D to the situations you discussed in Exercise A. Two of them correspond to the same situation.**

F **Work in pairs. Role-play two situations.**

Student A: Turn to page 132. Student B: Turn to page 140.

USEFUL LANGUAGE

ASKING FOR REPETITION

Sorry, could you repeat that?

I didn't (quite) catch that.

Could you speak up, please?

Could you say that again, please?

ASKING FOR CLARIFICATION

What do you mean by ...?

What does ... mean?

Could you clarify that?

CHECKING INFORMATION

Would/Could you spell that, please?

Can I read that back to you?

PROBLEMS WITH UNDERSTANDING

Sorry, I'm not with you.

Sorry, I don't follow you.

Sorry, I'm not sure I know what you mean.

ASKING FOR FURTHER INFORMATION

Could you give me some more details, please?

Could you be a bit more specific?

Could you explain that in more detail?

TECHNICAL PROBLEMS

Sorry, it's a bad line. Can I call you back?

It's a terrible connection.

I'm afraid I'll have to get back to you later.

Sorry, we were cut off.

SUMMARISING THE CALL

Let me go over what we've agreed.

Let me just summarise ...

1

Case study

The price of success

Poor communications are affecting the performance of a fast-growing electronics company

Background

Based in Seattle, US, W.C. Hooper Inc. (WCH) is a manufacturer and distributor of hi-tech electronic products, ranging from executive toys to state-of-the-art digital cameras. The company has grown rapidly in the last 20 years and until recently, its performance has been excellent. However, problems have arisen concerning communications, both internal and external, and these are beginning to impact on the efficiency of the business. A new Communications Director, Betty Friedman, has been hired, and one of her tasks is to improve communications in the company.

A product defect

A weakness in the company's communications was highlighted by the following incident. What mistakes do you think were made in the way this problem was handled? How could they be remedied?

About three months ago, a customer found a fault in WCH's most up-to-date, multi-functional cell phone. Her phone became very hot after being recharged and it burned her hand. 'It was so hot, I thought it would explode,' she said. The customer complained to the Customer Service Department, who sent her a replacement phone. The employee dealing with the complaint did not inform either the Marketing or R&D Departments about the fault. After this incident, there were a number of similar complaints. As a result of bad publicity, the phone was withdrawn from the market.

Lawrence Discount Stores

Another incident a few weeks ago showed that internal communications in the company were not working well. Read about the problem and discuss the reason(s) why WCH lost an important customer.

Richard Lawrence, one of WCH's best and oldest customers, phoned William Hooper about the company's new digital camera, the EX-120. He told Hooper that he'd probably be placing an order for 5,000 of the products in the next few weeks. Hooper passed on this information by phone to the Sales Manager. When Lawrence sent in the order five weeks later, the Sales Manager sent him an e-mail saying that unfortunately the new product was out of stock. Lawrence complained to Hooper, who asked the Sales Manager why he hadn't given priority to Lawrence's order. The manager replied, 'I was waiting for him to confirm his order. I didn't realise that his order had to be given priority.'

The new Communications Director

Betty Friedman, the new Communications Director, hired a firm of consultants, Ward Associates, to analyse the communications problems in the company and to come up with recommendations for improvement. Read this extract from the report.

1 Internal communications

Problem:
Communications between Directors and Heads of Department need to be improved.

Recommendations:

- Heads of Department should send weekly reports to the Board of Directors. This would enable Directors to keep in touch with key developments in the company.
- A new manager should be appointed to be in charge of key accounts, such as the Lawrence Discount Stores account. He/She would ensure that key customers were given personal attention.

2 Sales reps/Head Office

Problem:
Head Office is not receiving information quickly from sales representatives. This has resulted in delays in processing orders and insufficient information about customers.

Recommendation:
Issue all sales reps with BlackBerry devices and instruct reps to send daily reports to the Sales Department.

3 Customer Services Department

Problem:
The department needs a new procedure for dealing with product complaints.

Recommendation:
Any complaint about a product which has health and safety implications should be forwarded immediately to the following departments: Marketing, Research and Development, Public Relations.

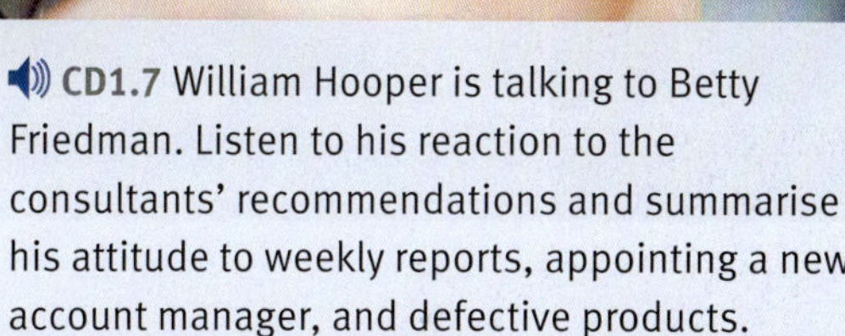

CD1.7 William Hooper is talking to Betty Friedman. Listen to his reaction to the consultants' recommendations and summarise his attitude to weekly reports, appointing a new account manager, and defective products.

CD1.8 Listen to Joanna Merkowitz, a sales representative, talking to Betty Friedman about the consultants' recommendations. Why is she against giving daily reports? Why does she enjoy her job so much?

Task

1. Work in small groups. You are members of the Board of Directors. Discuss each of the consultants' recommendations. Decide whether you agree or disagree with each recommendation, noting down your reasons.
2. Consider any other ideas that your group has to improve communications in WCH.

*Watch the Case study commentary on the **DVD-ROM**.*

Writing

As Communications Director at WCH, write a follow-up e-mail to the Head of Ward Associates, summarising the decisions you have taken, with your reasons.

Writing file page 127

UNIT 2

International marketing

'In marketing, there are those who satisfy needs and those who create wants.'
Juan Carlos Castillo, American academic

OVERVIEW

STARTING UP

A **What brands do you know that are marketed internationally? Think of one brand in each of these categories which is marketed internationally.**

cars   clothing   cosmetics   electrical equipment   soft drinks

B **Answer these questions for each brand you listed in Exercise A.**

1 What is its country of origin?
2 What is its brand image?
3 What is the target market/segment?
4 What sort of advertising campaigns does the brand use? (Are they standardised or adapted to local markets?)
5 What is the current slogan?

C **What are the most famous international brands in your country? What sort of image do they have a) at home, and b) abroad?**

VOCABULARY
Marketing word partnerships

A **Complete each group of word partnerships (1–5) with the correct word from the box.**

brand	customer	market	marketing	product

1 .... mix
strategy
plan

2 .... adaptation
penetration
segmentation

3 .... placement
portfolio
feature

4 .... profile
retention
base

5 .... positioning
identity
extension

B **Choose the correct word partnership from each group in Exercise A to complete these definitions.**

1 When entering a new market, a SWOT analysis (strengths/weaknesses/opportunities/threats) is conducted on a product, service or company before deciding on a ....
2 It may also be necessary to carry out a STEP analysis (sociological/technological/economic/political) of a new geographical market in order to decide if changes are to be made for ....
3 The USP (unique selling point) is the .... which makes it different from its competitors.
4 Part of building up a .... is analysing the buying habits of consumers.
5 .... is how a product is placed (up-market, mid-market, budget) in relation to rival products.

C **Look at these groups of words and phrases. Find the odd one out in each group.**

1 a) growing market b) developing market c) expanding market d) declining market
2 a) questionnaire b) focus group c) promotion d) survey
3 a) market sector b) market research c) market segment d) market niche
4 a) international market b) overseas market c) domestic market d) worldwide market
5 a) launch a product b) introduce a product c) bring out a product d) withdraw a product
6 a) special offer b) free sample c) discount d) slogan
7 a) retailer b) distributor c) wholesaler d) exporter

D **Discuss these questions.**

1 What are some of the problems companies may face when they try to internationalise a brand? (For example, brand names)
2 What are some of the advantages/drawbacks of standardised global advertising?
3 Why do some brands/products fail in other countries? Can you give any examples?
4 Give an example of an expanding market in your country.
5 Give some examples of products or services which are targeted at niche markets.
6 What's the difference between a retailer and a wholesaler?

READING

Italian luxury

A Answer these questions.

1 What do the following have in common: Gucci, Chanel, Calvin Klein, Louis Vuitton, Christian Dior, Versace, Giorgio Armani, Ralph Lauren, Prada, Yves Saint Laurent?

2 Which countries tend to make the world's most desirable luxury brands?

3 What would you buy if money was no object?

B Read the article below quickly and complete this information.

Tod's group HQ – where?	 1
Key products	 2
Chairman	 3
Competitors that Chairman admires	 4
New markets	 5
Objective in next five years	 6

FT

Diego Della Valle: Italian atmosphere is central to Tod's global expansion

by Vincent Boland

It is not too difficult, in the high-ceilinged elegance of Palazzo Della Valle on the Corso Venezia in Milan, to be seduced by the charms of a certain kind of Italian lifestyle. Here is the headquarters of Tod's Group, which has become a powerhouse in the marketing of that vision to the world's wealthy and discerning.

The atmosphere is deliberate: where some Italian fashion houses have expanded ever further into the realms of celebrity and glamour, Tod's is anchored as firmly as it can be to its family roots and its traditional, hand-made, century-old heritage.

Its signature products – shoes and bags – are made of leather, a raw material that has remained almost unchanged since it was first discovered. A new advertising campaign will take the company back to basics, with a focus on Italian families and their lifestyles – actual Italian families, however rich and privileged – rather than on celebrities.

'The Italian lifestyle is in our DNA, and in our group, we believe in our DNA,' says Diego Della Valle, the Chairman and Chief Executive of Tod's Group.

This image is especially important in new markets, such as China and India, he says. In common with other luxury-goods makers, he is intent on capturing consumers in those markets who aspire to the same sense of the Italian lifestyle as do customers in more mature markets. 'A luxury-goods company has to have control of its image,' he says. 'For Tod's, the thing is to communicate this tradition, the generations of work that have gone into our products. For us, it's an absolute priority.'

To achieve it, one must put quality before quantity, and one must maintain the group's traditions even as it globalises, which it has been doing fairly relentlessly in the past decade.

The challenge is to marry tradition with modernity in a way that not all Italian luxury-goods and fashion producers have managed. Tod's has done it, Mr Della Valle says, by maintaining one key vision: 'We're a luxury-goods company, not a fashion company.'

This distinction between fashion and luxury is central to Mr Della Valle's global ambitions. The two have different products and ought to have different strategies, he says. The competitors he admires most, he says, are Louis Vuitton, Hermès and Chanel.

Mr Della Valle says that the goal in the next five years is 'to complete the globalisation' of Tod's, for which he has been laying the groundwork. 'I'd like Tod's to be much bigger than it is now, without diluting the brand,' he says.

He expects China and India to account for as much as 25 per cent of revenues by then, because the growth potential is much higher than in more traditional markets. 'There is a much bigger appetite for luxury goods in those markets than in mature markets, and day by day more people are coming into this market.'

But as for China as a competing producer, Mr Della Valle is sceptical about its ability to produce luxury goods. 'It lacks the structure of small companies, the tradition, the concept of excellence' that Italian luxury-goods producers have inherited and which they must maintain as a competitive advantage, he says. '"Made in Italy" doesn't necessarily mean expensive goods,' he says. 'It means excellent goods.'

C Read the article again and correct this summary.

Tod's Group wishes to convey the charms of the Italian lifestyle to the world's rich. To do this, it focuses on celebrity and glamour, and its new advertising campaign will feature Italian celebrities. The Chairman says he wants to expand into India and China to capture consumers there who appreciate the Italian lifestyle. To enter such big markets, Tod's will need to think about quantity as well as quality.

Tod's is primarily a fashion company and needs to be much bigger. China and India have more possibility for growth than Tod's traditional markets. The Chairman is worried because China will be able to produce luxury goods more cheaply. In future, Tod's will look to lower production costs by manufacturing in low-cost countries.

D Match words from each column to make word partnerships. Then check your answers in the article.

1 competitive	a) markets
2 traditional	b) markets
3 raw	c) advantage
4 mature	d) materials
5 global	e) ambition

E Discuss these questions.

1. What products do you know that rely on their heritage and cultural background?
2. In a recession, do you think companies such as Tod's should manufacture in low-cost countries rather than at home? What are the advantages and disadvantages of this?
3. Would you ever buy a fake luxury product?
4. Do you agree that designer luxury goods are always higher quality than non-designer goods?

LISTENING
How to market internationally

A CD1.9 Listen to Svend Hollensen, Professor of International Marketing at the University of South Denmark, and answer these questions.

1. Which two marketing strategies does he mention?
2. What does he say about a) the OneCafé company, and b) Lux?

Svend Hollensen

B CD1.10 Darrell Kofkin is Chief Executive of the Global Marketing Network, a training organisation which offers qualifications in international marketing. Listen to the interview and complete the gaps in these two extracts.

... a new curriculum that enables ....[1] worldwide to have the latest ....[2], the latest ....[3] and ....[4], to enable them to become ....[5] marketers.

So our students are asked to write a ....[6], develop a ....[7], develop a ....[8], write a ....[9], present an ....[10] – just as they would do in the workplace. Because we know in talking to employers ....[11] that they want marketing professionals that have the ....[12] and skills required of today's demanding ....[13] environment.

Darrell Kofkin

LANGUAGE REVIEW

Noun compounds and noun phrases

- A compound noun is two nouns together. Noun compounds are common in business because they are shorter and more convenient than noun phrases. For example:
  a market survey rather than *a survey into the market*
  a product design brief rather than *a brief for the design of a product*
- Longer noun phrases are also common. They may consist of adverbs, adjectives and compound noun. This pattern is typical:

adverb	adjective/*-ing* participle	noun	head noun
highly	confidential	sales	report
	excellent	sponsorship	deal
	expanding	customer	base

➡ ***Grammar reference*** page 146

A **Find noun phrases in the article on page 16 which have similar meanings to these phrases.**

1 a programme of activities over a period of time with the aim of persuading the public to buy a product (paragraph 3)

2 the person who has the highest position in a company (paragraph 4)

3 the makers of clothes, shoes, etc. in new and changing styles (paragraph 7)

4 an organisation that makes expensive things bought for comfort and pleasure, not for basic needs (paragraph 7)

5 possibility for future development and expansion (paragraph 10)

B **Cross out the word in each group which does not make a compound noun with the word in bold.**

1 **marketing** campaign / budget / leader / strategy

2 **market** leader / survey / check / sector

3 **product** market / range / features / launch

4 **advertising** campaign / exchange / agency / slogan

5 **brand** awareness / loyalty / image / contract

6 **sales** figures / conditions / forecast / targets

7 **price** promotion / rise / product / range

C **Write the words in each of these noun phrases in the correct order.**

1 advertising impressive campaign really

2 customer department new relations

3 competitive mobile highly market phone

4 successful product incredibly launch

5 customer base loyal

6 thorough extremely report sales

7 brilliant absolutely campaign global

8 competitive increasingly marketing environment

D CD1.11 **Listen and check your answers.**

SKILLS

Brainstorming

A **Brainstorming is a useful way of generating creative ideas in meetings. Decide which of these tips are good advice and which ones you disagree with. Then compare your answers with a partner.**

1 Explain the purpose of the meeting clearly.
2 Ask each person to speak in turn, starting with the most senior.
3 Announce the time limit for the meeting.
4 Avoid criticising or judging ideas during the session.
5 Encourage ideas, however unusual they may be.
6 Don't interrupt when people are offering suggestions.
7 Make sure everyone keeps to the point.
8 Don't spend time on details.

B CD1.12 **Listen to the first part of a brainstorming meeting between Martin Thomas, the Marketing Director, who chairs the meeting, and three other members of the Marketing Department at Business Solutions Limited: Carol Rueckert, Caroline Holloway and Guillem Rojas. Then answer these questions.**

1 What do they want to achieve at the meeting?
2 What three locations are suggested?

C CD1.13 **Now listen to the rest of the meeting and answer these questions.**

1 What types of accommodation does Carol suggest?
2 What suggestions are made concerning the free time of delegates?

D **Match the comments made by the participants to the headings in the Useful language box below. Some comments can be put under more than one heading.**

1 ... so the purpose of the meeting this morning is to ...
2 Yeah, it sounds great.
3 ... have you got any ideas for where we can have this?
4 OK, anyone else?
5 That's great. Any other ideas, any options?
6 I think it's a great city ...
7 Good idea, yeah.
8 That's an excellent suggestion, yeah, that's great.
9 Yeah, any other ideas about what we ... what we can do?
10 That's true.

E **Choose one of these situations and hold a brainstorming meeting.**

1 Your company has developed a new sports or music magazine. Brainstorm ideas for an advertising campaign.
2 Your company will shortly be receiving a visit from some important Chinese businesspeople who wish to set up a joint venture with your firm. Brainstorm ideas for a suitable programme for the three Chinese visitors.

USEFUL LANGUAGE

STATING OBJECTIVES

The purpose of the meeting this morning is to ...

What we need to achieve today is ...

Our objective here is to ...

EXPRESSING ENTHUSIASM

That's great!

That's the best idea I've heard for a long time.

That's an excellent suggestion.

ENCOURAGING CONTRIBUTIONS

Don't hold back.

Say whatever comes to mind.

Any other ideas?

At this stage, we want all your ideas, however crazy you think they are.

AGREEING

Yes, that's a good idea because ...

Absolutely, because ...

Exactly, because ...

You're (absolutely) right because ...

Case study 2

HENRI-CLAUDE COSMETICS

Creating a global brand

A successful French cosmetics company plans to go global

Background

Henri-Claude Cosmetics (HCC), a French cosmetics and personal-care company, has created a highly successful eau-de-cologne for men under the brand name *Physique*. This is the company's best-selling men's fragrance and the best-known brand in their product portfolio. HCC is now planning an international campaign for *Physique* early next year. It intends a high-profile launch in 10 countries, which will enable the brand to achieve international recognition. The theme of the campaign will be '*Physique* for the Urban Man'.

A global ambassador – a celebrity in the arts world – will be chosen to lead the campaign.

Key features of *Physique*

Based on redwood and cedar, with citrus and spices, *Physique* has a fresh, woody, long-lasting aroma.

- It has five other secret ingredients, known to only a small number of senior managers.
- The scent is very appealing to women. Men who use *Physique* say they feel confident, attractive and sophisticated.
- Its target audience in France is ambitious, career-minded men in the 30–40 age range.

The eau-de-cologne is positioned as a premium fragrance. It is priced at the top end of the market.

CD1.14 Listen to a conversation between Carla Fernández, Global Marketing Manager, and Pierre Martin, Chief Executive of HCC. They are talking about the results of research carried out in overseas markets concerning the international launch of *Physique*. Make notes on the following aspects of the product:

- target audience
- brand image
- name
- positioning
- packaging
- slogan

PRODUCT DETAILS – *PHYSIQUE*

Product shape: Tall, rounded bottle, solid appearance. Black, with the brand name in the centre. Silver top. Screw top or spray.

Average retail prices:

40ml	$60
75ml	$75
100ml	$95
125ml	$110

The price places *Physique* in the top ten most expensive male fragrances.

Distribution in France: sold exclusively in *parfumeries* (specialised stores for cosmetics and toiletries) and in shops in top hotels.

Promotion: Commercials on French television; radio spots; full-page advertisements in prestigious magazines, e.g. *Paris Match*, *Marie Claire*, etc.

Special promotions at high-class events such as Longchamp racing stadium, and in embassies and duty-free shops at the airports.

Words associated with *Physique* by consumers (in order of frequency): masculine, sensual, sophisticated, elegant, energetic, alluring, spicy, glamorous, individualistic.

Quotation from sales literature: '*Physique* man is confident, ambitious and resilient. He is at home in any city and enjoys the challenge of urban life. He has a lot of creative energy, travels widely and is optimistic about the future.'

Preparation for the international marketing launch

Having received the results of research in a number of potential overseas markets, the Marketing Department of HCC has organised a meeting to brainstorm ideas for the global marketing strategy of *Physique*.

Task

You are members of the Marketing Department of HCC.

1. Work in groups and brainstorm the points listed in the rough notes. One person in each group should take notes. Then meet as one group and select some of the best ideas for further study.
2. In your groups, devise a one-minute television commercial for the international launch. Using a storyboard*, present the ideas of your group to your colleagues. Then as one group, choose the best commercial. If necessary, take a vote.

* A series of pictures showing the sequence of scenes (setting, action, dialogue) of a TV commercial. A storyboard helps marketing staff to visualise the concept for the commercial.

BRAINSTORMING SESSION

1. **Which 10 countries should be chosen for the launch?**
2. **Does *Physique* need a new name? If so, what?**
3. **Should *Physique* continue be targeted at the 30–40 age group? If not, what age group should it target?**
4. **Should *Physique* continue to be positioned as a premium fragrance, or should HCC market it as a mass fragrance, with a different pricing structure?**
5. **The container of *Physique* must be changed. How should the new container look? Plan the new packaging (shape, design, materials).**
6. **Price: Are the present pricing levels appropriate? Should HCC offer a cheaper version of *Physique* for emerging markets?**
7. **Distribution: Should HCC continue to sell the fragrance in exclusive outlets in overseas markets, or should it use a wider variety of outlets? If so, what sort of outlets should it choose?**
8. **Promotion: Who should be the international ambassador(s) for the brand? What special promotions could HCC organise in the overseas markets?**
9. ***Physique* needs a new slogan. Ideas?**
10. **Manufacture: Is it now time to manufacture the fragrance in low-cost countries? If so, which countries would be suitable?**

Watch the Case study commentary on the ***DVD-ROM.***

Writing

As a member of the Marketing Department of HCC, write the action minutes for the brainstorming session you attended.

Writing file page 130

UNIT **3**

Building relationships

'If you destroy a bridge, be sure you can swim.'
African (Swahili) proverb

OVERVIEW

VOCABULARY
Describing relations

LISTENING
Business partnerships

READING
Business networks in China

LANGUAGE REVIEW
Multi-word verbs

SKILLS
Networking

CASE STUDY
Al-Munir Hotel and Spa Group

STARTING UP

A **Work in pairs. Ask each other the questions in the quiz. Then turn to page 132 to find out how good you are at building relationships.**

1 YOU ARE IN A ROOM WITH A GROUP OF PEOPLE WHO DON'T KNOW EACH OTHER. DO YOU:
   a) introduce yourself?
   b) introduce a topic of conversation?
   c) wait for someone to say something?

2 WHEN YOU ARE INTRODUCED TO PEOPLE, DO YOU REMEMBER THEIR:
   a) name?
   b) face?
   c) clothes?

3 ON FESTIVE OCCASIONS, E.G. NEW YEAR, DO YOU:
   a) send greeting cards to everyone you know?
   b) reply only to cards received?
   c) send e-mails?

4 DO YOU THINK SMALL TALK IS:
   a) enjoyable?
   b) a waste of time?
   c) difficult to do well?

5 DO YOU PREFER:
   a) to socialise with colleagues only if you have to?
   b) to socialise often with colleagues?
   c) not to socialise with colleagues?

6 DO YOU LIKE TO HAVE CONVERSATIONS WITH:
   a) people who share your interests?
   b) almost anyone?
   c) people who are your social equals?

B **You are going to listen to Gillian Baker, Business Relations Manager with an international training organisation, talking about how companies can build strong business relationships. What factors do you think she will mention?**

C CD1.15 **Listen to the interview and check the predictions you made in Exercise B.**

D **What are the most important relationships for you a) at your place of work/study, b) outside your place of work/study? Why?**

VOCABULARY
Describing relations

A **Complete the table below with these verbs, which are often used with the word *relations*.**

~~break off~~ ~~build up~~ cement cultivate cut off damage develop disrupt encourage establish foster improve jeopardise maintain promote restore resume sever sour strengthen undermine

Positive meaning	Negative meaning
build up relations	break off relations

B **Choose the correct verb in each sentence.**

1 Sales staff who are impolite to customers *disrupt / damage* the reputation of a company.

2 We are planning to *promote / establish* branch offices in Spain next year.

3 By merging with a US company, we greatly *strengthened / maintained* our sales force.

4 Relations with customers have been *fostered / undermined* recently by poor after-sales service.

5 Thanks to a new communications system, we are *souring / improving* relations with suppliers.

6 A strike at our factory last year *resumed / disrupted* production for several weeks.

7 We could not agree on several points, so we *broke off / cut off* talks regarding a joint venture.

8 The success of our new product launch was *cemented / jeopardised* by an unimaginative advertising campaign.

9 In order to gain market share in China, we are *building up / cutting off* relationships with local agents.

10 Business relations between the two countries have been *severed / fostered* by official visits and trade delegations.

C **Match these sentence halves. Then make five more sentences with the verbs in Exercises A and B.**

1 Widespread rumours of a hostile takeover bid are certain

2 The Accounts Department's very slow payment of invoices

3 The long-term contracts, which will run for the next five years,

4 The excellent relations the company enjoys with the local community

5 As a result of the government's imposition of currency controls,

a) are a credit to its highly effective PR Department.

b) have cemented relations between the two companies.

c) its close relations with several major foreign investors have been jeopardised.

d) is causing stormy relations with some of the company's suppliers.

e) to strain relations between the two leading French software companies.

See the **DVD-ROM** for the *i-Glossary*.

D **Give an example of a company you know which is good at building relationships with its customers. How do they do this?**

LISTENING

Business partnerships

Alison Ward

A CD1.16 **Alison Ward is Head of Global Corporate Responsibility at Cadbury, the chocolate maker. Listen to the first part of the interview and complete this information about Cadbury's Cocoa Partnership.**

Launched	........................[1]
% Cadbury cocoa beans from Ghana	........................[2]
% yield from the land	........................[3]
Average age of farmers	........................[4]
Cadbury partners in Ghana	........................[5]

B CD1.17 **Listen to the second part and complete these extracts with up to three words in each gap.**

1 Well, we're really proud that we've achieved .... for our Cadbury Dairy Milk brand ...

2 So it means that people around the world can now make an .... and ...

3 Fairtrade's an interesting marque in that it's not only .... in consumer markets – it's very well .... – but it also has great power back in ....

C CD1.18 **Listen to the final part and answer these questions.**

1 What other partnership does Cadbury have?

2 What does Alison say about the changes in the supply chain with that partnership?

*Watch the interview on the **DVD-ROM**.*

D **Think of any other partnerships similar to that of Cadbury and the farmers from Ghana. Tell your colleague about it.**

READING

Business networks in China

A **Where can you meet people to build good business relations?**

B **Read the article on the opposite page quickly and say who these people are.**

1 Li Ka-shing 2 Gary Wang 3 Helen Wong 4 Zhou Junjun 5 Andrew Grant

C **Read the article again. Which paragraph:**

1 begins by talking about the origins of *guanxi*?

2 gives examples of what can be achieved if you have connections?

3 talks about how *guanxi* is changing?

4 talks about top connections made at MBA programmes within China?

5 talks about how a business started through connections made at a European business school?

6 talks about networking through multinational companies?

7 talks about Chinese businesspeople wanting something in return for connections?

8 suggests that making connections might take time and effort?

D **Answer these questions.**

1 What is *guanxi*?

2 What examples are given of things you can achieve if you have good *guanxi*?

3 What can Western companies do if they are involved in informal groups?

4 How is *guanxi* changing?

5 Why does Ogilvy Public Relations Worldwide hold annual parties for previous employees?

E Find words or phrases in the article which mean the following.

1 using or taking what you need from a supply of something (paragraph 2)

2 when someone always supports someone or something (paragraph 3)

3 being responsible for what you do and willing to explain it or accept criticism (paragraph 3)

4 a moral or legal duty to do something (paragraph 3)

5 people you know who can help you, especially because they are in positions of power (paragraph 4)

6 talking to other people who do similar work in order to help each other (paragraph 6)

7 determination to keep trying to do something difficult (paragraph 7)

F Discuss these questions.

1 What advice would you give to someone trying to develop business relationships in China?

2 A foreign company is opening a branch in your country. What factors should it consider?

3 In your experience, are certain nationalities better at building relationships than others? If so, which ones?

How East is meeting West

by Frederik Balfour

Guanxi. It's the first word any businessperson learns upon arriving in China. Loosely translated, *guanxi* means "connections" and it is the key to everything: securing a business license, landing a distribution deal, even finding that special colonial villa in Shanghai. Fortunes have been made and lost based on whether the seeker has good or bad *guanxi*.

Now, like so many things in China, the old notion of *guanxi* is starting to make room for the new. Businesspeople—local and foreign—are tapping into emerging networks that revolve around shared work experiences or taking business classes together. Networking that once happened in private rooms at smart restaurants now goes on in plain view—at wine tastings for the nouveau riche, say, or at Davos-style get-togethers such as the annual China Entrepreneurs Forum held annually at China's Yabuli ski resort. By tapping into these informal groups, Western companies can theoretically improve their understanding of the marketplace, hire the best talent, and find potential business partners.

Guanxi goes back thousands of years and is based on traditional values of loyalty, accountability, and obligation—the notion that if somebody does you a favor, you will be expected to repay it one day. One of Asia's most successful businessmen, Hong Kong billionaire Li Ka-shing, has used his *guanxi* particularly astutely over the years, in the process winning valuable licenses and permission to build huge real-estate developments. Playing the *guanxi* game is still imperative, especially for foreign investors.

Many of China's networkers meet through an American or European MBA program. Gary Wang attended INSEAD, the famous French business school outside Paris. Today, he runs a YouTube wannabe called Tudou that was built largely on connections made at business school. A fellow student who worked at Ogilvy & Mather Worldwide helped out with public relations. And another INSEAD graduate, Helen Wong, a partner at Granite Global Ventures, helped Wang raise $8.5 million after a friend heard him speak at the China Europe International Business School (CEIBS) in Shanghai. "Without knowing all these people through INSEAD," says Wang, "Tudou probably never would have happened."

Executive MBA programs, all the rage now in China, have become *Guanxi* Central. Targeted at senior executives and high-powered entrepreneurs, the programs are attracting some of China's most successful businesspeople. "It's important to have friends in different industries and meet people from different cities," says Zhou Junjun, who runs the Chinese operations of a South Korean systems company and did an Executive MBA at the Cheung Kong Graduate School of Business in Beijing.

Multinational companies, of course, provide rich opportunities for networking, too. Ogilvy Public Relations Worldwide holds an annual party for former employees, many of whom now work for the company's clients, including Lenovo, Johnson & Johnson, and solar-panel maker Suntek. McKinsey has plenty of alumni who have moved into senior posts at major companies and start-ups. "Obviously, they became a valuable network for us," says Andrew Grant, who runs the firm's China practice in Shanghai.

If one thing has remained the same for foreigners in China, it is this: cracking the *guanxi* code still takes hard work and perseverance. Networking at an alumni barbecue or wine tasting goes only so far when trying to build relationships of any lasting value. After the first 30 minutes at these functions, say people who have attended, foreigners and locals almost invariably break off into separate groups.

What's more, Chinese businesspeople are more experienced and globally savvy than they were just a few years ago. They're looking for business connections who can help them expand outside China or get their company listed on a foreign exchange. "People want something more professional and strategic from their relationships," says Li Yifei, Viacom's chief representative in China. "They want to know how good your *guanxi* is back home."

from *Business Week*

LANGUAGE REVIEW

Multi-word verbs

Multi-word verbs are particularly common in spoken English. They are made with a verb and particles such as *at, away, down* and *off*. Four types are:

1. Without an object
   *Networking now **goes on** in plain view.*
2. With an object – separable
   *We'll **draw up** a new contract. / We'll **draw a** new contract **up**.*
3. With an object – inseparable
   *They're **looking for** business connections.*
4. With two particles
   *I'm really **looking forward to** meeting you next week.*

➡ ***Grammar reference*** page 147

A 🔊 CD1.19 **Two executives are talking about building relationships with clients. Put the conversation in the correct order. Then listen and check your answers.**

- ☐ a) They were both annoyed. My contact thought I had let him down, and his boss simply decided not to turn up at the meeting. We'd set up a meeting in Brussels by e-mail, but he called it off at the last minute. I'd already checked in at the hotel.
- ☐ b) Oh, what went wrong?
- ☐ c) Well, I'm going to carry on working until about six. We could meet after that.
- ☐ d) How did you turn it round?
- ☐ e) It's fine now, but at the start of the year, it was disastrous.
- 1 f) So, how's the relationship with Toyota going?
- ☐ g) Well, I went over my contact's head and went directly to his boss at Toyota Motors Europe. I was really trying to clinch a deal.
- ☐ h) Glad it worked out. Anyway, are you free for a drink later?
- ☐ i) Well, I had to build up my relationship with my original contact again. At first, he kept putting me off. But eventually we met up and I focused on our relationship, not the next sale. Now we get on really well and sometimes play golf together.
- ☐ j) Was he annoyed?

B **Underline all the multiword verbs in the conversation in Exercise A. Then decide which of them has a similar meaning to each of these verb phrases.**

1. have a friendly relationship
2. registered
3. make stronger
4. change something into something successful
5. postponing/delaying
6. appear/arrive somewhere
7. disappoint
8. arrange
9. continue
10. cancelled

C **Rephrase these comments using the multiword verbs from Exercise B.**

1. We can't hold the meeting tomorrow.
   *We'll have to **call off** the meeting tomorrow.*
2. They've postponed the presentation until Thursday.
3. I'm sorry I've disappointed you.
4. She's arranged the conference call for nine o'clock.
5. This is a crucial meeting. Make sure you arrive on time.
6. Everyone continued working as if nothing had happened.
7. You'll need to register at the Hilton around four o'clock.
8. I have a good relationship with my new boss.

SKILLS

Networking

A CD1.20 **Networking is an essential way of establishing good business relationships. Listen to the first conversation and say whether these statements are true or false. Correct the false ones.**

1 Howard Clark's company is probably less successful this year than last year.

2 Howard's company does not have time to redesign the website itself.

3 Judy Masters thinks that Howard will have no problems contacting Martin Englemann.

B CD1.21 **Listen to the second, telephone conversation, then answer these questions.**

1 Why does the website need redesigning?

2 How does Martin Engelmann react to Howard's offer to redesign the website?

C **Now listen to both conversations again and complete these extracts.**

CD1.20

1 Hello. Haven't we .... somewhere before?

2 Maybe I could .... there. I know someone who's a top-class web designer [...] I'm sure he'd be interested. Why .... him?

3 Great. You haven't got his phone number, ...?

4 Yep ... 07825 300646. Can I .... your name when I call him?

5 OK, I'll .... him. Thanks very much ....

CD1.21

6 I was .... your name by Judy Masters.

7 I was wondering ... well ... would you be .... in helping us to redesign it?

8 Can I suggest .... at our office, say, at the end of the month?

D **Work in pairs and role-play these two situations.**

1 The US owner of an up-market chain of restaurants phones a Canadian supplier of shellfish. The supplier was recommended by a friend of the owner.

2 A conference entitled 'Entry strategies for overseas markets' gives participants an opportunity to do some networking.

Student A: Turn to page 133.
Student B: Turn to page 142.

USEFUL LANGUAGE

MENTIONING PEOPLE YOU KNOW

I was given your name by Judy Masters.

Anna Kaufmann suggested I gave you a call.

A colleague/friend/acquaintance mentioned your name.

GIVING ADVICE

Why don't you give him a call?

You could meet our Systems Manager.

REFERRING TO PREVIOUS MEETINGS

Haven't we met somewhere before?

We both went to that presentation.

I think we met some time ago.

ASKING FOR HELP/CONTACTS

Can I mention your name when I call him?

She mentioned that you might be able to help me.

Have you got his phone number, by any chance?

Do you have his contact details?

ESTABLISHING COMMON INTERESTS

We have something in common. We're both interested in ...

I see we're in the same line of business.

We both do similar work. / We have similar interests.

Are you in sales or product development?

3 Case study

Al-Munir Hotel and Spa Group

An Arab hotel group wishes to build customer loyalty by getting to know its visitors better and encouraging them to return to its hotels

Background

Vanessa Schultz, recently appointed Director of Customer Relations, has been hired by the Al-Munir Hotel and Spa Group to improve the group's customer relations. The group has a number of hotels in Oman and the United Arab Emirates. Vanessa Schultz's first task is to focus on building better relationships with the guests who use the hotels, especially with those who may become frequent visitors. The challenges facing the hotel group are exemplified by the following facts. In the last five years:

- group turnover has fallen by 22%
- the group's room occupancy rate has dropped from 81% to 62%
- customer surveys have indicated increasing dissatisfaction with the hotels
- the retention rate of guests has fallen from 25% to 8%
- there seems to be little customer loyalty to the hotel group
- recent reviews have reduced two of the hotels' rating from four stars to three.

Vanessa Schultz realises that she and her colleagues must come up with a plan for building long-term relationships with guests. Discuss the possible reasons for the disappointing trends noted above.

Look at the results of a customer satisfaction survey on the right. What conclusions should Vanessa Schultz draw from them?

Vanessa Schultz has used the services of Abd Al-Halim Hamdi, a local consultant specialising in hotel management, to find out why many guests do not return to stay at the hotels on a regular basis. Hamdi carried out a survey of guests by telephone and written questionnaires and is now reporting his findings to Vanessa Schultz.

What do you think will be the main reasons why guests do not return to the hotel?

Results of Customer Satisfaction Survey

(Average scores for responses from customers completing the questionnaire this year)

Key: 5 = outstanding, 4 = good, 3 = average, 2 = below average, 1 = poor

Category	Score
Location	5
Rooms	4
Amenities *	3
Service	2
Staff **	2
Information ***	1
Value for money	3

* Amenities include such things as a restaurant, café, spa, gym, business centre, swimming pool, crèche, concierge.

** Respondents were asked to grade staff in terms of their helpfulness, enthusiasm and knowledge.

*** This refers to the information about the hotel provided in rooms, and about sites and attractions in the region.

CD1.22 Listen to the conversation and check if your reasons are the same as the ones that Hamdi gives to Vanessa Schultz.

Vanessa Schultz has called a meeting which will be attended by members of the Guest Relations and Marketing Departments. This is the agenda for the meeting.

1 How can the Al-Munir Group make guests feel 'special' and 'highly valued'?
2 What can the group do to a) reward loyal customers, and b) persuade guests who have stayed once to return?
3 What can be done to make staff more motivated and customer-orientated in their approach to their work?
4 What questions should the management be asking in order to gather information for an accurate, up-to-date profile of each guest? For example: How did the guest find out about the hotel?
5 How can the group maintain its relationship with guests once they have left its hotels?
6 What other actions can the group take to improve customer loyalty, increase the average scores in the next customer satisfaction survey and get back its four-star rating?

Task

Work in small groups. You are members of either the Guest Relations or Marketing Departments.

1 Prepare for the meeting by discussing each item on the agenda. One of you should lead the discussion and note down your ideas.
2 Meet as one group. One person should play the role of Head of Guest Relations.
3 Share your ideas on each item of the agenda.
4 Agree on an action plan which you will present to the Board of Directors of the Al-Munir Group at their next meeting.

Watch the Case study commentary on the ***DVD-ROM.***

Writing

Write a sales letter to Marion Wise, a businesswoman who has stayed frequently at Al-Munir hotels and is one of the group's most loyal customers. Describe a special offer which you are making to a small group of your priority customers. Make the letter as personalised as possible.

→ *Writing file* page 126

1 Doing business internationally

Drew Corporation, based in Dallas, USA, is an international group supplying food products to the retail trade. It is currently holding its annual planning conference in Mauritius. One of the discussion sessions, entitled 'Succeeding in new markets', is attended by some of the company's top executives. The leader of the session has asked participants to work in small groups and either talk about or provide notes on a recent overseas assignment, focusing on any cultural problems they encountered in their work. In one of the groups, Bob Hewitt talks about an assignment in China, Christina Novak provides notes about her work experience in India and Melissa Petrides writes about a business trip to Russia.

A CD1.23 **You are going to hear Bob Hewitt talking about a recent new venture in China. Listen and answer these questions.**

1. Why didn't Bob make more use of David Li's business experience?
2. What does Bob mean when he says, 'we expected to get a foothold in the market pretty quickly'?
3. What conclusion did Bob come to concerning the future of Munchem restaurants in China?

B CD1.23 **Listen again and note down the mistakes Bob made because of his lack of knowledge of the Chinese market.**

Task 1

Rank the mistakes you noted in Exercise B according to how important you think they were (1 = the most important). Check your answers with the suggested ranking on page 139.

C **How would you prepare for a business trip to a country you had never visited before?**

D CD1.24 **You are going to hear Christina Novak talking about a recent trip to India. She had never done business there before. Listen and answer these questions.**

1. Why did Christina go to India?
2. What do you learn about Mumbai Enterprises?
3. What event helped to improve relations between Christina and the President of Mumbai Enterprises? Explain your answer.

E CD1.24 **Listen again and note down the cultural mistakes that Christina made.**

Task 2 What lessons can be learned about Indian business culture from Christina's experience? Check your answers on page 139.

F **Melissa wrote her impressions of a recent business trip to Russia in her blog. Read the blog below, then, in small groups, analyse and note down the cultural differences which created misunderstanding between Melissa and Georgy Volkov.**

G 🔊 CD1.25 **Listen to Galina Koznov, an expert on doing business in Russia. Compare her comments on what Melissa wrote with the points you noted in Exercise F.**

Task 3 Write a response to Melissa's blog, advising her on the best way to do business in Russia.

MY VISIT TO RUSSIA

Melissa Petrides

June 1 Met Georgy Volkov, President of Mika. Asked him for a five-year sales forecast for the products we're supplying him. 'Can't do that,' he said. 'We need to get permissions and certificates first from Ministry of Trade, tax authorities, local municipalities, customs, etc. It'll take us a long while.'

June 7 Asked Georgy how it was going with the permissions and certificates. He didn't seem pleased with my question. Wonder if I upset him. 'You must understand, Melissa, it takes a long time to set up a joint venture in Russia.'

June 8–10 Great weekend at Georgy's dacha in the countryside. Went fishing, then shared a sauna with him and his wife and had a wonderful meal (lots of caviar). Didn't talk business at all.

June 11 Difficult meeting with G and colleagues. I talked about our fantastic range of organic food products. 'We can't sell them over here. No chance at all. They'll be too expensive, customers won't buy them,' he said. I was shocked.

June 15 Very tricky meeting. We needed to take legal advice about the joint venture. I suggested using Goodman and Parker, who have a branch in Moscow. We've worked with them in many countries and they're very trustworthy. Georgy wasn't interested. 'I don't know anyone there, plus they'll charge us a lot and we'll get nothing from them. Let us use my old schoolfriend Mikhail Popov. He works for a small law firm. They'll give us good advice and they won't charge very much.'

June 18 Time for me to fly back to Dallas. G had fixed up an appointment for us to see the Minister of Trade. Would have meant missing my flight, so asked our Moscow Branch Manager, Pat Sanderson, to accompany G to the meeting instead. G not at all pleased, but I wasn't willing to cancel my flight at such short notice.

June 20 Pat Sanderson called. Meeting not successful. He didn't see the Minister of Trade, but only low-level officials in that department. G very unhappy. He told Pat, 'I worked hard to set up the meeting with the Minister. My reputation will suffer because Melissa couldn't attend the meeting. It'll take me a long time to get back in favour with the Minister.'

UNIT **A** # Revision

1 Communication

VOCABULARY

Choose the best word to complete each sentence.

1 Liam is a very *articulate / responsive* speaker. He expresses his ideas clearly and effectively.

2 The product presentation was *rambling / sensitive*. It included a lot of useless information, and no one really understood the point.

3 Your talk is limited to 10 minutes, so you need to be *responsive / succinct*. If you don't stick to the point, you won't have time to say everything.

4 Bill is *extrovert / focused*, so he really enjoys giving presentations. He loves being the centre of attention and talking to people.

5 I'm afraid I still don't know anything about the launch. The Marketing Manager gave a presentation about it, but he wasn't very *hesitant / coherent*. I don't think he was prepared.

6 I've asked Elise to attend the meeting. She's very *persuasive / inhibited*, and I think she can get a good deal for us.

7 I really enjoy listening to Pietro negotiate. He's *reserved / eloquent* and knows the business very well, so he speaks with great authority.

8 To be a *fluent / concise* speaker, you need to practise speaking so that your words flow naturally.

9 Veejay *interrupted / confused* Simon's talk and asked several questions. He should have waited until Simon had finished.

10 Let's not *clarify / digress* from the main point. We haven't got much time.

11 Speakers can *explain / engage* the audience by telling interesting personal stories and by making eye contact.

12 You have to concentrate and *listen / ramble* to the questions the audience asks.

IDIOMS

Complete the conversation below with the words in the box.

bush	grapevine	loop	mouth	picture	stick	wall	wavelength

A: Have you seen Marco today?

B: No. Why?

A: Oh, I just wondered.

B: Don't beat about the ....[1]. Why are you asking?

A: Well, I heard on the ....[2] that he's been promoted.

B: Really? Are you sure you didn't get the wrong end of the ....[3]?

A: That's why I asked if you'd seen Marco. I want to get it straight from the horse's ....[4].

B: Why don't you ask Rolf? He'll know.

A: Rolf? Talking to Rolf is like talking to a brick ....[5]. We're never on the same ....[6].

B: OK, how about Lea? I'm sure Marco's keeping her in the ....[7].

A: Yeah, good idea. I'm sure Lea will put me in the ....[8]. Thanks for the suggestion!

SKILLS

Match the halves of the expressions.

1	Sorry, could you	a)	'a long time'?
2	I didn't quite	b)	you spell that, please?
3	Could you speak	c)	catch that.
4	Could you say	d)	what we've agreed.
5	Would	e)	you back?
6	Sorry, I'm not	f)	I know what you mean.
7	What do you mean by	g)	repeat that?
8	What does	h)	up, please?
9	Sorry, I	i)	that again, please?
10	Sorry, I'm not sure	j)	with you.
11	I'll have	k)	'too expensive' mean?
12	Can I call	l)	to get back to you later.
13	Could you be	m)	don't follow you.
14	Let me go over	n)	a bit more specific?

2 International marketing

VOCABULARY

Match the words to make common word partnerships.

1	marketing	a)	penetration
2	market	b)	retention
3	product	c)	goods
4	customer	d)	market
5	brand	e)	feature
6	free	f)	materials
7	expanding	g)	group
8	focus	h)	sample
9	raw	i)	name
10	designer	j)	strategy

NOUN COMPOUNDS AND NOUN PHRASES

Put the words in the correct order to make sentences.

1 product / launching / really / We're / a / impressive / range
2 good / forecasts / The / are / sales / very
3 increase / want / awareness / We / to / brand
4 thorough / doing / We're / market / extremely / research
5 successful / created / They / a / advertising / hugely / campaign
6 introduced / We've / just / card / a / customer / new / loyalty
7 thought / absolutely / He / an / of / brilliant / slogan / advertising
8 shopping / They're / highly / entering / online / the / competitive / market

SKILLS

Complete the sentences below with the words in the box.

absolutely achieve back best great mind purpose stage suggest think

1 The .... of the meeting this morning is to plan next month's launch.
2 What we need to .... today is an agreement on the budget.
3 I don't .... we could move the launch to next month, do you?
4 Can I .... that we schedule a meeting for early next week?
5 That's .... !
6 That's the .... idea I've heard for a long time.
7 Don't hold ....
8 Say whatever comes to ....
9 At this ...., we want all your ideas, however crazy you think they are.
10 You're .... right.

3 Building relationships

VOCABULARY

Circle the odd verb or verb phrase out in each group.

1 break off cement sever end
2 create damage jeopardise hurt
3 build up strengthen begin grow
4 foster maintain look after endanger
5 develop promise encourage promote
6 disrupt improve cultivate make better
7 restore resume establish restart
8 undermine sour weaken allow

MULTIWORD VERBS

Match the sentence halves.

1 We arrived at 7.58 and the train set
2 Let's set
3 I need to catch
4 Alicia drew
5 I was looking for
6 I'm looking
7 I'm going to carry
8 I need to switch

a) forward to seeing you next week.
b) up the new contract while we continued discussing the schedule.
c) off at eight o'clock. We barely made it!
d) up with Freda – she's way ahead of me.
e) on the printer. Is that OK with you?
f) on working until I finish.
g) Ramon this morning, but I didn't see him.
h) up a meeting for Tuesday.

WRITING

Read the note and the background information. Write an e-mail of 75–100 words from Tom Jordan to João Pereira. Say who advised you to e-mail and why you're writing; explain your work and suggest a meeting.

> Tom,
> If you want to talk to someone about Brazil's petroleum industry, e-mail João Pereira (jdp44@brazchem.com). He can probably give you some facts and figures. Tell him that Judy Milligan suggested you get in touch. I worked with João in Dubai a few years ago.
> Best,
> Judy

Information about you:

- job – a business journalist
- current project – research on how various industries are coping with the current economic climate
- plan – produce a documentary film for TV
- Judy Milligan – old friend of yours
- travel plans – you'll be in São Paulo next month

Cultures 1: Doing business internationally

Complete the sentences below with the words in the box.

direct	flexible	local	patient	product	relax	reliable	rip-off

1 It's important to listen to people who have .... knowledge.

2 The .... has to be right for the market.

3 You have to get the price right. Having a product that's high-end is OK, but if people think it's a ...., that's a real problem.

4 If you want to have a good reputation, you have to be .... and do what you say you'll do.

5 It's important to be .... when you're negotiating. In many cultures, it takes time build a relationship before you can talk business.

6 When you do business in Russia, it's important to .... and socialise.

7 The extent to which people are .... varies considerably across cultures. In some places, you have to pay careful attention even to understand if the person is saying yes. In other places, people may seem very abrupt when they say what's on their mind.

8 It's extremely important to be .... when doing business internationally.

Small talk

Objectives

Speaking

- Can engage in extended conversation in a clearly participatory fashion on most general topics.
- Can use stock phrases to gain time and keep the turn whilst formulating what to say.
- Can initiate, maintain and end discourse naturally with effective turn-taking.

Listening

- Can follow much of an everyday conversation if speakers avoid very idiomatic usage.
- Can understand main points and check comprehension by using contextual clues.

Lesson deliverable

To participate in an activity to practise small talk in a business context.

Performance review

To review your own progress and performance against your objectives at the end of the lesson.

A SPEAKING

A colleague is preparing to attend an international conference. What tips and advice would you give on the following topics.

- Making small talk
- Dealing with communication problems
- The importance of body language
- Strategies to keep a conversation moving

B READING

What potential differences in cultural behaviour does each of these comments highlight? Compare similarities or differences in approach to your own culture.

1 Every time there was a short silence, my colleague had to say something. He was talking about nothing. It was very annoying.

2 I started talking about football, but he did not seem very interested, so I changed the subject to the weather. That must be safe I thought, but he excused himself and went to speak to someone else. I couldn't understand it.

3 When he said he was interested in my products, I gave him the 'thumbs up' sign and he looked at me shocked. I don't know why I didn't get the contract.

4 People in the group seemed happy to stand really close to each other, but it made me feel uncomfortable.

C LISTENING

1 BSA1.1.1 Listen to the first conversation and answer these questions.

1 How does Jeff introduce himself to Professor Chaudri?

2 How does Jeff react to a question about his personal life?

3 How does Professor Chaudri handle Jeff's reaction?

4 Why does Professor Chaudri want George's phone number?

2 BSA1.1.2 Listen to the second conversation and answer these questions.

1 How does Chizuko react when Wayne greets her? Why do you think this is?

2 How does Jeff stop Wayne talking about meeting Ms Hayashi before?

3 How does Jeff offer to help Ms Hayashi?

3 BSA1.1.3 Listen to the third conversation and answer these questions.

1 Who finds it difficult to join in the conversation? Why do you think this is?

2 How do the others try to help this person?

3 Who does not seem to be aware of Mr Chen's difficulty?

4 Listen to the three conversations again and make notes of useful language you can use when you are participating in small talk.

Task

Pre-task: Discussion

In pairs, discuss the strategies you can use to introduce yourself confidently to a person or group of people who are already chatting. What would be good questions to break the ice? Suggest some suitable topics to talk about with someone new.

Part 1: Preparation

Context: You are going to attend an international conference. You met some of the people at the conference last year. Your aim is to find potential overseas business contacts and reconnect with some you've already met.

1 **Work in two groups, A and B. Within your group, half of you attended the conference last year and will know some people from the other group. The rest of you will be attending for the first time. Assign roles.**

2 **In your groups, plan and practise how you are going to make conversation with members of the other group. Think about the following points.**
- How to introduce yourselves to new people and those you have met before
- How to introduce someone else into the conversation to make sure everyone participates
- How to ask for help/advice/information from people you meet and give helpful information when asked.
- If you wish, choose a question that might embarrass or be uncomfortable for the people you meet. Don't be afraid to ask questions that may be difficult in a social situation. Think about how to deal with tricky situations, how to change the subject smoothly, or how to exit a conversation politely.

Part 2: Small talk

The two groups meet at lunchtime during the conference. Each person from Group A finds someone from Group B and spends a few minutes talking to that person and trying to find the help, advice and information he or she requires. Then introduce another person into the conversation and make sure that they participate fully.

Part 3: Reporting back

Return to your original group and report how your meetings went and what you achieved from the conversations.

D PEER REVIEW

Look at the objectives again at the beginning of the lesson and think about the conversations you had.

- Were you able to engage in extended conversation on most topics?
- Could you use stock phrases to gain time and keep the conversation going whilst formulating what to say?
- How did your partner(s) perform?
- What observations would you make about your partner's body language?
- What can you and your partner(s) do to improve your skills?

E SELF-ASSESSMENT

Write 120–140 words about your performance. Think about:

- how well you achieved the objective
- feedback from your partners
- tricky situations you faced
- how body language affected the conversations
- what you can do to improve

F PROFESSIONAL DEVELOPMENT AND PERFORMANCE GOALS

Think of opportunities you can exploit to practise and improve your skills both inside and outside the classroom.

Write a few sentences about ways of improving your small-talk skills.

1.2 E-mails

Objectives

Writing

- Can write an e-mail, giving some detail of work-related news and events.
- Can respond to work-related e-mails, clearly addressing the sender's points and arguments.
- Can respond effectively to e-mails requesting work-related information.

Reading

Can infer the meaning of words from context in work-related documents on familiar topics.

Lesson deliverable

To write two e-mails giving detailed information in a work-related context.

Performance review

To review your own progress and performance against your objectives at the end of the lesson.

A SPEAKING

In pairs or small groups, discuss the headline below. How would you answer the question? Why?

Is e-mail better than face-to-face meetings for problem solving in international teams?

B LISTENING AND WRITING

1 **BSA1.2.4 Listen to John Harrison talking to a journalist.**

   1 Write the three big advantages that John Harrison describes.

   2 Work in pairs. Discuss these three big advantages. How far do you agree? Why?

2 **In an article, John Harrison lists some strategies. Discuss these with a partner.**

Strategies for writing effective e-mails about project problems

1. Attach additional documents which make the nature of a problem clear
2. Flag what has been done successfully and do not concentrate only on problems
3. Explain the current problem clearly
4. Confirm consequences of problem(s)
5. Give clear recommendations
6. Acknowledge the difficulty of finding a solution to complex problems

C READING

1 **Paul Tuck is leading an international project to implement standard software across a global organisation. This project has sub-projects in two countries. Read the two e-mails and complete the summary below.**

Sub-project summary

	Italy	Poland
Current status and problems		
Recommended solutions		

1

From: Elio

To: Paul

Subject: Project update

Dear Paul

Just to update you on the status of the project. We're currently running on schedule in Italy, but I'm worried. To be honest, I don't think we will be able to keep it up. One project member is leaving the company next month and we have no replacement. We're also running into a busy time with local initiatives and this will definitely impact our ability to deliver. As we discussed last month, extending the project deadline by two months at this stage would be sensible and my clear recommendations are to go for this.

To pick up at the meeting next week.

Elio

2

From: Slawek

To: Paul

Subject: Project review urgently needed

Dear Paul

Please find a detailed project update attached from the organisation in Poland. As you will see, we have run up against technical problems: we can't get the new software to function in a stable way here and this means we have cost issues and are falling further behind schedule.

In terms of solutions, if we want to hit the deadline, which we need to do in Poland with other projects starting soon, then we need to invest more in resources now and buy more consulting hours to get the current problems solved. I realise this will not be popular, but we need to invest to work things out.

I think it would be useful to have a 1:1 in advance of the project team meeting next week. Would you have a second tomorrow to catch up?

Slawek

2 Work in pairs. Re-read the list of strategies in Exercise B2 and find examples of them in the two e-mails. Not all strategies are included.

D WRITING

Write a response to Elio's e-mail about the Italian project. Use strategies learnt in Exercise B2. Turn to page vi for a model answer.

Task

E-mail 1

You are working on an international project. You have to send a regular e-mail to the project leader with a brief update of project achievements together with any problems and solutions.

1 **Work in two groups. Think about:**
- the name and scope of your project
- the name of the project leader who needs this report
- which achievements you want to list
- which problems you want to mention and how much detail to give about each problem
- what ideas to suggest for solutions
- how to propose the best way of continuing the discussion

2 **Then in pairs within your group write the e-mail. Think about:**
- how to start the e-mail and explain its objective
- where to put the paragraphs
- how to conclude

3 **Give your e-mail to a pair from the other group.**

E-mail 2

1 **Work in pairs. Read the e-mail you have been given and write a reply. Think about:**
- how to respond to any project achievements listed
- how to respond to any problems and solutions
- how to continue the discussion (by e-mail, phone, 1:1, etc.)

2 **When you have finished, give your reply back to the pair from the other group.**

E PEER REVIEW

In small groups, evaluate the e-mails you received:

- Were they clear, professional and polite?
- Did they set out the problem clearly?
- Did they outline possible consequences and solutions?

F SELF-ASSESSMENT

Look at the e-mails you wrote and received in this lesson and look at the lesson objectives. Write a list of language and strategies that you used effectively.

G PROFESSIONAL DEVELOPMENT AND PERFORMANCE GOALS

Find two recent examples of e-mails you have received asking for detailed information. How can you use the skills you have learnt and practised in this section to respond effectively? Complete the sentences to create an action plan.

1 To be clearer, one thing I will do to improve is ...

2 To have more influence and impact, I will ...

3 To ensure I come across as polite and professional, I will ...

UNIT 4

Success

'It is not enough to succeed. Others must be seen to fail.'
Gore Vidal, US writer

OVERVIEW

VOCABULARY
Prefixes

listening
Successful businesses

READING
Carlos Slim

LANGUAGE REVIEW
Present and past tenses

SKILLS
Negotiating

CASE STUDY
Kensington United

STARTING UP

charisma
dedication
discipline
drive
imagination
looks
luck
money
nepotism
ruthlessness

A **What makes people successful? Add four more words to the list in the box on the left. Then choose the five most important.**

B **Talk about a person you know who is successful. Why are they successful?**

C **What are the best indicators of an individual's level of success? How important are the following in your culture?**

exotic holidays	cosmetic surgery	chauffeur-driven car(s)
designer clothes	expensive jewellery	mixing with famous people
pedigree pets	luxury home(s)	exclusive club membership
trophy partner	domestic help	having your name in the media

brand
customer
headquarters
innovation
leader
people
profit
shares
subsidiaries
workforce

D **Complete these statements with the words from the box on the left. Then discuss with a partner which three statements are the best indicators of a successful business.**

A successful business ...

1 is always making money and increasing its ....
2 is often the market ....
3 is moving forward and interested in ....
4 has a motivated ....
5 has a loyal .... base.
6 has a world-famous .... and an instantly recognisable logo.
7 issues .... which are worth millions on the stock market.
8 has its .... in a prestigious location.
9 has branches and .... all over the world.
10 treats its employees well and is ....-orientated.

VOCABULARY
Prefixes

A **Read this news report and identify nine common prefixes.**

example: multinational

Rabbit, the successful mobile phone company, has renamed itself ChitChat Media as part of its effort to establish itself worldwide. Although some industry commentators see the name change as risky and an indication of their overconfidence, the company continues to outperform all its rivals in the competitive telecoms market. In a statement, co-founder and CEO Markus Danton said that it was an exciting time for the company and that its achievements had been underestimated in the past. He went on to say, 'We are an ultramodern company taking the next logical step to achieve our aim of becoming the leading company in the sector worldwide.'

He denied reports of problems in the recently entered Asian markets, claiming journalists had been misinformed. His ex-business partner Darius Schnell, who left the company less than three months ago, was not available for comment. Many experts feel Mr Schnell's contributions to the success of the company have been devalued in recent press reports since his hasty exit last November.

B **Match the prefixes in Exercise A to these meanings.**

1 too much
2 better / more than
3 badly
4 extremely
5 former
6 opposite
7 with
8 too little
9 again

C **Cross out the word in each group that does not follow the prefix in bold.**

1 **under** perform / rate / charge / ~~profit~~
2 **co** producer / worker / boss / author
3 **re** launch / engineer / locate / decide
4 **over** spend / lose / estimate / supply
5 **mis** manage / judge / look / calculate
6 **out** win / produce / bid / class
7 **ultra** efficient / cautious / modern / big
8 **ex** boss / director / employee / staff
9 **de** merge / grow / nationalise / regulate

D **Complete these sentences with words from Exercise C in the correct form.**

1 Several sales staff underperformed last year and didn't meet their targets.
2 Smith and Turner were the two .... of the report.
3 We will .... our product as soon as we have finished the modifications.
4 Sales were very disappointing. We .... the number of people who would buy our product in Asia.
5 Because the company has been .... for years, we are close to bankruptcy.
6 It was an expensive acquisition. They had to .... their rivals to take over the company.
7 Our .... factory has state-of-the-art machinery.
8 My .... was impossible to work with, so I left the company.
9 There is much more competition in .... financial markets.

E **Discuss these statements.**

1 Outselling your rivals is the best indicator of success.
2 Mismanagement is the biggest cause of business failure.
3 Rebranding is often a pointless exercise.
4 Underfunding and overstaffing are the quickest way to failure.
5 Undercutting the competition is a dangerous business strategy.

See the ***DVD-ROM*** *for the i-Glossary.*

LISTENING
Successful businesses

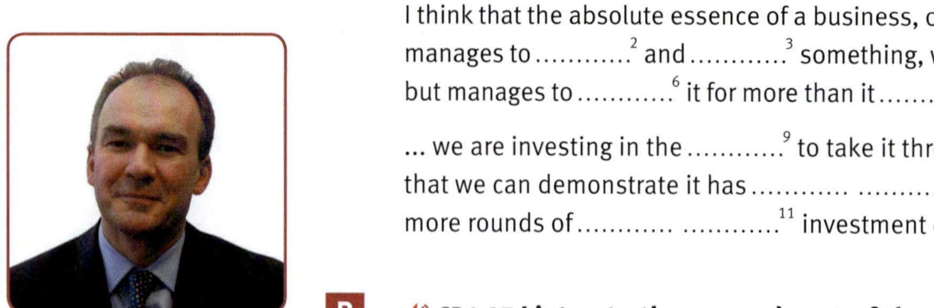

Tom Hockaday

A CD1.26 **Isis Innovation is a technology development company owned by the University of Oxford. Listen to Tom Hockaday, its Managing Director, talking about the essential qualities of a successful business and complete the gaps in these two extracts.**

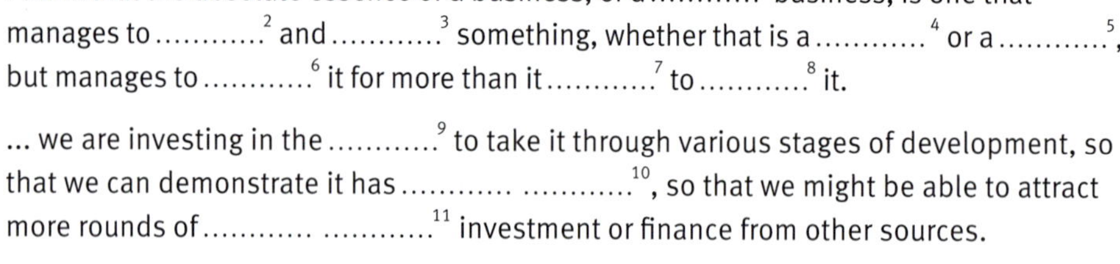

I think that the absolute essence of a business, or a ....[1] business, is one that manages to ....[2] and ....[3] something, whether that is a ....[4] or a ....[5], but manages to ....[6] it for more than it ....[7] to ....[8] it.

... we are investing in the ....[9] to take it through various stages of development, so that we can demonstrate it has ....[10], so that we might be able to attract more rounds of ....[11] investment or finance from other sources.

B CD1.27 **Listen to the second part of the interview and summarise in a short paragraph what Tom says about Natural Motion – the type of company it is, what it does and the reasons for its success.**

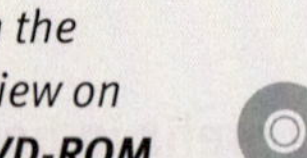

Watch the interview on the ***DVD-ROM.***

C CD1.28 **Listen to the final part of the interview and answer these questions.**

1 Which types of business does Tom expect to succeed in the near future?
2 Which four examples does he give?

READING
Carlos Slim

A **Read the article on the opposite page and correct the six mistakes in this paragraph about Carlos Slim.**

Carlos Slim is probably the richest man you have ever heard of. The major influences on his life were his father, Julián, who was born in Mexico, and Jean Paul Getty. He studied finance at Harvard University and on graduating set up as a stockbroker. He made a lot Of money in the Mexican recession of 1982, selling his assets in the middle of the crisis. In 1990, Slim gained control of Telmex, which owns 90% of Mexican telephone lines and is the largest part of Slim's empire. Slim is also involved in charity through his Carso Foundation.

B **Match the words on the left with words on the right to form word partnerships. Then check your answers in the article.**

1	business	a)	spree
2	economic	b)	acumen
3	annual	c)	recession
4	retail	d)	point
5	turning	e)	sales
6	buying	f)	outlets
7	global	g)	crisis

C **Complete this text with the word partnerships from Exercise B.**

In 2008, influenced by China's success and its appetite for commodities, shipowners went on a ....[1], and ....[2] of vessels reached an all-time high. The ....[3] came the following year with the housing crisis, credit crunch and ....[4] in the United States, which led to a ....[5]. Orders for ships dried up, and department stores and ....[6] throughout the world had empty shelves. However, business is recovering and there has been a transformation of the industry from one that relied almost exclusively on a shipowner's innate ....[7] to today's highly sophisticated finance-based industry.

D **If you had Carlos Slim's money, what kind of businesses would you buy? What kind of lifestyle would you lead?**

Profile: Carlos Slim

by James Quinn

Carlos Slim is either the world's richest or second-richest man, with a fortune estimated to be in excess of $67bn. Possibly the richest man you've never heard of, until recently his influence had largely been restricted to his native Latin America, where his sprawling family empire controls more than 200 companies, spanning everything from banking and retail to telecoms, road-building and restaurants. But given the size of his fortune, he was unlikely to stay local for long. In recent years, he has begun to stretch his increasingly long tentacles north of the border and into the United States, and this week took the American intelligentsia somewhat by surprise by revealing plans to inject $250m into the *New York Times*.

Slim puts his success down to his admiration for his father Julián – who emigrated from the Lebanon aged 14 and made his fortune investing in property in the 1910–17 Mexican revolution – and to American oil billionaire Jean Paul Getty. Slim learned of Getty's business acumen as a young boy and has gone on to mirror his ability to make money.

Aged 11, he invested in government saving bonds, keeping a detailed ledger to track all of his purchases. By 15, he had bought a very small shareholding in Banco Nacional de México – then the largest bank in Mexico, and one to which he has recently been linked with buying, as the current owner Citigroup looks to divest some of its assets.

While studying civil engineering at university in Mexico City, he realised the way to make money was from investing in companies, and so set up on his own as a stockbroker on graduation, working 14-hour days.

It was not until the Mexican recession of 1982 that Slim really began to make some money, taking advantage of a nationwide 'fire sale' of assets by local and foreign investors alike, looking to sell in the midst of one of the country's worst economic crises.

The period led to the formation of one of the key parts of Slim's empire – Grupo Carso, which today has annual sales of $8.5bn a year and owns retail outlets such as Sanborns and Sears, as well as a wide range of manufacturing businesses.

Eight years later, in 1990, came the second major turning point in Slim's career when Mexico decided to privatise its national telecoms company. Slim went head to head with America's Southwestern Bell, France Telecom and as many as 35 other domestic investors, but managed to seize control of Telmex.

Some 90 per cent of the telephone lines in Mexico are today operated by Telmex. But it is the low-cost mobile phone network América Móvil, which he also controls, which has grown to be the most substantial part of his empire, opening up other parts of Latin America to mobile telephony. It now operates in 11 countries, including Brazil, Ecuador and Guatemala.

Many commentators believe that his recent buying spree is part of a desire to replicate what he did in Mexico in the 1980s on a world stage, taking advantage of the global recession by investing in distressed assets at knock-down prices while he can.

In spite of his obvious wealth, he remains frugal in his tastes, and is often seen wearing a plastic-effect wristwatch which doubles as a calculator. His clothes tend to be bought from the many retailers his empire owns.

Over the next four years, he has committed to spend $10bn through his charitable Carso Foundation, whose main aim is to fight marginalisation and poverty by investing in health, education and employment.

from *The Telegraph*

LANGUAGE REVIEW

Present and past tenses

Complete the rules with the words *present simple, present continuous, present perfect, past perfect* or *past simple.*

1 We use the .... to describe actions and situations which are generally true.
*Carlos Slim **is** worth about $67bn.*

2 We use the .... to describe completed actions or events which took place at a particular time or over a period of time in the past.
*Slim **bought** Telmex in 1990.*

3 We use the .... to describe current or temporary situations.
*Petrol **is getting** more expensive by the week.*
*At the moment, Slim **is writing** a book about his family.*

4 We use the .... to describe life experiences, the present results of past actions or to announce news.
*The company **has done** well recently.*
*In recent years, Slim **has devolved** power to his family.*

5 We use the .... to describe an action which is completed before a time in the past.
*The office **had closed** by the time we got there.*

➡ ***Grammar reference*** page 147

A **Label the tenses in these sentences based on the article on page 39 and say why those tenses are used.**

1 In recent years, Slim has begun to stretch his tentacles north.

2 Aged 11, he invested in government saving bonds.

3 He remains frugal in his tastes.

4 By 15, he had bought a very small shareholding in Banco Nacional de México.

5 Slim is currently looking at investing in distressed assets.

B **Write an article about Apple for a business magazine. Use these notes, putting the verbs in brackets into appropriate tenses.**

THE COMPANY

- (*reinvent*) the personal computer with the Macintosh in 1980s
- (*have*) highest brand loyalty of any computer manufacturer
- (*operate*) more than 250 retail stores
- (*have*) informal culture

HISTORY

- (*start*) in Cupertino, California, April 1, 1976
- October 23, 2001: (*introduce*) the iPod digital music player
- Since it was formed 1976, (*employ*) over 75,000 people worldwide

RECENT EVENTS

- Recently (*rank*) first as most admired company overall in Fortune survey
- People in survey by CoolBrands recently (*vote*) the iPhone as world's coolest brand
- September 28, 2009 downloads from App Store (*surpass*) 2 billion

WHAT IT IS DOING NOW

- Currently (*experience*) the greatest expansion in its history
- Now (*focus*) on its software more than ever
- At time of writing, (*offer*) students a free iPod Touch with the purchase of a MacBook

C **Research Carlos Slim on the Internet and write a final paragraph for the article on page 39 saying what he is doing now.**

SKILLS

Negotiating

A **Three key skills in negotiating are:**

1 bargaining

2 checking understanding

3 signalling (drawing attention to what you're about to say).

Study the examples of each in the Useful language box below.

B CD1.29 **Listen to a negotiation between an exporter of Turkish rugs and the Head Buyer of a chain of department stores. Answer these questions.**

1 What agreement do the exporter and buyer reach concerning a) quantity, and b) discount?

2 What delivery date does the buyer want? Is she sure to get what she wants?

C CD1.29 **Listen again and complete these sentences.**

1 If you place an order for only 50 rugs, we can offer you a .... of 5% ...

2 'Supposing we increased our order for your .... rugs, what discount would you give us?'
'Well, what sort of quantity do you have ....?'

3 'OK, if we ordered 100 rugs, made in Esme, would you .... the discount?'
'No, not double it, but we'd be .... to increase it to 7%. That's pretty generous I'd say.'
'That sounds fairly ....'

4 'Could you get the rugs to us by the end of this month?'
'Mmm, that's .... – I honestly don't know.'

5 I'd like to make a .... I'd be .... to place an order for 150 standard rugs if you could give us a discount of 10% ...

6 OK, if I'm certain we can supply you that quantity by the end of the month, you've got .... We'll give you 10% off .... for that amount.

D **Look at the audio script on page** 157 **and find an example each of checking understanding and signalling language.**

E **Role-play this situation.**

A Spanish manufacturer has produced a new range of expensive leather briefcases. A Swiss retailer is considering placing an order for 300 of each design. The Sales Manager and Chief Buyer negotiate the contract.

Student A: Turn to page 133.
Student B: Turn to page 142.

USEFUL LANGUAGE

BARGAINING

If you increase your order, we'll give you a bigger discount.

We can deliver by that date, providing we have the goods in stock.

If we lowered the price, would you be prepared to increase your order?

CHECKING UNDERSTANDING

Sorry, could you repeat that?

Are you saying you don't have that quantity in stock?

So what you're saying is you'll ...

SIGNALLING

I'd like to make a suggestion. I think we should leave this point and come back to it later.

I want to ask a question. How are we going to pay for this?

4 Case study

A major English football club needs to agree a new sponsorship deal to ensure its continuing success

Background

Kensington United is one of the great success stories in English football. Today, it is in second place in the Premier Division and has reached the third round of the European Champions League competition. The club regularly attracts over 40,000 spectators at its home matches, and its Italian manager, Marco Conti, is adored by fans. Kensington United is also a commercial success and is very profitable.

What has brought about its success? Firstly, Marco Conti had a clear strategy for the team from the start. He developed young players who had come through the club's youth training scheme. The team was also strengthened by one or two carefully chosen foreign players.

CD1.30 Listen to an interview on *Sportsline*, a weekly TV programme focusing on football. The presenter talks to a football manager about Kensington United. Take notes of the key points.

Current situation

Kensington's current four-year sponsorship deal with an insurance company is about to finish. Ingrid Tauber, the club's Commercial Director, is considering a new and better deal with Universal Communications plc, the powerful media group. It is not only the increased money from sponsorship which appeals to Kensington United, however. Universal Communications' broad range of business activities would offer many other opportunities to increase revenue.

Universal Communications is interested in Kensington because the club's success has brought it over four million fans in the UK and 40 million in Asia. Kensington played a friendly match recently in India, which was shown on television. Another friendly match in China attracted a TV audience of over 250 million. The team's popularity in those countries would help Universal Communications to boost sales of its mobile phones in Asia.

Representatives of Kensington United and Universal Communications are meeting shortly to discuss a possible sponsorship deal.

Task

You are members of the negotiating team of either Kensington United (turn to page 133) or Universal Communications (turn to page 141).

1 Read your role card and prepare for the negotiation. Work out your objectives, priorities, strategy and tactics. Think carefully about what concessions you are willing to make. An agenda has been prepared (see right).

2 Do the negotiation.

AGENDA

Date: 10 May Time: 10 a.m.
Venue: Conference room, Kensington Football Ground

1 Total value of the contract
2 Timing of payments
3 Advertising
4 Control of players and club activities
5 Control of spectators
6 Official supplier of Kensington football boots
7 Other commercial opportunities
8 Fringe benefits for players
9 Other points

CD1.31 Listen to the excerpt from the radio programme *Sporting World*. How does it affect the result of your negotiation?

Watch the Case study commentary on the ***DVD-ROM.***

Writing

If the negotiation was successful, write a press release from the point of view of either Kensington United or Universal Communications outlining the main points of the agreement and the benefits to the organisation you represent. The tone and style of the message should express pleasure and optimism.

OR

If the negotiation was unsuccessful, write a letter to your opposite number in the negotiation expressing your regret that you were unable to make a deal. However, you should indicate that you might be willing to reopen negotiations in the future, as clearly there could be areas of mutual benefit.

➜ *Writing file* pages 126 and 128

UNIT **5**

Job satisfaction

'A man can stand anything except a succession of ordinary days.'
Johan Wolfgang Goethe (1749–1832), German writer

OVERVIEW

STARTING UP

A **Which of these factors would motivate you to work harder? Choose your top five and rank them in order of priority. Explain your priorities.**

bonus	more responsibility	working for a successful company
bigger salary	threat of redundancy	better working environment
commission	hard-working boss	promotion opportunities
praise	supportive colleagues	more time off
important job title	perks	more flexible working hours

B CD2.1, 2.2, 2.3 **Listen to three people talking about their motivation at work. Which of the factors in Exercise A do they mention? Who do/would you agree with?**

C **Discuss these questions.**

1. For what reasons might you change jobs? How often do you expect to do so in your lifetime? Is changing jobs often a sign of success in your culture?
2. A recent US survey showed children preferred parents to go out and earn money rather than spend more time with them. What does this show, in your opinion?
3. Would you prefer a male or female boss? Why?

D **Turn to page 134 and do the quiz 'Are you in danger of burning out?'.**

VOCABULARY

Synonyms and word-building

A **Look at the sentences below. Underline the words or phrases which can be replaced with an item from the box without a change in meaning.**

assessment breakdown empowerment fringe benefits red tape remuneration severance payment ~~take industrial action~~

1 If employees become too discontent, they may go on strike. *take industrial action*

2 Most people like to have control over their work and therefore put autonomy near the top of their list of motivating factors.

3 Dealing with bureaucracy is a very time-consuming, demotivating problem which affects large businesses and organisations.

4 Overwork can lead to burnout if not spotted early.

5 Many job satisfaction studies, perhaps surprisingly, have found that often a compensation package is not the most motivating factor for many employees.

6 Offering perks rather than a salary increase can be a way of retaining employees in traditionally high staff turnover industries.

7 He received a very generous golden handshake when he left the company.

8 One way for managers to monitor and develop staff is by using appraisal interviews.

B **Complete each of these sentences with a word formed from the verb on the left. Sometimes you will need to use a negative form.**

1 a) The survey showed that staff working flexible hours were more *satisfied* with their jobs than those working fixed hours.

b) Low pay and poor working conditions create .... workers.

c) Small European companies are top of job .... league tables.

motivate

2 a) What are the strongest .... factors in people's lives?

b) Workers become .... if they work long hours for low pay.

c) What was your .... for becoming a salesperson?

frustrate

3 a) You could see the .... building up in the workforce.

b) I find talking to him .... because he never listens.

c) I felt so .... with their attitude that I decided to resign.

recognise

4 a) Employees are more likely to change jobs if they feel their work is .... or that others take credit for it.

b) Because of her people skills, she was able to achieve .... and respect at the company.

c) The company .... his lifelong service on retirement with a formal dinner and a substantial golden handshake.

C **Discuss these questions.**

1 What do you find satisfying and frustrating about your work or studies?

2 How true do you think these statements are?

a) There is no such thing as company loyalty these days.

b) Only successful people can have a good work–life balance.

c) Job satisfaction is about personality, not external factors.

d) Job satisfaction increases with age.

e) Improvements in technology lead to greater job satisfaction.

f) Job sharing and job rotation are not good for motivation.

g) People who work from home tend to work harder than people who don't.

LISTENING
Staff motivation

Madalyn Brooks

Watch the *interview on the* ***DVD-ROM.***

A CD2.4 **Listen to Madalyn Brooks, Director of Human Resources at Procter & Gamble (UK), and answer these questions.**

1 What is the key to a successful business?

2 What are the two main ways in which Procter & Gamble drives job satisfaction?

B CD2.5 **Madalyn says that job priorities have changed in three areas over the last years. Listen to the second part of the interview and take notes on what she says under these headings.**

1 flexibility

2 the drive for personal learning and growth

3 working for socially responsible organisations

C CD2.6 **Listen to Madalyn talking about what people want. Do not take notes while listening. Afterwards, write down in one minute as many things as you can remember that people want. Compare your answers with a partner. Who remembered the most things?**

READING
Working for the best companies

A **You are going to read an article from** *The* ***Sunday Times*** **survey** ***The 100 Best Companies To Work For.*** **What would you look for in your ideal company?**

B **Work in pairs.**

Student A: Read Article A on the opposite page.
Student B: Turn to page 135 and read Article B.

Choose five points that you think make the company in your article a good one to work for. Take notes on those points and then tell your partner, without looking back at the article.

C **Ask your partner questions about their company, so that you can work out together whether these statements are true or false (M = Marriott Hotels International, K = KPMG).**

1 Over 70% of staff at K and M think that their training is of great benefit.

2 M scores lower on opportunities for personal growth than K.

3 Less than half the staff in M and K earn more than £35,000.

4 M and K both offer childcare vouchers and contributory pensions.

5 K has more than double the annual sales of M.

6 K employs a higher percentage of women than M.

7 M and K have a fairly similar-size workforce.

8 More than half the staff in M and K earn £15,000 or more.

D **In pairs, look at Article A to find word partnerships with** ***basic, role, performance*** **and** ***paternity.*** **Then look at Article B to find word partnerships with** ***career, childcare, medical*** **and** ***pension.***

Article A

Marriott Hotels International

Hospitality and lodging

Annual sales	£550m
Staff numbers	11,157
Male/female ratio	48:52
Average age	31
Staff turnover	36%
Earning £35,000+	4%
Typical job	Food and beverage associate

Marriott checks in ten places higher up our list this year thanks to its five-star treatment of staff. Employees award the family-run hospitality business the highest positive score in our survey – 76% – for loving their work here.

It may not be the biggest payer (three-quarters of workers get a basic salary of £15,000 or less), but staff have fun (83%), think the job is good for their personal growth (77%) and are happy with the balance between work and home life (66%).

Employees also feel they can make a difference in the organisation (73%), make a valuable contribution to its success (76%) and are excited about where the company is going (69%).

The worldwide group, which employs more than 11,000 staff, ranks second out of all 20 organisations on questions about what staff think of the company and their colleagues and third for their positive views of managers.

There is a culture of respect and recognition, and there is training specifically on teamwork, a quality prized by the company. Marriott even uses psychosometric testing to assess how well managers align to its nine core organisational competencies. Staff say that senior managers truly live the values of the organisation (71%), help them fulfil their potential and motivate them to give their best every day (71% and 70%, both top scores). They say the managers are excellent role models and regularly show appreciation, winning positive scores of 69% and 75% respectively, results bettered in both cases by only one other firm.

The company, where the average length of service for general managers is 17 years, likes to promote from within. Its performance review process creates a development plan for every member of staff and identifies their training needs. On-the-job training is a key feature of development, and there are NVQ programmes for accredited qualifications, with staff saying this training is of great benefit to them (72%).

Rewards for outstanding contribution and long service, plus an annual staff appreciation week and quarterly social activities, reinforce the value Marriott places on its people. In the year to August 2008, the firm spent £355,000 on fun events for employees, who go out of their way to help each other (76%).

Staff have free use of the hotel leisure clubs and access to a confidential helpline if they have any personal worries. All this helps promote a strong sense of wellbeing. Stress isn't a problem (76%), workers say they are not under so much pressure they can't concentrate (72%) or that they can't perform well (70%, the second-highest score).

Benefits include between 20 and 25 days' basic holiday, two weeks' paternity leave on 90% of pay, childcare vouchers, dental insurance, critical illness cover, life assurance and a contributory pension. Employees say Marriott is run on strong principles (75%) by an inspirational boss (71%), and that they are proud to work for it (79%).

E **In pairs, complete these sentences with some of the word partnerships from Exercise D.**

1 You need to compare various .... policies online.

2 The government's new .... is designed to prevent widespread old-age poverty.

3 Ask Human Resources for the proper forms a month before your ....

4 Many fathers do not take up their .... entitlement.

5 .... does not include overtime, bonuses, commission or travel allowance.

F **In groups, discuss which company you would prefer to work for and why.**

LANGUAGE REVIEW

Passives

- We use the passive when we are not interested in who performs an action or it is not necessary to know.
  *Information about the takeover **had been leaked** to the press.*
- We often use it to describe processes and procedures because we are more interested in the process itself than who carries it out.
  *The bottles **are filled** before the labels are put on.*
- We use the passive to write in a more formal style because it is less personal than the active. It is often used in reports, minutes and business correspondence.
  *Your application **has been forwarded** to the Human Resources Department.*

➡ *Grammar reference* page 148

A **Match each tense or verb form (1–8) to the appropriate extract (a–h).**

1 present simple
2 past simple
3 present perfect
4 past perfect
5 present continuous
6 future simple
7 modal verbs with passives
8 passive infinitives

a) The report stated that more employees *should be encouraged* to provide feedback on management.
b) Employees felt their jobs *had been made* more interesting through training.
c) The minutes *are* always *taken* by a member of HR.
d) The survey stated that employees become unhappy when they feel that their concerns *are being ignored* by management.
e) The performance reviews *were carried out* over the summer.
f) They were happy *to be accepted* on the fast-track programme.
g) Employees *will* now *be expected* to act on the reviewers' suggestions as soon as possible.
h) Bonuses and other incentive programmes *have been cut* since the recession.

B **Complete this extract with passive forms of the verbs in brackets.**

Over time, job satisfaction ....[1] (*define*) in a number of ways. Edwin Locke said that job satisfaction ....[2] (*determine*) by the difference between what one wants in a job and what one has in a job. Herzberg states that satisfaction and dissatisfaction ....[3] (*drive*) by different things – motivation and 'hygiene' factors (such as pay), respectively. Motivation ....[4] (*can / see*) as an inner force that drives people to perform. One of the most famous ways of measuring job satisfaction is the Minnesota Job Satisfaction Questionnaire, which ....[5] (*create*) in 1963. Some researchers say that people who ....[6] (*satisfy*) with life tend to ....[7] (*satisfy*) with their job.

C **Read these notes for four sections of a report on employee satisfaction. Then write sentences, using the passive, to include in the report.**

example: *Questionnaires were distributed to all departments.*

PROCEDURE
- Distribute anonymous employee satisfaction questionnaires: all departments
- Interview union representatives
- Hold meeting with all Heads of Department

PRESENT PROBLEMS
- Management ignore suggestions/ complaints
- Not encourage staff to take on new tasks

MEASURES TO IMPROVE JOB SATISFACTION SINCE APRIL
- Encourage staff to do various tasks
- Adopt open-door policy

RECOMMENDATIONS
- Introduce new performance reviews for managers from 1 December
- Carry out research into new employee incentive programme

SKILLS

Cold-calling

A **A headhunter is a person who finds people with the right skills and experience to do a job, then tries to persuade them to leave their present job. Headhunting often involves cold-calling. When you cold-call, you telephone or visit someone you have never met before and try to sell them something or persuade them to do something. Discuss these questions.**

1 What qualities and skills do you think a headhunter needs to be successful in their job?

2 Do you think that headhunting is an ethical occupation?

B CD2.7 **Patricia Evans, a headhunter, calls Enid Wong concerning a job opportunity. Listen to the conversation and answer these questions.**

1 What is the purpose of Patricia Evans's call?

2 Was the call successful? Why? / Why not?

C CD2.7 **Listen to the conversation again and complete these sentences.**

1 I was given .... by Edward Zhang, I believe you know him quite well.

2 He suggested .... you. He thought you might be interested in a .... that's become .... at KB Financial Services.

3 Would you like to meet to find out .... about the job?

4 I don't think there's .... in us meeting, I'm very happy in this job ...

5 OK, I quite understand. Can you recommend anyone I could contact and .... them .... about the job?

6 Great, ... that. My number's 020 7644 8981.

D CD2.8 **Listen to another conversation in which Patricia Evans calls Federico González. What does Patricia say about the position and the company to interest Federico? What do they decide to do next?**

E **Look at the audio script of the second conversation on page 158. Underline the expressions that Patricia uses to a) persuade Federico to consider the offer, and b) deal with Federico's objections.**

F **Role-play this situation.**

Barnard Media is looking for a television producer to be in charge of its business programmes. It has hired a headhunter to find a suitable candidate for the job.

Student A: Turn to page 141.
Student B: Turn to page 143.

USEFUL LANGUAGE

COLD-CALLING

Hello, Mr/Mrs/Ms X. My name's ...

I work for Y. I was given your name by ...

SOUNDING PEOPLE OUT

Z suggested I call you. He/She thought you might be interested in ...

I was wondering if you'd be interested in ...

Would you like some information about ... ?

PERSUADING CANDIDATES TO CONSIDER THE OFFER

KB is offering a top salary and great benefits.

It's well over six figures.

It's a very attractive part of the package.

They give staff a substantial bonus – well above the industry average.

Why don't we get together? If you're still interested ...

DEALING WITH OBJECTIONS

People often say that to me, but ...

There's another thing you should bear in mind.

You can look at this in another way.

I take your point, but ...

SHOWING INTEREST

Perhaps we could discuss this face to face?

Can you give me some more details?

I'd like some time to think about this.

5

Case study

Just good friends?

A software company with a 'long hours' culture needs to ensure that staff relationships don't damage behaviour at work

Background

Patrick McGuire, CEO of San Diego-based Techno21, is facing a problem caused by the highly competitive nature of the IT industry. Recently, employees have been working much longer hours than previously and often over weekends. As a result, a number of staff have developed close, personal relationships with each other. Patrick has begun to think that the company may need to introduce a policy to give these employees guidelines concerning their behaviour at work.

Techno21 is a young company with a very relaxed atmosphere, and staff are encouraged to socialise during their free time.

Discuss the advantages and disadvantages of working in this kind of environment.

Relationships at work: three cases

Patrick McGuire's assistant has prepared notes on three cases in which personal relationships have affected staff performance and morale. Read about the cases in preparation for a meeting on managing relationships at work.

1 Promotion application of Judith Fisher

Peter Walters, the Chief Financial Officer, had a close relationship with one of his staff, Judith Fisher, but they broke up. A few months later, Walters had to choose someone to be promoted to be his deputy. Judith Fisher was one of three candidates. She didn't get the job. She claims now that it was because she'd had a personal relationship with Walters which had gone sour. According to her, this was Walters's way of taking revenge. Patrick McGuire and Veronica Simpson (HR Director) took no action. Judith is now threatening to take legal action against the company.

2 The sales conference

At the company's international sales conference, Brad Johnson, a sales manager, met Erica Stewart for the first time. He attended all the discussion groups she was in and always sat at her table at lunch. He texted her repeatedly, inviting her to have a drink or dinner with him. He was clearly very impressed with her.

When they both got back to Head Office, Brad Johnson asked for Erica to be transferred to his sales team. Erica went to see Veronica Simpson in order to reject Johnson's request. However, Veronica strongly advised Erica not to turn down the transfer, saying: 'Brad thinks you have the personal qualities to be a brilliant salesperson. He needs bright young people to strengthen his team and he thinks you're the right person to join his team.' Erica is confused and cannot decide what to do.

3 The loving couple

About a year ago, two colleagues, Lisa Davis and Steffan Olsen, became romantically involved.
They kept their relationship secret – or so they thought. However, the other members of their team suspected something was going on. The team noticed that, at meetings, Lisa and Steffan always supported each other's opinions. Also, they would give each other loving looks or be more tactile than was normal among employees. Their behaviour upset the rest of the team.
A representative of the group talked to the team leader and asked her to do something about it.

CD2.9 Patrick McGuire has come up with a proposal which he wants to discuss with Veronica Simpson. Listen and take notes.

Discussion document

Patrick McGuire's assistant has sent an e-mail outlining the points to be discussed at the next HR meeting.

To: HR Staff
From: Kate Mann
Subject: Tuesday's HR meeting

1 Did we make the right decision concerning Peter Walters and Judith Fisher? What further action, if any, should we take?
2 Did Veronica give Erica Stewart good advice? What should Erica do now?
3 How should the team leader deal with the issue of Lisa and Steffan? She has asked for guidance from HR.
4 Which of Patrick's four options is best for the company?
5 How can we avoid someone gaining an unfair advantage by having a close relationship with a colleague or boss? What action can we take if this happens?

Task

You are members of Techno21's HR Department.

1 In small groups, discuss the questions in the e-mail and note down what action to take in each case.
2 Meet as one group. Try to agree on what decisions to take concerning the questions. One of you should take the role of Veronica and chair the meeting.

Watch the Case study commentary on the ***DVD-ROM.***

Writing

As a member of the HR Department, write a set of guidelines on relationships at work for discussion at the next board meeting.

→ *Writing file* page 129

UNIT 6

Risk

'He who doesn't take risks, doesn't drink champagne.'
Alexander Lebed (1950–2002), Russian general and politician

OVERVIEW

STARTING UP

A **Are you a risk-taker? What risks have you taken?**

B **Which item in each of the categories below carries the most and the least risk? Explain why.**

Travel	Lifestyle	Money	Shopping
car	drinking alcohol	property	online
plane	poor diet	stocks and shares	mail order
train	smoking	savings account	private sales
ship	jogging	cash	auction

C **What sort of risks do businesses face (for example: financial risks, environmental risks)? Can you give some examples?**

VOCABULARY
Describing risk

A **The verbs in the box are used when talking about risk. Check their meanings and put them under the appropriate heading in the table below.**

anticipate calculate eliminate encounter estimate evaluate ~~face~~ foresee gauge identify measure minimise prioritise reduce spread weigh up

predict	meet	assess	manage
	face		

B **Match these sentence halves from newspaper extracts.**

1 During the credit crunch, many businesses ...
2 We can reduce risk ...
3 Trying to minimise risk ...
4 It is impossible to ...
5 It is difficult to foresee the risks ...
6 Actuaries calculate risk ...
7 It is important to consider ...

a) the risks involved when sending staff to work in dangerous locations.
b) in order to advise insurance companies.
c) involved in setting up a new business.
d) eliminate all risk when entering a new market.
e) faced the risk of running out of money.
f) by spreading our lending across more markets.
g) is an important part of business strategy.

C **These adjectives can be used with the word *risk*. Complete them with the missing vowels.**

1 s l _ g h t
2 g r _ _ t
3 m _ n _ s c _ l _
4 c _ n s _ d _ r _ b l _
5 p _ t _ n t _ _ l
6 _ m m _ d _ _ t _
7 h _ g _
8 r _ m _ t _
9 s _ r _ _ _ s
10 n _ g l _ g _ b l _
11 s _ g n _ f _ c _ n t
12 _ m m _ n _ n t
13 s _ b s t _ n t _ _ l
14 t _ r r _ b l _
15 t r _ m _ n d _ _ s

D **Of the adjectives in Exercise C, which describe:**

1 a high level of risk? a low level?
2 a possible future risk? a risk in the very near future?

E **In pairs, talk about the types and levels of risks facing some of the following.**

1 your company/institution
2 a major company/industry in your country
3 your city/town/country
4 a foreign country

See the ***DVD-ROM*** for the i-Glossary.

LISTENING
Managing risks

A CD2.10 **Listen to Steve Fowler, Managing Director of the Institute of Risk Management, and give one example of internal risk and one example of external risk.**

Steve Fowler

B CD2.10 **Listen again and complete the chart.**

C CD2.11 **Listen to the second part of the interview. What are the five key steps to risk management?**

D CD2.12 **Listen to the final part. Which three examples does Steve give of organisations or industries that failed to manage risk? What does he say about each example?**

Watch the interview on the ***DVD-ROM.***

E **Look at the audio scripts on pages** 158–159. **Underline the key words and phrases that Steve uses to structure his answers. Compare your answers with a partner.**

READING
Insuring trade risks

A **Answer these questions.**

1 What things do you and your family insure against?

2 What sort of things do big international companies need to insure against?

B **Read the article on the opposite page quickly and, in as few words as possible, say what the main point of the article is.**

C **Read the article again and answer these questions.**

1 How did the insurance industry start?

2 What do reinsurers do?

3 How do the two examples of major losses in paragraphs 7 and 8 illustrate this quote?

'Countries with an underdeveloped system of insurance suffer immeasurably more from major catastrophes than those where a good part of the material losses can be covered by professional risk carriers.'

D **In your own words, summarise the key points in the numbered examples (1–3) in the article.**

E **Find words in the article which mean the following.**

1 when the maker of a product is responsible for any injury that the product causes (paragraph 4)

2 money that a court orders someone to pay to someone else (paragraph 5)

3 the collection of all policies held by an insurer (paragraph 6)

4 the total combined risks that could be involved in a single loss event (paragraph 7)

5 a terrible event that causes a lot of destruction and suffering (paragraph 9)

F **Complete these sentences with words from Exercise E.**

1 They are being sued for .... by clients who they advised to invest in an insurance company that went bankrupt.

2 The defect in her car caused the accident, and she is suing the company for product ....

3 The region was devastated by a natural ....

4 It's safer to spread your liability by holding a .... of risks.

5 An .... of risk happens when there is a concentration of risks that might give rise to very large losses from a single event.

G **Without looking back at the article, match the words on the left to the phrases on the right to make expressions.**

1	bear	a)	the way
2	spring	b)	the brunt
3	meet	c)	to mind
4	pave	d)	the risks
5	spread	e)	a need

H **Match the expressions in Exercise G to their meanings.**

1 immediately think of something

2 make it possible for something to happen in the future

3 suffer the worst part of something unpleasant

4 reduce the chance of a large loss by sharing risks

5 be good enough to do what someone needs, wants or expects

I **In the next 30 years, which types of risk do you think will become a) more significant, and b) less significant?**

FT

Internationalisation – risk or opportunity?

by Torsten Jeworrek

The internationalisation of the economy is not as recent as the buzzword *globalisation* would have us believe. In fact, it was internationalisation that paved the way for the beginnings of the insurance industry back in the fourteenth century, as shipowners sought to protect the increasing value of their ships and cargoes.

Even today, the complex nature of risks emanating from international trade is one of the insurance industry's most difficult challenges and one that affects all classes of business, as the following examples show:

1 More than 90 per cent of all world trade is transported by sea or other waterways. The largest container ships today, with cargoes of up to 13,000 containers, may be worth far in excess of $1bn. However, even this concentration of value is small compared with that found at the world's great container ports, such as Singapore or Hamburg, which act as depots to goods worth tens of billions of dollars every day.

2 The outsourcing of production sites to low-wage countries does not just reduce costs. It can also reducethe quality of the goods produced. Defective products can result in recall costs or even product liability costs. Recent examples of recalls that spring to mind include toys coated with lead paint and toothpaste contaminated with the antifreeze diethylene glycol.

3 Liability losses can reach extreme proportions when pharmaceutical products cause dangerous side effects in patients. National law in the country where the products are sold plays a key role in this connection. The US, in particular, has seen some extremely high awards for damages.

Insurance companies that cover such large risks need a secondary market where they can place them. Reinsurers assume this function. Sharing the load among several carriers helps to spread the risks. The diversification effects achieved by spreading risks across different regions and classes of business allows reinsurers to balance their portfolios and realise a level of capital efficiency that enables them to cover their clients' risks – and ultimately those of the insured – at a reasonable price.

Extreme losses in the past show just how important the reinsurer's role is. One of the biggest loss events in the history of insurance was on September 11, 2001. The attack on the World Trade Center in New York was a prime example of the complexity of today's risks, with an accumulation of losses across a range of insurance classes such as fire, business interruption, liability, life and health, and compounded by significant capital market losses.

The insurance of large and accumulation risks is a definite advantage for the sustainable development of economies. In countries where insurance is not very far advanced, it is the vulnerable economies and above all the inhabitants that have to bear the brunt of these losses. The tsunami of 2004 not only brought immense human suffering but also caused losses of over US$ 10bn. As the insurance density in the regions affected is still very low, the insurance industry only covered a small percentage of these losses, less than US$ 1bn.

Countries with an underdeveloped system of insurance suffer immeasurably more from major catastrophes than those where a good part of the material losses can be covered by professional risk carriers.

The global economy is increasingly networked and interconnected. Risks are becoming ever more complex, and the insurance industry has to develop new concepts for its clients in order to meet their need for risk cover in this changed environment.

LANGUAGE REVIEW

Adverbs of degree

- We can use adverbs to strengthen the meaning of adjectives.
  *The US has seen some **extremely high** awards for damages.*
- We can also use them to soften the meaning.
  *The report was **slightly critical**.*

➡ ***Grammar reference*** page 148

A **Which of these adverbs strengthen the adjective which follow and which soften it?**

a bit entirely exceptionally extremely fairly fully highly increasingly
moderately quite rather reasonably slightly somewhat totally very

B **Complete these dialogues with a suitable adverb.**

1 'What were your sales results like last year?'

'........... good. I made my targets with two months to spare.'

2 'What's your new CEO like?

'Extremely talented and .... intelligent. She brings out the best in people.'

3 'Do you really think we should invest in an .... volatile market?'

'Well, first of all we should stay calm and review what we already own.'

4 'What did you think of the HR Director's presentation?'

'To be honest, I don't think she was .... prepared. She seemed to be reading it most of the time.'

5 'Are you confident that the merger will go ahead?'

'........... confident, although we still need a few more meetings to sort out one or two problems.'

C **In pairs, create short dialogues using some of the phrases below.**

example: A: *Last month's sales figures seem wrong.*
B: *I think they're fairly accurate, but I'll check if you like.*

fairly accurate	deeply disappointed
incredibly well-prepared	slightly damaged
absolutely awful	totally unrealistic
severely criticised	superbly presented
badly misjudged	thoroughly enjoyed

SKILLS

Reaching agreement

A CD2.13 **Following the brainstorming meeting in Unit 2 (page 19), the team meets again to finalise plans for the sales conference. Listen to the authentic meeting and note down what they agreed about these items.**

1 Location
2 Workshop activities
3 Dinner
4 Month

B **Match these expressions from the meeting to the appropriate heading in the Useful language box below. (Some headings are not used.) Use the audio script on page 159 to check the context of each expression.**

1 Now, just to sum up, we've looked at ...

2 ... I think it's a really great place ...

3 So can we all agree, then, that we go with Florence?

4 ... I think that most of the time we'll be spending indoors.

5 Now, what about the activities?

6 What did you come up with, Carol, for the actual workshops?

7 I thought it might be a good idea to use role play ...

8 I think some kind of interaction is a good idea ...

9 OK, so we go with the workshops, then?

10 Well, I don't know about role plays, though.

11 ... I was thinking maybe something like, you know, a simple quiz ...

12 Exactly.

13 ... yeah, that's a brilliant idea ...

C **You are managers of a national newspaper. Consider this situation.**

One of your top foreign correspondents, Mike Harris, has been reporting on events in a country at war. To get his story, he went behind enemy lines and was kidnapped. In the operation to rescue him, one of the rescue team was killed and two were seriously injured.

Harris is known to be one of the best foreign correspondents in the world. However, he has been widely criticised in the national press because of the 'unnecessary risks' he took to get his story. He had been advised by local officials that it was extremely unwise to go into such hostile territory, but he ignored their warning.

Hold a meeting to decide:

a) how to deal with the criticisms, which are harming your newspaper's image;

b) whether to discipline Mike Harris for his behaviour.

USEFUL LANGUAGE

ASKING FOR OPINIONS
How do you feel about this?
Do you have strong feelings about this?
What's your view on this?

GIVING OPINIONS
Well, I'm sorry to say, I think ...
Well, unfortunately, we're going to have to ...
I can't see what the problem is.

AGREEING
I think I agree with you there.
I couldn't agree with you more.
Absolutely!/Exactly!

DISAGREEING
Hold on now, don't you think ...
I can't go along with that.
Sorry, I can't agree with you.

ADDING A CONDITION
I agree, providing we can ...
We can do that as long as ...
That's OK if ...

MAKING SUGGESTIONS
What about if we ...
How about ...
I think we should / ought to ...

EMPHASISING
I don't want to repeat myself, but ...
I'm sorry to go on about this, but ...
I do think this is really important.

SUMMARISING
So, we've agreed that ...
I'll just sum up what we've agreed.
OK, let me recap ...

Winton Carter Mining

A mining company assesses the risks involved in a new joint venture

Background

Winton Carter Mining (WCM) is a dynamic Canadian mining company. It has announced that it will be going public early next year. Valued at C$85 million, the company has mining interests in Africa and has been highly successful in exploiting copper, cobalt and bauxite deposits in the more politically stable countries in the region. WCM's offer is bound to appeal to those investors who are willing to take risks in return for high profits.

Discuss the risks and hazards that foreign mining companies could face when exploiting mineral deposits in Africa – for example, political instability.

Mining groups victim to African uncertainty

by William MacNamara

Under the jungles of countries such as Guinea, where soldiers killed 157 demonstrators last week, and Congo, struggling to recover from civil war, lie some of the richest unexploited mineral deposits. Yet exploiting those deposits poses problems that scare off most of the companies best able to develop them.

Traditional sources of metals – Australia, Chile, South Africa, Russia – still have abundant reserves. But as they are gradually exhausted, many in the industry believe Africa's volatile mining frontiers will have to take over.

A difficult decision

When a company goes public, it prepares a prospectus which gives information about the company to investors. The prospectus aims to persuade the public to buy shares in the company. WCM has the opportunity of setting up a joint venture in an African country with the state run mining company, ATZ. WCM is considering whether to sign a contract with ATZ. The Chief Executive Officer and the Chief Financial Officer of WCM must decide whether to mention this project in their prospectus.

1 **What are the advantages and disadvantages of mentioning the African project in WCM's prospectus?**

2 **What do you think they will decide to do?**

CD2.14 Listen to the discussion between Daniel Habersham, CEO, and Denise Couture, CFO. What do they decide to do? Do you think they made the right decision?

Task

You are directors of WCM. Work in groups of four or five.

1 Each of you has done some research into the mining industry in the African country. Each of you reads one of the documents and reports on its contents to the other directors at the meeting.

Director 1: Turn to page 136.
Director 2: Turn to page 134.
Director 3: Turn to page 135.
Director 4: Turn to page 140.
Director 5: Turn to page 142.

2 Evaluate each risk according to the following scale:
very high high medium low risk-free

3 Join with the other groups. Report on your discussion. Then make a final decision as one group whether or not to continue negotiations with ATZ.

4 Decide whether to include information about the African project in your company's prospectus.

Watch the Case study commentary on the ***DVD-ROM.***

Writing

As members of the board of WCM, write a report for the CEO analysing the options you considered. Make recommendations on what WCM should do.

➡ *Writing file* page 131

2 Working in new markets

Curtis Knight is a public relations firm, based in Switzerland. A growing part of its work involves helping countries to promote themselves as tourist or business destinations. For example, it represents countries at a semi-official level in forums such as trade conferences and tourism promotion fairs, handling the way the country is advertised and promoted.

A **What would be useful to know if you wanted to do business in Kazakhstan?**

B CD2.15 **An executive from Curtis Knight is giving a presentation about Kazakhstan to a group of businesspeople at a trade conference. Listen to the first part of his presentation and make notes under these headings.**

General information

- Population
- Land area
- Ethnicity
- First contacts

Verbal/Non-verbal communication

- Space between speakers
- Eye contact
- Handshakes
- Voice

C **Read the extract on the opposite page from a brochure about business in Kazakhstan and answer these questions.**

1. What is the dress code for men and women in Kazakhstan?
2. What attitude do Kazakhstanis have towards punctuality? Can you give an example?
3. Who makes the decisions in most companies in Kazakhstan? Why is this the case?
4. List three qualities that Kazakhstani staff would look for in an expatriate manager.
5. Which two styles of management would be effective in Kazakhstan? What kind of manager would you prefer to work under?
6. What's the best way of developing a personal relationship with a business contact in Kazakhstan?
7. List three things that would characterise a social evening in Kazakhstan.

D **Discuss these questions.**

1. What information in the presentation and brochure extract surprised you?
2. What would you find difficult to deal with if you were doing business in Kazakhstan?
3. What questions would you like to ask someone who is an expert on Kazakhstan?

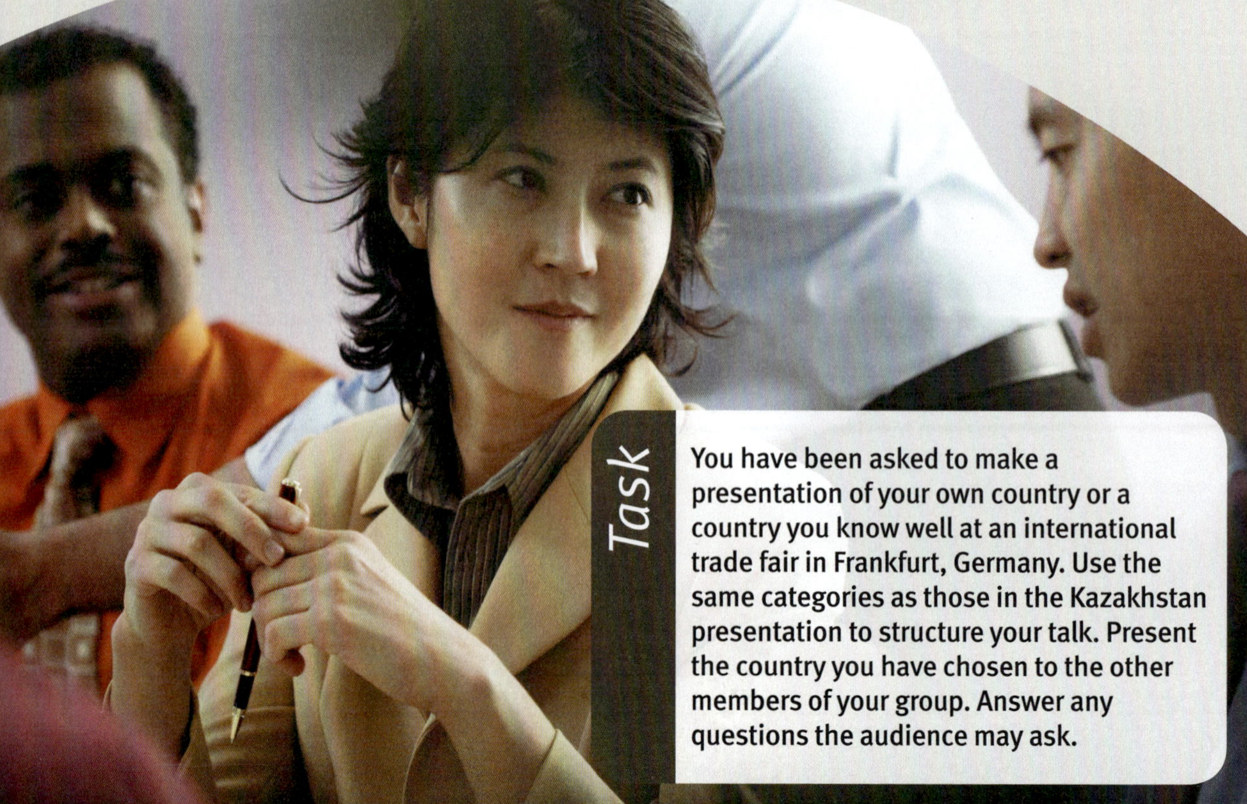

Task

You have been asked to make a presentation of your own country or a country you know well at an international trade fair in Frankfurt, Germany. Use the same categories as those in the Kazakhstan presentation to structure your talk. Present the country you have chosen to the other members of your group. Answer any questions the audience may ask.

Business culture in Kazakhstan

Dress, punctuality and formality

Men tend to dress conservatively in business. They usually wear black or dark trousers and a white or light shirt. However, Kazakhstani women often dress very fashionably. They like to wear the latest designer clothes.

In formal office situations, Kazakhstanis use first and family names.

Regarding punctuality and meeting deadlines, they tend to be more relaxed than in some other countries. For example, if you want to see an official, you can just 'drop in' during working hours. It is unlikely anyone would ask if you have an appointment.

Business cards are very important, as they show your status and position. Your job title should be on your card, and it is helpful if the wording is in Russian on one side and English on the other.

Decision-making in the workplace

In most businesses, it is true to say that the boss makes most of the decisions. This is probably a result of the Soviet system, where obedience was considered to be an important quality in an employee. If staff want answers or feedback, they generally go to their supervisor. Hierarchy is very important in all businesses, and senior people are shown great respect.

Qualities of a supervisor or manager

If you have to manage local Kazakhstani staff, they will expect you to have certain qualities and will respond well if you possess them. They will want you to be knowledgeable, to show leadership qualities and to be approachable. The last quality is very important. If you are approachable, local staff are much more likely to share their ideas with you.

There are two types of manager who are likely to be respected by local staff. The first kind is decisive and gives clear leadership. The second type is 'people-oriented'.

Relationship-building

Creating good relationships is as important here as in other countries. You need to get the trust of your business contact before getting down to business. Once again, you should bear in mind the importance of talking about the right things at the beginning of your relationship. The things that matter to most Kazakhstanis are family, children and health.

Socialising

During a job or after making a deal, you will probably have a social evening with your Kazakhstani contact. You should expect to eat a lot of food and to be offered a variety of drinks. There will also be many toasts during the meal. Kazakhstanis love to make toasts!

Conclusion

There are outstanding opportunities for investment in most sectors of the economy, and now is the time to build up relationships with Kazakhstanis working in the same area as you.

UNIT **B** # Revision

4 Success

VOCABULARY

Choose the correct prefix to complete each word in bold.

1 We finished building our new *multi- / ultra-* **modern** offices earlier this year.

2 The sales team *out / under* **performed** last year. We simply have to sell more, or we're going to have serious problems.

3 The government is going to *ex / de* **regulate** the industry next year.

4 We *over / mis* **spent** by about €100,000 last quarter, so we need to save money this quarter.

5 Hiram and I *re- / co-* **taught** a training session last month. He talked about sales, and I talked about marketing.

6 We're going to *re / de* **name** the product so it's more appealing to the new market.

7 I *mis / co-* **judged** Leon. I thought he was doing a terrible job, but this has been our most successful year.

8 With its fine workmanship and expensive materials, this range of furniture *under / out* **classes** the competition.

9 The *ex- / over* **director** predicted the company would fail when he left, but it didn't.

10 We have a truly *ultra / multi* **national** company, with staff from over 50 different countries.

SKILLS

Complete the conversation below with the correct form of the words in the box.

ask	be	deliver	give	have	increase	leave	lower	make	plan	repeat	say

Anton We'd like to place an order for 100,000.

Lo Chi If you ....[1] your order, we'll ....[2] you a bigger discount.

Anton By 12 April?

Lo Chi Sorry, could you ....[3] that?

Anton With a bigger order – more than 100,000 – can you make the delivery date of 12 April?

Lo Chi We can ....[4] by that date, providing we ....[5] the order today.

Anton I'm not sure.

Lo Chi If we ....[6] the price, would you be able to increase your order to 150,000?

Anton Are you ....[7] you have that quantity in stock?

Lo Chi Well, no, not today.

Anton So what you're saying ....[8] you can have 150,000 ready for 12 April, but you don't have stock today?

Lo Chi Yes, that's right.

Anton I want to ....[9] a question. How are you ....[10] to produce and deliver 150,000 in time for 12 April? The shipping will take at least three days.

Lo Chi Yes, I hadn't thought of that.

Anton I'd like to ....[11] a suggestion. I think we should ....[12] the question of quantity and come back to it later.

WRITING

Imagine that the negotiation in Skills didn't reach a conclusion. Write a polite e-mail of 90–110 words from Anton to Lo Chi. Use these notes to suggest a solution.

- Order size and scheduling problem; possible solution?
  50,000 3 April
  50,000 10 April
  50,000 17 April
- Allows good delivery time, lower item price

5 Job satisfaction

VOCABULARY

1 Match the words and phrases (1–8) to those with a similar meaning (a–h).

1	appraisal	a)	fringe benefits
2	take industrial action	b)	breakdown
3	autonomy	c)	empowerment
4	bureaucracy	d)	go on strike
5	burnout	e)	assessment
6	a compensation package	f)	severance payment
7	perks	g)	remuneration
8	golden handshake	h)	red tape

2 Complete each sentence with a word formed from the verb in brackets.

1 We feel a lot of .... (*frustrate*) with the new computer system.
2 I'm really .... (*satisfy*) with my current workload. I can get everything done on time.
3 His manager .... (*recognise*) that there was a problem and offered a reasonable solution.
4 One big .... (*motivate*) factor for me is the travel.
5 It's .... (*frustrate*) not being able to catch Simon at his desk.
6 The new warehouse manager has received a lot of .... (*recognise*) for his good safety performance.

PASSIVES

Rewrite these sentences in the passive.

1 The management has cut the working week to 30 hours since the downturn.
2 I gave my team a new assignment.
3 The management are listening to the employees.
4 The new regulations caused a lot of change.
5 We should encourage customers to give feedback.
6 Ben in IT always sets up new e-mail addresses.
7 We carried out some important maintenance overnight.
8 We will expect the new workers to speak good English.

WRITING

Write a set of guidelines (175–200 words) for managers to deal with their team in a positive way. Write them as answers to these questions.

1 What should I do if I think someone is overworking and getting burnt out?

2 How can I motivate staff who complain that they are underpaid?

3 What should I do if a member of staff arrives at work late every day?

6 Risk

VOCABULARY

1 Complete the sentences below with the correct form of the words in the box.

anticipate eliminate encounter estimate identify prioritise spread weigh up

1 We're .... a downturn next year, so we're being cautious this year.

2 We've .... the pros and cons and decided that the risk is too great.

3 Can you .... the items in the budget? What's the most important expense? What's the least important?

4 Palmer has .... a way to reduce risk that nobody else thought of.

5 We've reduced risk by .... our lending across more markets.

6 We .... the cost of opening a new office to be more than a million pounds. We think it's too risky.

7 The risk of not hiring a local manager is that we'll .... problems with the local staff as a result.

8 We can't completely .... risk, but we can reduce it.

2 Circle the odd word out in each group.

1 slight minuscule negligible immediate

2 remote considerable serious imminent

3 terrible tremendous potential huge

4 significant minimal substantial great

ADVERBS OF DEGREE

Choose the best word to complete each sentence.

1 We've done *exceptionally / moderately* well this year. For the past five years, we've sold about 200,000 units a year, but we've already shifted 450,000 this year!

2 The employee happiness scores were 3/10 two years ago, 4/10 last year, and 5/10 this year, so our workers are becoming *entirely / increasingly* happy.

3 The flight delays and cancellations *totally / slightly* ruined our conference. We were supposed to have 1,200 delegates, but only about 150 were able to attend.

4 Entering the German market looks *a bit / extremely* risky, but I don't think we'll encounter any major problems. Let's do it.

5 He's been working successfully in top management for more than 20 years, so he's *fairly / fully* qualified to run the company.

6 We've sold 50,000 a year for the past five years, so I think increasing your sales target to 350,000 next year is *highly / reasonably* ambitious.

SKILLS

Match the sentence halves.

1	I can't see what	a)	feelings about this?
2	Do you have strong	b)	agree with you more.
3	How do you	c)	really important.
4	I think	d)	the problem is.
5	I couldn't	e)	can't agree with you.
6	I'll just sum up	f)	what we've agreed.
7	Sorry, I	g)	I agree with you there.
8	I do think this is	h)	feel about this?

Cultures 2: Working in new markets

Complete the sentences below with the words in the box.

decision-making   dress   eye contact   formality   leadership quality   punctuality
shaking hands   socialising

1 .... in the Spanish corporate workplace is fairly conservative. Men usually wear dark suits and avoid flashy colours.

2 South Americans are fairly relaxed about .... In fact, quite often meetings don't start at the agreed time.

3 There's a lot of .... in Japanese business settings. Bowing of is crucial importance, there are rituals surrounding the exchange of business cards, and people are seated in meetings according to company hierarchy.

4 In some cultures, ... is done almost entirely by bosses. However, Swedish businesspeople tend to value consensus and compromise.

5 .... is an important part of doing business in Russia. The time you spend getting to know your colleagues while eating, drinking and relaxing is considered extremely important.

6 Being approachable is an important .... in Kazakhstan.

7 For American businesspeople, good .... shows that you're confident and honest. However, in some cultures, too much eye contact can be a sign of disrespect.

8 .... is becoming more common for business and professional women in Egypt, but it's better to wait for a woman to take the initiative.

2.1 Business skills

Negotiations

Objectives

Speaking

- Can participate in ongoing dialogue during a negotiation.
- Can summarise a negotiating position at the end of a negotiation in some detail.

Lesson deliverable

To participate in a business negotiation and negotiate pay and working conditions.

Performance review

To review your own progress and performance against the lesson objectives at the end of the lesson.

A SPEAKING 1

1 Which of these benefits and working conditions do you value most in a job? Choose three and add one of your own. Then compare your answers with a partner.

job appraisals   peer review   annual salary increase
performance-related pay   flexi-time   induction training
opportunities for promotion   inspirational boss
own desk   free parking   sports facilities   fun events
positive atmosphere   pension scheme

2 What other benefits can you negotiate with your employer that are not related to salary?

3 Have you ever negotiated your salary? Is there a good time to ask for a rise?

B SPEAKING 2

Role-play negotiating a salary rise with an employer.

Student A: Turn to page vi.

Student B: Turn to page vii.

When you have finished, discuss the success of your negotiation with another pair. Which was the most successful salary negotiation? Why?

C LISTENING 1

1 BSA2.1.5 Listen to Agata talking to her Sales Manager, Alan. Decide if the sentences are true (T) or false (F).

1. Agata would like a 10% increase after working for the company for ten months.
2. Agata's sales are almost twice Kumar's.
3. Alan suggests that Agata does more training.
4. Kumar has been promoted to Sales Manager.

2 BSA2.1.6 Listen and answer the questions about Agata's performance.

1. How does Alan justify Kumar's promotion?
2. What benefits does Alan point out that are not pay-related?
3. What benefits would Agata have after three years?
4. What is Alan's proposal?

3 Discuss these questions.

1. What do you think of Agata's negotiating style?
2. What would you do differently from Agata and Alan?

D USEFUL LANGUAGE

Match the list of useful language for negotiations (1–7) to the sentences (a–j). Some functions are used more than once.

1. Open question ....a)....
2. Softening ....
3. Signalling and making suggestions ....
4. Stating a negotiating position ....
5. Checking understanding ....
6. Pointing out the benefits ....
7. Summarising ....

a How has it been from your point of view?

b Well, to be honest, I was hoping you'd pay a little more.

c Sorry, I didn't catch that.

d If I did some sales training, I'm sure I'd bring in even more clients!

e Let's look at this another way.

f So, what you're saying is ...

g Right. Let's see what we've got so far.

h I'd like to feel more valued and I'd like to be able to save for the future.

i I'd like to make a proposal. I think we should ...

j So, to sum up, I'll work from home, ...

E LISTENING 2

1 BSA2.1.7 **Listen to the final part of the negotiation. Which expressions from section D are used?**

2 BSA2.1.7 **Listen again and complete Agata's e-mail summarising the discussion on page vii. Use one word in each space.**

Task

Pre-task: Context

Work in pairs. It is six months later and Agata has the opportunity to renegotiate her salary and working conditions. How might the situation be different now for both parties?

Part 1: Preparation

Work in two groups, A and B. Group A: you are Agata, the Key Account Manager. Turn to page viii. Group B: you are the Sales Manager. Turn to page ix.

Read your role cards. Then discuss the questions below and try to anticipate the other party's negotiating position.

Note: Alan has now left the company and the Assistant Sales Manager has recently been promoted to Sales Manager. He/She has no record of the conversation that took place six months ago.

- What should Agata, the employee's, approach be?
- What is the company's attitude likely to be?
- What information or questions could each side prepare?

Part 2: Negotiation

Work in A/B pairs: one Key Account Manager and one Sales Manager. State your positions, ask questions and confirm what you agree at the end.

Part 3: Reporting back

Regroup with another pair. Discuss the outcome of your negotiations. Which was the most successful negotiation? Why? When you have finished, report back to the rest of the class.

Extra Practice: DVD clips and Worksheets 12 & 13

F PEER REVIEW

Work with your partner from Part 2 of the Task. Discuss the following questions and give feedback.

- Did you achieve a win-win outcome? Why? / Why not? What was it more difficult to achieve in this kind of negotiation?
- Did everyone understand the same agreement and conditions? Which action points need to be clarified?
- How could you improve the outcome if you were going to negotiate again?

G SELF-ASSESSMENT

Look again at the lesson objectives and reflect on the feedback from your teacher and colleagues.

- Which learning objectives did you achieve?
- Which expressions did you use from the recordings?
- What would you still need to improve when negotiating a salary or working conditions?

H PROFESSIONAL DEVELOPMENT AND PERFORMANCE GOALS

If you recorded part(s) of your negotiation in class, listen to it before your next class.

Write down examples of conditional sentences that you both used.

Or, work with your partner outside class and record part(s) of your negotiation.

2.2 Business skills

Teleconferences

Objectives

Speaking
Can participate in teleconferences using fixed expressions for self-introduction and turn-taking.

Writing
Can write detailed notes from a phone conversation.

Listening
Can follow a natural group discussion, but may find it difficult to participate effectively.

Lesson deliverable
To plan, prepare and participate in a teleconference meeting in a business context and write a short follow-up document.

Performance review
To review your own progress and performance against the lesson objectives at the end of the lesson.

A SPEAKING 1

1 **Work in pairs. Discuss what you think the following quotation means.**

'*I don't answer the phone. I get the feeling whenever I do that there will be someone on the other end.*'
Fred Couples

2 **Work in pairs. Brainstorm the differences between a meeting and a conference call. Consider:**

- the challenges of effective communication in a meeting and a conference call
- communicating in another language in a teleconference call
- how you would prepare for a teleconference call in another language

B LISTENING

1 BSA2.2.8 **Listen to extracts from a teleconference between employees of a large international charity called No to Poverty.**

1 Work in groups. What difficulties do the participants in the teleconference call experience during the call?

2 BSA2.2.8 **Listen again. How effective was Frances King as the call leader? What strategies does she use to manage the call?**

3 BSA2.2.8 **Listen again. Write the expressions from the conference call in the correct part of the table. Write any additional expressions that you think would be useful.**

Identifying yourself to your fellow callers	
Checking who is on the call	
Taking turns to speak	
Keeping the meeting on track	
Ending the meeting	

C SPEAKING 2

Work in groups of four. Reconstruct the teleconference call at No to Poverty. Use the useful expressions in the table above and the following planning document to help you.

PLANNING		
Teleconference meeting		
Participants		
Name	Position	Location
Objective(s)		
Decision(s)		
Action points		

Task

Pre-task: Brainstorm

In groups of four, brainstorm charities that you care about most.

- Why are they important to you personally?
- Why is it important for individuals and organisations to support these charities?
- Using any resources you have in class, what information can you find out about them?
- Summarise what you know about them to the group.

Part 1: Preparation

Your company has decided to donate some money from its profits to two charities. You are going into a teleconference call with your international colleagues to discuss and agree which two charities your company will support.

In your group of four:

- Decide on a meeting leader.
- Discuss strategies to overcome any communication problems.
- Complete the teleconference planning document. Use the charities you discussed in the Pre-task.

TELECONFERENCE PLANNING
Objective(s)
Names of preferred charities: 1 2 3 4
Agree which two charities out of the four to support.
Decision(s)
Action points

Part 2: Taking part in a teleconference

1 **Turn to page viii and distribute the role cards within the group.**

Role-play the teleconference, paying attention to the difficulties indicated on the role card. Explain your choice of charity and give reasons why the company should select your choice.

Meeting leader: Make sure the other participants keep to the point. Manage any interruptions and make sure everyone gets a chance to speak. Invite participants to give their opinions. Summarise the action points at the end.

Other participants: Make sure you take turns effectively and listen to one another.

All participants: Make some notes during the meeting to help you with the follow-up task below.

2 **After you have finished the meeting, fill in the Decision(s) and Action points sections of the document above.**

Extra Practice: DVD clip and Worksheet 14

D PEER REVIEW

1 **In your groups, read the documents each of you produced after your teleconference meeting. Are the details the same? If not, what differences are there? What does this tell you about the success of your communication as a group?**

2 **Give feedback to the people in your group. Think about the lesson objectives and these questions.**

   1 How successful was the teleconference? Think about handling interruptions, dealing with people going off the topic and making sure everyone contributed.
   2 What did each person do well?
   3 What points for development can you suggest?

E SELF-ASSESSMENT

Write 120–140 words about your performance. Think about:

- feedback from other participants
- the lesson objectives
- what you did well or could have done better
- your role in the meeting (leading or just participating)

F PROFESSIONAL DEVELOPMENT AND PERFORMANCE GOALS

Now think about the next time you participate in, or lead, a teleconference at work. Complete these sentences.

1 Before the teleconference call, I will ....
2 During the teleconference call, I will ....
3 If there are communication difficulties, I will ....
4 After the teleconference call, I will ....

UNIT 7

Management styles

'In my house, I'm the boss. My wife is just the decision-maker.'
Woody Allen, American writer, director, actor and comedian

OVERVIEW

STARTING UP

A Which of these statements do you agree with? Explain your reasons.

Managers should:

1. know when your birthday is.
2. know where you are and what you're doing at all times during working hours.
3. not criticise or praise.
4. not interfere in disagreements between members of staff.
5. not ask people to do things they're not prepared to do themselves.
6. be available at all times to give staff advice and support.
7. keep their distance from staff and not get involved in socialising outside work.
8. use polite language at all times.
9. work longer hours than their staff.
10. comment on the personal appearance of their staff.

B What is the role of a manager? Choose your top three roles from the following and explain your ideas.

- motivator
- mediator
- leader
- problem-solver
- monitor
- decision-maker
- friend
- organiser
- role model

Can you connect the roles above to the points you discussed in Exercise A?

C How important are these factors in judging the success of a manager?

- the loyalty of staff
- achievement of results
- popularity with their superiors

VOCABULARY

Management qualities

A **Give the opposite meaning for each of these adjectives, using the prefixes *in-*, *ir-*, *un-*, *il-* or *dis-*. Then provide the noun forms.**

1 considerate
inconsiderate, consideration
2 competent
3 creative
4 diplomatic
5 efficient
6 flexible
7 inspiring
8 logical
9 loyal
10 organised
11 decisive
12 responsible
13 sociable
14 supportive

B CD2.16 **Mark the stress on the positive adjective and noun forms in Exercise A. Listen and check your answers.**

C **Choose the four best qualities of a manager using the adjectives in Exercise A and rank them in order of importance (1 = most important). Then choose the four worst qualities and rank them (1 = worst).**

D **Match these pairs of contrasting management styles.**

1 autocratic
2 centralising
3 directive
4 empowering
5 hands-on
6 task-orientated

a) collaborative
b) controlling
c) delegating
d) democratic
e) people-orientated
f) laissez-faire

E **Discuss these questions.**

1 Which management style(s) would you like to experience / have you experienced?
2 How would you describe your own management style? If you are not a manager, what do you think your management style would be?
3 What qualities do you think you possess or lack?

See the ***DVD-ROM*** *for the i-Glossary.*

LISTENING

Successful managers

A CD2.17 **Laurie Mullins is the author of *Management and Organisational Behaviour*. Listen to the first part of the interview. Which two factors influence the managerial function today, and what are the two examples that Laurie gives of these factors?**

B CD2.18 **Listen to the second part. Which six managerial philosophies does Laurie mention?**

Laurie Mullins

Watch the interview on the ***DVD-ROM.***

C CD2.19 **Listen to the final part and complete these extracts.**

Some managers believe in the need for ....[1] and control through an ....[2] system of central control, formal organisation ....[3], systems of ....[4], and the belief that it's natural for people to try to get away with what they can ...

Other managers believe in the integration of ....[5] and ....[6] goals and that people can be ....[7] to the goals of the organisation, in which case they will exercise self-...........[8] and self-...........[9].

D **In groups, answer this question.**

Which management style do you think gets the best out of people?

READING
Management styles

A **Discuss these questions.**

1 What do you like or dislike about the management style in your organisation?

2 What would your ideal workplace be like?

B **Work in pairs.**

Student A: Read the article on the opposite page about Anna Wintour, Chief Executive of *Vogue*, the fashion magazine.

Student B: Turn to page 145 and read the article about Jim Buckmaster, CEO of Craigslist, the Internet company.

Read your article quickly and decide which of these statements are true for the CEO you read about.

They ...

1 think most meetings are a waste of time.

2 are good at making decisions quickly and firmly.

3 want people to know who is the boss.

4 think artificial deadlines are stressful.

5 believe in hiring the best staff they can.

6 think their staff feel happy working there.

C **Read your article again. In pairs, compare and contrast the styles of the two CEOs.**

D **Which of these adjectives do you think describe Anna Wintour?**

approachable demanding perfectionist ruthless volatile

E **Match the adjectives in the box to the definitions below.**

anti-authoritarian approachable demanding perfectionist ruthless self-motivated talented volatile

1 not caring if you have to harm others to get what you want

2 not satisfied with anything unless it is exactly right

3 having a natural ability to do something well

4 wanting to achieve something by themselves

5 against forcing people to obey strict rules

6 friendly and easy to talk to

7 expecting a lot of time and effort from others

8 liable to suddenly become angry

F **Complete this paragraph with adjectives from Exercise E.**

At my last company, the managers were remote and not at all ....[1]. They were hard to get to know. The only one who showed any emotion was the CEO, who had a ....[2] temper. He was completely ruthless and didn't care about his staff at all. He acted like a dictator. He had a ....[3] management style, insisting that everything was exactly right. He was also very demanding, making us work really unsociable hours. In my new company, the managers are good communicators, decision-making is open and transparent and the style is ....[4]. Management is by consensus. All the staff are ....[5] and experts in their own fields. They are ....[6] and trusted to work without supervision.

Student A

Anna Wintour

60 Minutes' Morley Safer interviews *Vogue*'s Editor in her first lengthy U.S. T.V. profile.

She is said to be the most powerful woman in fashion and she does nothing to dispel that belief. Her name is Anna Wintour, a name that strikes terror in some and loathing in others. It should also be said she commands a loyal band of friends and admirers.

"The blurb on your unauthorized biography reads 'She's ambitious, driven, needy, a perfectionist'. Accurate?" *60 Minutes* correspondent Morley Safer asked Wintour.

"Well, I am very driven by what I do. I am certainly very competitive. I like people who represent the best of what they do, and if that turns you into a perfectionist, then maybe I am," Wintour replied.

Wintour is involved in every detail of the magazine: the clothes, editing the pictures and articles. She is decisive, impatient, and bears a look that says "I'm the boss, and you're boring."

"An editor in the final analysis is a kind of dictator—a magazine is not a democracy?" Safer asked.

"It's a group of people coming together and presenting ideas from which I pick what I think is the best mix for each particular issue, but in the end, the final decision has to be mine," Wintour explained. "We're here to work. There's on-duty time and off-duty time, and we're drawn together by our passion for the magazine. If one comes across sometimes as being cold or brusque, it's simply because I'm striving for the best."

"It's not like a tea party here. We work very hard," *Vogue*'s Editor-at-large Andre Leon Talley told Safer. Asked what kind of boss she is, Talley told Safer, "Let's say that Anna can be intimidating. I think that's her armor, to intimidate. To give the people the sense that she is in charge. She is not a person who's going to show you her emotions ever. She's like a doctor, when she's looking at your work, it's like a medical analysis."

Vogue Creative Director Grace Coddington says, "I think she enjoys not being completely approachable, you know. Just her office is very intimidating, right? You have to walk about a mile into the office before you get to her desk, and I'm sure it's intentional."

from *CBS*

G **Discuss these questions.**

1 What are the advantages and disadvantages of each style of management described in the articles?

2 Would you rather work for a male or female manager? Describe your ideal manager.

3 Do you agree with Buckmaster that most meetings are a waste of time?

LANGUAGE REVIEW
Text reference

- In written English, we often use pronouns to avoid repeating words and phrases when it is already clear what we are talking about.
  *We need the report urgently – **it's** got to be sent to head office.*
- Writers sometimes use *we* to refer to themselves and the readers together.
  *As **we** saw in Episode 1 …*
- We sometimes use *it* as an 'empty' subject with no real meaning.
  ***It's** nine o'clock.*
- We can use *it, this, that, these* and *those* to refer back or forward to something in a text, or outside the text itself.
  *Most French senior management were educated at the Grandes Écoles. **These** colleges champion an intellectual rigour in their students. **This** produces a highly educated management population.*
- We can use *they* to avoid saying *he* or *she*, especially after indefinite words like *anyone, no one, somebody*, etc.
  *Someone's been trying to phone us all morning, but **they** can't get through.*

➡ *Grammar reference* page 149

A **Look at the Jim Buckmaster article on page 145 and say what all the words in red refer to.**

B **Look at the first paragraph of the Anna Wintour article on page 69 and find an example of *it* as an 'empty' subject.**

C **Look at the Anna Wintour article again and underline all the examples of text reference. Use this checklist to help you.**

- pronouns
- possessive adjectives or pronouns
- *it, this, that, these* and *those*

D **Say what all the words you underlined in Exercise C refer to.**

E **Read this paragraph and say what *the former* and *the latter* refer to.**

Wintour's critics describe her management style as autocratic, whilst her supporters label it perfectionist. The former believe she is ruthlessly determined, whereas the latter would rather say she is focused on excellence.

F **Write a profile of a manager you know or are interested in.**

SKILLS
Presentations

A 🔊 CD2.20, 2.21 **Jason Harding, Sales Manager of the drinks company Quench Products, is giving a presentation to some customers. Listen to both parts of the presentation and answer these questions.**

1. What is the name of the product?
2. When will it be launched?
3. What are its unique selling points?
4. What will the audience take away with them?

B CD2.20 Listen to the first part of the presentation again and complete these extracts.

1 I'm going to tell you about our new iced tea that'll be .... early next March.

2 What is Quench Iced Tea? What are its ....?

3 The fact that we offer it in .... will give it a definite .... over the competition.

4 I want to .... that. In other words, it's got a ....

5 This will undoubtedly appeal to ....-........... .... And that's a major .... of our product.

C CD2.21 Listen to the second part again and complete these extracts.

1 ....[a] the tea itself. As you know, our company uses only ....-...........[b] tea ...

2 Please take a look at the ....

3 What does this ....[a]? It ....[b] that once again, we're offering customers ....[c].

4 You can see from the slide that the bottles are ....[a], very ....-...........[b] and ....[c]. They'll really ....[d] on the shelf.

5 So to ....[a], we're offering customers a unique, delicious, thirst-quenching product. A product that'll ....[b] to different tastes and which has ....[c]. It'll [...] be supported by a ....[d].

D Match each extract in Exercises B and C to a heading in the Useful language box below.

E Prepare a presentation about a product you have bought recently. Try to persuade your audience to buy it.

USEFUL LANGUAGE

STATING THE PURPOSE
The purpose of my talk today is to ...
What I want to do today is to ...
My main objective today is to ...

INVOLVING THE AUDIENCE
What are its main selling points?
As I'm sure you all know, ...
As you are aware ...

PERSUADING
It will give us an edge over the competition.
This will undoubtedly appeal to ...
It has many outstanding features.

EMPHASISING
I'd just like to highlight ...
I want to stress that ...
I'd like to emphasise that ...

CHANGING THE SUBJECT
Moving on to ...
OK, now I'll talk about ...
Right, turning now to ...

REFERRING TO VISUALS
Let's look at the chart.
Let me draw your attention to the slide.
Please take a look at the visual.

DISCUSSING IMPLICATIONS
What this means is ...
The consequence of this is ...
This has resulted in ...

EXEMPLIFYING
For instance ...
Let me give you an example.
Let me give you an interesting statistic.

A multinational electronics company must choose a new manager with the right management style to lead an international project team

Background

Niel Selig and Pedar Lind founded their electronics company (S&L) in Copenhagen, Denmark, in 1985. They developed the company by making top-of-the-range electronics products for higher-income groups. The products have a classical look, innovative designs and a distinctive appearance. A highly successful company, S&L has expanded internationally and now has over 500 stores worldwide.

Six months ago, an international team was assembled to carry out a project. Consisting of 16 members, the team was instructed to conduct a survey of S&L's customer service to retail outlets in six major European countries.

Unfortunately, the project has run into difficulties. Deadlines for submitting reports have been missed, and morale in the project team is low. It has become apparent that the present Project Manager, Paul Johnstone, does not have the right style to manage the team. It has been decided, therefore, to replace him with someone else within the organisation who has a more suitable management style.

Management style of Paul Johnstone

You are directors of S&L. You interviewed three members of the project team about Paul's style of management.

CD2.22, 2.23, 2.24 Work in small groups. Listen to the comments and note down the strengths and weaknesses of his style, using these categories.

- Personality
- Communication
- Goal-setting
- Decision-making
- Monitoring performance
- Giving feedback

Replacing the Project Manager

The Directors of S&L have talked informally to several candidates who are interested in taking over from Paul Johnstone. The candidates were asked to note down their management style.

Read the descriptions of their style on the opposite page.

Manager 1: Ruth

Sales Manager, Central Europe

I'm strong, self-confident, sociable.
I have high expectations of co-workers.

My job:

- To give clear, detailed instructions which must be carried out. I'm not interested in explanations if the work isn't done.
- It's important to give clear goals for each member of staff.
- Deadlines must be met at all costs. I won't accept excuses.
- I'm a hands-on manager. I check all the time to make sure staff are doing their job properly.
- I'm a good listener, but then I tell people what to do.
- Dealing with multinational staff is difficult. You have to tell them your management style and what you expect from them.
- I'm a decisive person, but if I make a mistake, I admit it.

Staff appraisal interviews: Every three months. I discuss my team's weaknesses and strengths.

My strengths: Leadership, achieving targets

My personality: A workaholic; tough, fair, ambitious. I like new challenges.

Manager 2: Eduardo

Manager, New Business

I'm a people person – friendly, loyal, extrovert.

My job:

- To make sure that my staff really enjoy coming to work.
- I hold a lot of team meetings, formal and informal.
- I always try to get everyone to agree before we make any decisions. It's time-consuming, but that's my style.
- I don't set goals. I talk to staff, and we agree on what goals they must achieve.
- I don't want the word *decisive* to define my style, as I prefer to make decisions in a group.
- I'm very good at sorting out staff problems. It's the part of my job that I enjoy the most.
- Dealing with international staff is no problem, as I treat everyone as individuals.

Staff appraisal interviews: Once a year. I check with all staff each week to see if everything's OK.

My strengths: Organised, a good listener, excellent interpersonal skills

My personality: Warm, understanding – very important to be liked by my team

Manager 3: Kazuo

Manager, Business Support Unit

I'm hard-working, democratic and loyal.

My job:

- To achieve the objectives and goals of the company.
- To ensure that each person in the department understands our goals and shares in decision-making.
- I believe the company is more important than the individual. It is essential never to let the company down.
- Hold many meetings, no time limit. Always consult staff on all decisions.
- Do not permit disagreement/arguments. We want harmony at all times.
- Discuss aims with the team and set realistic targets.
- I work six days a week, sometimes seven. I expect staff to do the same.
- People should feel ashamed if they don't meet company targets.
- I want to learn how to manage multicultural groups successfully.

Staff appraisal interviews: Every quarter

My strengths: Organising ability, getting the job done, loyalty to the company

My personality: Quiet, determined, focused on results

Manager 4: Martina

Manager, IT Department

I'm ambitious, trusting and responsible.

My job:

- To organise people so that they get the work done.
- I set goals, after agreement with my people. I then give them responsibility and authority to get the job done. They have to decide how to do it. Their job? To carry out my instructions – to the letter!
- My priority is to make the right decisions, as quickly as possible, then get staff to put them into practice.
- I use the bonus system to motivate my team. Everyone is motivated by money.

Staff appraisal interviews: Once a year. To be honest, they're usually a waste of time. I want a weekly update from each member of staff on how they're achieving their goals.

My strengths: Organising, leading teams, motivating, getting the job done

My personality: Tenacious, demanding, tough on the outside – but soft inside!

Task

1. Work in groups of four. You are Directors of S&L. Each of you chooses a different candidate. Make a persuasive presentation of your candidate to the other members of your group.
2. Working individually, rank the four candidates in terms of their suitability for the position of Project Manager. Number 1 would be your first choice, number 4 the least suitable candidate.
3. Working as a group, compare your decisions and choose one candidate to be the new Project Manager.
4. Make a presentation to another group outlining the strengths and weaknesses of each candidate and stating your choice of candidate, with your reasons.

Watch the Case study commentary on the ***DVD-ROM.***

Writing

As one of the Directors, write a short report to the Board of Directors recommending your preferred candidate as the new Project Manager. Give reasons for your decision. Use these headings:

- Introduction
- Summary of shortlisted candidates
- Recommendation with reasons

➡ *Writing file* page 131

UNIT 8

Team building

'Strength lies in differences, not in similarities.'
Stephen Covey, US author and management consultant

OVERVIEW

STARTING UP

A **Think of at least two advantages and two disadvantages of working in teams.**

B **For each category in this quiz, tick the three statements that most apply to you. Then read the explanations on page 136.**

What sort of team player are you?

Doers vs. Thinkers	Details vs. Ideas	Mind vs. Heart	Planners vs. Improvisers
a) I consider what I say.	**a)** I often come up with unusual solutions.	**a)** I like to think logically.	**a)** Meetings have to be prepared for carefully.
b) I contribute a lot in discussions.	**b)** It's important to be realistic.	**b)** I keep emotions out of decision-making.	**b)** I like surprises.
c) Action is more important than reflection.	**c)** People see me as a creative person.	**c)** I avoid confrontation.	**c)** I hate time-wasting at meetings.
d) I listen to others before I say anything.	**d)** I like practical solutions.	**d)** I sometimes tread on people's toes.	**d)** Too much time can be spent on preparation.
e) Discussion gives me energy and ideas.	**e)** You shouldn't overlook details.	**e)** Understanding people is as important as being right.	**e)** People say I'm a punctual person.
f) I don't say a lot at meetings.	**f)** You shouldn't get lost in details.	**f)** I care about other people's feelings.	**f)** I need a deadline to get me going.

C **Work in groups and compare your answers to Exercise B. Then discuss these questions.**

1 Do you think your group would make a good team, based on the results of the quiz? Why? / Why not?

2 Does a team always need a leader, and if so, should a team change its leader regularly?

3 Does tension between team members make a team more effective?

VOCABULARY
Prefixes

A Match the prefixes of the words (1–10) to their meanings (a–c).

Prefix	Meaning of prefix		
1 *mis*match	a) not	b) do badly	c) former
2 *pro*-European	a) opposite	b) in favour of	c) before
3 *pre*-event	a) not enough	b) against	c) before
4 *post*-activity	a) after	b) too much	c) not enough
5 *dis*connect	a) very	b) former	c) not
6 *ex*-military	a) opposite	b) former	c) after
7 *bi*lateral	a) against	b) after	c) two
8 *re*motivate	a) again	b) former	c) after
9 *multi*cultural	a) again	b) many	c) against
10 *hyper*link	a) not enough	b) very / more than usual	c) opposite

B Complete this web advert using the correct form of words from Exercise A.

ESPRIT DE CORPS – the last word in team building

Is your team letting itself and the company down?

- Do you have ....[1] teams and leaders?
- Do you have team members who feel ....[2] from each other?
- Do you need to energise and ....[3] a tired team?

We have the solution.

Choose from our wide range of team-building activity days and longer training and development programmes.
Having worked for some of the world's largest and best-known international companies, ...[4] teams are a speciality. Staffed by many ....[5] personnel, we know what makes teams work.
Before making any recommendations, we will visit you for a ....[6] consultation to find out your exact requirements.
After completing the event/programme, we will hold a ....[7] feedback and debriefing session and also supply a full written report (including expert advice and follow-up strategies).
Click on the ....[8] below to see the full range of events and programmes.

C Complete the final part of the advert from Exercise B with the verbs in the box.

breakdown	build	~~develop~~	inspire	maximise	reduce	stimulate

Esprit de Corps team-building events and programmes will help you and your company to:

- develop[1] loyalty and trust
- ....[2] potential
- ....[3] barriers
- ....[4] communication
- ....[5] creativity
- ....[6] relationships
- ....[7] staff turnover

D Add prefixes to these words to give their opposite meanings. Then use them to discuss the questions below.

1 communicative	6 focused	11 sociable
2 decisive	7 imaginative	12 stable
3 efficient	8 loyal	13 tolerant
4 enthusiastic	9 organised	14 patient
5 flexible	10 practical	

- Who is the best or worst person you have ever worked with? Explain why.
- What qualities could you contribute to a team? What qualities would the other members need to have to create an effective team?

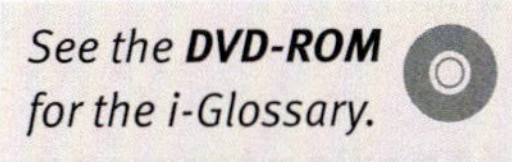

LISTENING
Building successful teams

Dan Collins

Watch the interview on the **DVD-ROM.**

A CD2.25 **Listen to the first part of an interview with Dan Collins, founder of team-building specialists Fresh group. According to Dan, what is a team, and what is a leader's role in a team?**

B CD2.26 **Listen to the second part. What kind of communication problems do people at work often have?**

C CD2.27 **Listen to the third part. Work in pairs. Which four team roles does Dan mention? Take notes on what he says about each role.**

D CD2.28 **Listen to the final part. What does Dan say about the attitudes to teams and how they are led in a) Europe and the US, and b) India and China?**

E **You have to set up a team for a very important project. Choose four people you know and say why they would make a good team.**

READING
New ways of team building

A **You are going to read an article entitled *Recipes for team building*. What do you think are the advantages of sending teams on cookery courses?**

B **Read the article on the opposite page quickly and check if your answers to Exercise A were mentioned. What other advantages were mentioned?**

C **Scan the article to find (where mentioned):**

1 all the cookery schools 2 their clients 3 their locations

D **Read the article again and answer these questions.**

1 Who are these people? Summarise the points they make in the article.

a) Anna Venturi c) Christi Strauss e) Rosalind Rathouse

b) Masele Siatu'u d) Richard Pash f) Letizia Tufari

2 Apart from running team-building courses, what else do some corporate cookery schools do? Why is this successful?

E **Without looking at the article, complete these word partnerships.**

1 f _ _ t _ _ team spirit

2 break down b _ r r _ _ _ s

3 joint v _ n _ _ r _

4 client h o _ p _ t _ _ _ _ _

5 income s t _ _ _ m

F **Answer these questions.**

1 Would you like to attend a cookery course as part of a team-building exercise? Why? / Why not?

2 What would you find difficult about working in a team?

3 Which sort of people make the worst team members?

4 If you could go on or design any team-building course, what would it be?

G **Write a short paragraph summarising the advantages of sending teams on a cookery course.**

FT

Recipes for team building

by Rhymer Rigby

When cutting-edge companies want to foster team spirit, relax or even entertain clients, breaking bread together is no longer enough – they now bake that bread themselves. Corporate cookery courses are the latest exercise in business bonding.

Venturi's Table claims to be the UK's only dedicated corporate cookery school. Anna Venturi, the London-based school's founder, says business is brisk, as teams from companies including Abbott Mead Vickers, Merrill Lynch and eBay head to Wandsworth to cook up a storm.

Ms Venturi says cooking appeals to companies because it brings people together: 'It's not competitive. We just want everyone to relax and have a good time. In fact, it's almost therapy. We get everyone, from directors to secretaries, from graduates to retirement dos.'

The team from Cereal Products Worldwide, a joint venture between Nestlé and General Mills, making mushroom ravioli, stuffed loin of pork and sweetened oranges with profiteroles in the kitchen at Venturi's Table, appears to prove Ms Venturi's point that cooking can build teams.

The group members are of mixed culinary abilities: some are dab hands in the kitchen; others have never caramelised an orange in their lives. Yet everyone happily pitches in – and slaving over a hot stove and piping chocolate custard into a profiterole helps to break down barriers. Masele Siatu'u, CPW's Human Resources Vice-President, says having your elbows in flour and eggs brings together fellow employees who are dispersed across the world.

This is the reason the company chose to send the team on a cookery course, says Christi Strauss, CPW Chief Executive. 'We look for something that cuts across ages and backgrounds and cultures. If we [played] golf, it would be great for good golfers, but not necessarily for anyone else.' With cookery, she says, anyone can take part and they can participate as much or little as they want. Plus there's a tasty meal on offer at the end of the day.

Richard Pash, a Marketing Manager at Mars and another Venturi customer, says cookery feels natural compared to some team-building activities. Constructing a bridge across a stream when there is a perfectly good one 50 metres away may seem a little pointless, but cooking a three-course meal you intend to sit down and eat certainly isn't. 'Unlike many courses we've been on, it's the opposite of contrived,' says Mr Pash.

Venturi's Table isn't the only company offering corporate cookery courses. The Cookery School at Little Portland Street in London has an increasing number of corporate clients who, says Principal Rosalind Rathouse, comprise about a third of its business. These include Investec, BP and Iron Mountain.

Many of the better-known cookery schools offer packages aimed at businesses. Mosimann's Academy allows teambuilders to be taught by the eponymous Anton, while the Lavender House in Norfolk and The Food and Wine Academy also cater for corporate cooks.

The Cookery School differentiates itself by working with psychologists who observe the team members as they cook before feeding back to the group. Organisations that want to see how teams work under different circumstances can ask for a stressful or confrontational kitchen. 'It becomes a microcosm of the workplace,' says Ms Rathouse.

Perhaps the most intriguing use of places like Venturi, however, is not as venues for team building but for client entertainment. Ms Venturi's daughter Letizia Tufari, who worked at Pfizer before joining her mother's business, says client hospitality is a growing income stream for Venturi. She says that for cash-rich, time-poor businesspeople, fine dining has become rather pedestrian. But cooking a three-course meal for oneself is more unusual.

LANGUAGE REVIEW

Modal perfect

The modal perfect is formed using **modal verb + *have* + past participle.**
*His presence **might have boosted** the team's performance.*

Two uses of the modal perfect are:

- criticising or commenting on past actions
  *You really **should have backed** up the files.*
  *We **needn't have hurried** to the airport, as the plane was late.*
- speculating about the past or present
  *I think the meeting **may have finished** now.*
  *I've phoned the office three times now. I think they **must have gone** home.*

➔ ***Grammar reference*** page 149

A **Answer *yes, no* or *not sure* to each of these questions.**

1 *They should have changed the team leader.*
Did they change the team leader?

2 *Alicia needn't have spent so much time on the report.*
Did Alicia spend too much time on the report?

3 *They could have prepared better if they'd had more time.*
Did they prepare as well as they wanted to?

4 *The team would have been stronger without him.*
Was the team as strong as it could be?

5 *The team may have made a decision by now.*
Has the team made a decision yet?

6 *Carlos shouldn't have spent all the budget on one team-building course.*
Did Carlos spend all the budget on one team-building course?

7 *The Chairman couldn't have prepared properly, as we lost the contract.*
Did the Chairman do enough preparation?

8 *I've lost my memory stick. I must have dropped it somewhere.*
Did I drop my memory stick somewhere?

B **Which of these statements use the modal perfect correctly? Suggest alternative modals for the incorrect statements.**

1 It's too late to sign the contract. You must have done it last week.

2 I'm a bit angry. You would have told me you had invited the entire team for dinner.

3 His behaviour yesterday could have ruined all the team spirit we have built up.

4 They bought the shares when they were cheap and sold them at their peak, so they needn't have made a lot of money.

5 Simone wasn't at the meeting. She might have been delayed at the airport.

6 You couldn't have booked a place on the June course because it was completely full.

7 She's made a lot of mistakes. She should have been very careless.

8 Abi was inspirational and a motivator. We must have made her team leader.

C **Role-play this situation in pairs. Use as many of these structures as possible: *should have / shouldn't have / could have / needn't have /* + past participle.**

Student A: You are a sales rep. You have just been on a three-day business trip. You:

- stayed in a five-star hotel
- ordered breakfast in your room
- drank most of the mini-bar
- phoned home from your room
- hired a top-of-the-range car
- had your clothes dry-cleaned by the hotel.

Defend your actions.

Student B: You are the Finance Director. You think the rep's expenses are excessive and are refusing to pay them.

SKILLS

Resolving conflict

A **Read these suggestions about ways of dealing with conflict. Put each of them under one of these headings: *Do* or *Don't*.**

1 Delay taking action if possible.
2 Get angry from time to time with difficult members.
3 Try to see the problem from the point of view of the team.
4 Be truthful about how you see the situation.
5 Encourage open and frank discussion.
6 Try to ignore tensions within the team.
7 Bring potential conflict and disagreement into the open.
8 Give special attention to team members who are creating problems.
9 Persist with 'impossible people' – you may win them over.
10 Try to find 'win–win' solutions.

B CD2.29 **Listen to the conversation between Karen, Head of Department, and Larissa. Which suggestions from Exercise A does Karen use to deal with the conflict between Larissa and her colleague, Sophie?**

C CD2.29 **Listen again and note down the phrases Karen uses to deal with the conflict. Add them to the appropriate sections in the Useful language box below.**

D **Work in pairs. Role-play this situation. Use phrases from the Useful language box to discuss the problems.**

A team of six multinational staff is managing a number of key accounts at an advertising agency. However, one of the team is unhappy. The employee is difficult to work with and uncooperative.

Student A: Turn to page 136.
Student B: Turn to page 134.

USEFUL LANGUAGE

EXPRESSING YOUR FEELINGS

My main concern is ...
What really worries me is ...
What concerns me is ...

MAKING SUGGESTIONS

One thing you could do is ...
It might be worth ...
It could be helpful if you ...

EXPRESSING SATISFACTION

Yes, that would be very helpful.
Yes, that's a good idea.
Mmm. I think that's the right approach to take.

EXPRESSING DISSATISFACTION

I don't think that would do much good.
I'm not sure that would work.
I don't think that's the answer.

SHOWING SYMPATHY

I know how you feel.
I understand what you're saying.
I can see where you're coming from, but ...

IDENTIFYING THE REAL PROBLEM

What's really bothering you?
What are you really worried about?
What's the real problem?

RESOLVING THE CONFLICT

How do you think we should deal with this?
What's the best approach, do you think?
What's your solution?

REVIEWING THE SITUATION

Let's look at this again in a few days'/weeks' time.
Let's meet next week and see how things are going.
Let's review this when the situation's a bit clearer.

Case study 8

Motivating the sales team

A kitchenware company is having problems with its sale staff

Background

Designer Kitchen Products (DKP) is based in Leicester, England. It sells a range of high-class kitchenware to stores across Europe. A year ago, the company hired a new Sales Manager, David Seymour, to improve the sales revenue and create a high-performing team.

However, since David Seymour's appointment, the sales team has not met its targets, and morale in the department is low. The management is disappointed with the results in the UK, as they are planning to expand into Asia in the near future. In addition, the management needs a high-performing sales team to successfully launch several exciting new kitchenware products early next year.

The sales team consists of a mix of nationalities, but they are not working well together. David Seymour is considering various actions to improve the team's performance. He is well aware that if he cannot motivate the team to raise its performance, his own job will be on the line.

Before taking stronger action to generate more sales revenue, David Seymour made some notes on the team. Read about David Seymour, then read the notes on the sales team on the opposite page.

David Seymour

When David Seymour was appointed Sales Manager of DKP, he was given the task of increasing the company's sales revenue by at least 20% and building up the sales team for further expansion in Europe. He has so far failed to achieve his main objective. To improve the sales team's performance, he now believes the team needs to be more motivated and to be set much more challenging sales targets. He would also like to have tighter control over the team and to upgrade their training.

CD2.30 Listen to a sales meeting chaired by David Seymour. He makes a proposal about training for the team and asks members to comment.

What do you learn about the team's problems?

David Seymour's plans

Read about David Seymour's plans below. Then, in pairs, discuss which plans you think will benefit sales or teambuilding.

- To meet the target of increasing sales by 20%, each member of the sales team will be expected to increase sales by 20% in their area.
- Commissions will be based entirely on the team's monthly performance. There will be no individual commissions.
- The sales representative with the biggest percentage increase in sales over a six-month period will be given a prize.
- Monthly sales figures for each member of the team will be posted on a board at the company's head office, e.g. 1 = top salesperson, 7 = least successful performer.
- Each month, I will choose the 'outstanding salesperson of the month'. His/Her photo will appear in the company newsletter.
- Staff will attend webinars (web seminars) about new products twice a month. There will also be much more use of video conferences run by me.
- Staff must send in weekly reports about their activities.
- I will organise an informal dinner with each member of the sales team in the near future.

THE SALES TEAM Code for sales areas in terms of sales potential

***** Outstanding **** Very good *** Good ** Average * Poor

HANK (Canadian)

Area: South-East/West **** **Age:** 36

Personality: Fun-loving, extrovert, sociable; most ambitious member of the team

Notes:

- Ranking: no. 3 in terms of sales revenue
- Exceeds 60% of monthly sales targets.
- Added five new accounts last year.
- Usually late sending in sales reports. Not good at paperwork.
- Argues a lot in meetings. Can be very disruptive.
- Thinks he could double sales if he had the West London area.
- Dislikes Max. Thinks meetings are mostly a waste of time.

SONIA (Italian)

Area: North-East ** **Age:** 28

Personality: Dynamic, self-centred, a workaholic

Notes:

- Ranking: no. 4 in terms of sales revenue
- Always meets monthly sales targets.
- Added six new accounts last year.
- Most talented salesperson in the team.
- Excellent communicator with customers.
- Team members respect her, but no one likes her.
- Thinks she is underpaid for her contribution to sales.

MAX (English)

Area: West London ***** **Age:** 52

Personality: Serious, reserved, some say 'unfriendly'

Notes:

- Ranking: no. 1 in terms of sales revenue
- Added two new accounts last year.
- Very successful in keeping existing customers happy, but slow to promote new products.
- Rarely meets his monthly sales targets. Excellent paperwork.
- Speaks a lot at meetings. Very influential.
- Has a close relationship with Natalya. Always supports her at meetings.
- Thinks his sales targets are far too high.

LAURA (American)

Area: Midlands *** **Age:** 38

Personality: Outgoing, speaks her mind, argumentative.

Notes:

- Ranking: no. 6 in terms of sales revenue
- Added three new accounts last year.
- Meets about 30% of her monthly sales targets.
- Says that in present economic conditions, her area should be downgraded to one star.
- Very hard-working, sends in excellent sales reports.
- Good relations with customers.
- Not a team player. Dislikes Natalya and Sonia.

NATALYA (Russian)

Area: North-West/Scotland ** **Age:** 26

Personality: Reserved, organised, determined

Notes:

- Ranking: no. 5 in terms of sales revenue
- Added four new accounts last year.
- Meets 50% of her monthly sales targets.
- Is steadily improving her sales ability. Reliable paperwork.
- Has some good ideas to improve sales, but lacks confidence.
- Always supports Max in meetings.
- Hank thinks Natalya has the wrong personality for sales.

CHANG (Chinese)

Area: West/Wales *** **Age:** 45

Personality: Likeable, cooperative, most hard-working member of the team

Notes:

- Ranking: no. 2 in terms of sales revenue
- Very consistent salesman. Generally exceeds all his monthly sales targets.
- Added five new accounts last year.
- Enjoys team meetings. Needs to improve presentations of new products.
- An excellent salesman. Very good paperwork.
- Can be too polite and not assertive enough in meetings.
- He has a strong Chinese accent when speaking.

Task

You are Directors of DKP. Work in groups of four. Choose a role. Director 1 leads the meeting.

Director 1: Turn to page 136. Director 3: Turn to page 138.
Director 2: Turn to page 142. Director 4: Turn to page 136.

1. Read your role cards and prepare for a meeting to resolve your company's teambuilding problems.
2. Make a list of the problems that are affecting the performance of the sales team.
3. Consider David Seymour's proposals. Decide which ones, if any, should be acted upon.
4. Discuss any other ideas you may have to improve the team's performance. Decide which of your suggestions should be put into effect.
5. Work out an action plan for the next six months.
6. If there is more than one group of directors, compare your action plans.

Watch the Case study commentary on the ***DVD-ROM.***

Writing

Either: As a director, write a letter to the Chief Executive of DKP outlining your solution to the problems.

Or: You are a sales manager. The behaviour of one of your salespeople is upsetting the other members of the team. Write a letter warning them about their conduct and indicating what improvements they should make in their behaviour.

Writing file page 126

UNIT **9**

Raising finance

'A bank is a place that will lend you money if you can prove that you don't need it.'
Bob Hope (1903–2003), American comedian

OVERVIEW

STARTING UP

A **What are the advantages and disadvantages for a private individual of borrowing money from these sources?**

1 a bank
2 a friend or colleague
3 a loan shark
4 a member of your family
5 a pawnbroker
6 a credit-card company

B **In what situations might someone use the sources of finance mentioned in Exercise A?**

example: *A loan shark if you have a poor credit rating*

C **What do you think these sayings mean? Do you agree with them?**

1 Money talks.
2 Don't put all your eggs in one basket.
3 You have to speculate to accumulate.
4 Don't throw good money after bad.
5 Lend your money and lose a friend.
6 Out of debt, out of danger.
7 He who pays the piper calls the tune.
8 Beggars can't be choosers.

D **What would you like to raise money for, and how would you do it?**

VOCABULARY
Financial terms

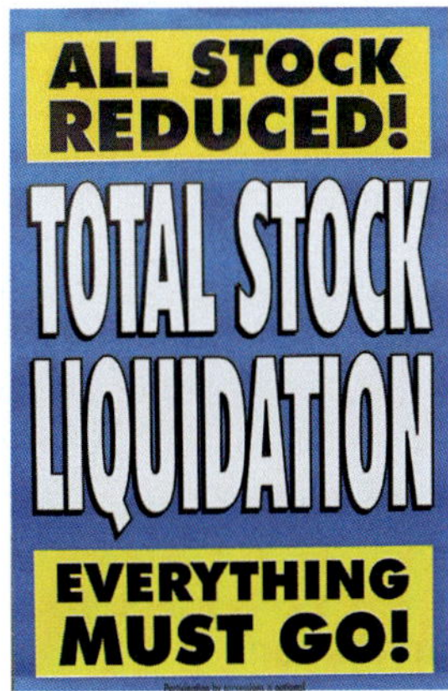

A Choose the correct word to complete each sentence.

1 Customers not paying on time often leads to .... problems.
   a) cashflow b) equity c) asset

2 Our state-of-the art machinery is our major ....
   a) possession b) asset c) equity

3 The .... rate on the loan was 12%.
   a) fee b) charge c) interest

4 They could not pay their debts and faced ....
   a) bankruptcy b) warranty c) overpayment

5 Sorbat has gone into .... with debts of about £20 million.
   a) indemnity b) investment c) administration

6 The finance a company raises from issuing shares rather than taking out loans is known as .... capital.
   a) equity b) dividend c) stock

7 The .... is the original amount of a loan not including any interest charged.
   a) instalment b) principal c) subsidy

8 A/An .... is a particular type of loan for the purchase of property.
   a) credit b) overdraft c) mortgage

9 If a company defaults on a loan, it means they miss a/an ....
   a) budget b) instalment c) collateral

10 Money lent to start-up businesses is known as risk or .... capital.
   a) share b) venture c) working

B Choose the correct words to complete each definition.

1 Being in the *red* / *black* means you are in credit.
2 A *loan* / *grant* is money which doesn't need to be repaid.
3 A *creditor* / *debtor* owes money.
4 *An interest* / *A dividend* payment is part of a profit paid to shareholders.
5 *Assets* / *Liabilities* are the total amounts of money owed by a business.
6 *An overdraft* / *A return* is the amount of profit made on an investment.
7 To go into *liquidation* / *debt* is when a company stops operating because of financial difficulties.
8 *A deposit* / *Collateral* is security for a loan in the form of assets which could be sold if the debt is unpaid.

C Discuss these statements.

1 Leasing machinery, vehicles, etc. makes more financial sense than buying them.
2 There should be more controls on access to credit.
3 Expanding fast means going into debt.
4 Declaring bankruptcy is a useful tool for clearing debts and starting again.
5 It is good practice to pay suppliers as late as possible and maximise any credit terms.
6 A successful business shouldn't need to raise a lot of finance.

LISTENING
Ways to raise money

Simon Davies

A CD3.1 **Simon Davies is Managing Director (Restructuring) at the Blackstone Group, a leading private equity firm. Listen to the first part of the interview and answer these questions.**

1 Which three ways of raising finance does he mention?

2 What are the advantages of:

a) private markets? b) public markets? c) borrowing money?

B CD3.2 **Listen to the second part and answer this question.**

What are the disadvantages of:

a) shares/equity? b) debt? c) public markets? d) private markets?

C CD3.3 **Listen to the final part. Simon says there are four reasons why finance has become a short-term business. What are they?**

D **In groups, discuss what you think about Warren Buffet's fund.**

READING
Finding finance

A **How can start-up companies raise money?**

B **Work in small groups. Before you read the article, check that you know the meanings of these terms. Use a dictionary if necessary.**

1 business angels
2 bank finance
3 equity finance
4 debt fundraising
5 venture capital funds

C **Work in pairs. Take notes on the key points of the article. Tell your partner about them and ask each other questions if you want clarification.**

Student A: Read the first half of the text up to line 57.
Student B: Read the second half of the text from line 58 to the end.

D **Read the whole article and answer these questions in pairs.**

1 What was the problem with some of the 'angel' networking clubs?
2 What was the advantage of London Business Angels?
3 How did Saha improve her ability to pitch to backers?
4 Who finally invested in Saha's company?
5 What is the problem with bank finance?
6 What is the position with debt funding and equity finance?
7 What is the problem with venture capital funds?

E **Find idioms in the first six paragraphs that mean the following.**

1 finish something you have started
2 a sudden or unexpected chance to do something that allows you to become successful in your job
3 reduce your chances of failure or loss by trying several possibilities instead of one
4 make sure you always know what is happening in a situation

F **Complete these sentences with the idioms in Exercise E.**

1 Do you think Isabella will .... this time?

2 There are hundreds of young musicians out there looking for a ....

3 It's a good idea to .... by applying to more than one MBA programme.

4 .... for information about the next fundraising event.

G **Discuss these questions.**

1 What questions would you ask Saha if you were an investor?

2 If you were setting up a business in your country, how would you raise the finance?

FT

No more easy money

by Jonathan Moules

Ambitious entrepreneurs are prepared to go the distance to get financial backing for their bright ideas. Sanchita Saha, founder of CitySocialising, a website to help people make new friends after relocating, travelled all the way to southern France.

This was not as pleasant an experience as it might seem. Once there, she spent months pitching to hundreds of potential investors to no avail, only to get a lucky break at the end.

First, she looked into 'angel' networking clubs, which provide entrepreneurs with access to large numbers of wealthy individuals interested in investing in early-stage ventures. However, she turned down a number of these for reasons of cost: they were charging £1,500 ($2,488) just to submit a business plan.

Eventually, she settled on London Business Angels, through which she could pitch to roughly 100 'angels'.

She also hedged her bets by securing a place on gateway2investment (g2i), a four-day programme to help ambitious entrepreneurs hone their pitching techniques, delivered by financial advisers Grant Thornton and backed by the London Development Agency.

'A lot of it is about networking – finding out who to talk to, who can help you, and keeping your ears to the ground,' she says.

Through LBA, Saha discovered a third scheme, called the European Border Investment Programme, which was running its own event in Nice.

Although it was a risk, she booked herself on a flight and found herself

pitching to another couple of hundred investors from across the European Union. Among those were a couple of Finnish investors who, together with five wealthy individuals at LBA, agreed to back Saha's business with a combined investment of £300,000.

Her work was not yet done, however, as she had to bring the disparate team together to form a syndicate with a lead investor, who would then become CitySocialising's Chairman.

'It was hard work and very stressful,' Saha admits. However, she is also one of the lucky ones.

Access to finance remains difficult for all sorts of companies, whether they are looking for rich individuals to take equity stakes, debt or venture capital.

Although bank finance is easier to get hold of than it was a year ago, the costs remain stubbornly high.

The latest quarterly research by the Federation of Small Businesses (FSB) found more than three-quarters of companies had seen the cost of their existing finance increase by up to 5 percentage points above the Bank of England's base rate.

Two-thirds of those in the FSB survey decided not to seek credit at the moment, which could suggest they are fearful of the cost.

The good news for start-ups is that the banks seem happier to lend to them, according to Stephen Alambritis at the FSB. 'That is a fresh approach,' he says.

Victoria Weisener, Programme Manager at g2i, is less optimistic about debt fundraising. 'What you hear is still the same: that people are lending, but we are not seeing any of that coming through,' she says.

She is similarly pessimistic about equity finance. 'While no one will say they are not actively investing, it is still pretty difficult to raise funds,' she says. 'Most of the activity is with business angels.'

Raising equity finance through venture capital funds is possible, but it is taking about twice as long as before the recession struck, according to Simon Cook, Chief Executive of venture capital firm DFJ Esprit, which has invested in some of Europe's most successful technology start-ups. In the past, both FeedBurner, the web-feed management system, and Skype, the Internet telephony service, have received backing from Cook's firm.

'Fundraising is taking longer and is slower, but funds are being raised,' he says.

LANGUAGE REVIEW
Dependent prepositions

Prepositions commonly occur after certain verbs, adjectives and nouns. Look at these examples from the article on page 85.

verbs	adjectives	nouns
DFJ Esprit has **invested in** technology start-ups.	They are **fearful of** the cost.	**Access to** finance ...
She spent months **pitching to** hundreds of investors.	She is less **optimistic about** debt fundraising.	Saha, **founder of** CitySocialising, ...

➡ ***Grammar reference*** page 150

A **Complete the extract from the article with suitable words and dependent prepositions from the box. Then look back to page 85 to check your answers.**

access to	investing in	looked into	pitch to	settled on	turned down

First, she ....[1] 'angel' networking clubs, which provide entrepreneurs with ....[2] large numbers of wealthy individuals interested in ....[3] early-stage ventures. However, she ....[4] a number of these for reasons of cost: they were charging £1,500 ($2,488) just to submit a business plan.

Eventually, she ....[5] London Business Angels, through which she could ....[6] roughly 100 'angels'.

B **Study the Grammar reference on page 150, then match these halves of sentences. They are all from newspaper articles or headlines.**

1. EFM, the struggling investment house, yesterday became vulnerable
2. The government refuses to take responsibility
3. Deputy Prime Minister invites Japan to invest
4. Does Lulu.com pose a serious threat
5. She is going to complain
6. The banks insisted
7. Our programme offers access
8. The new Director of Finance must be capable
9. Teenagers need to develop a healthy respect
10. All financial supervisors should be fully aware

a) for Dubai World's debt problems.
b) to the major publishing houses?
c) to takeover bids.
d) on being paid the interest on the loan.
e) to angel investors, venture firms and other private equity investors.
f) in high-tech sector.
g) of providing both financial and strategic direction.
h) about her solicitor.
i) of their responsibilities.
j) for money from an early age.

SKILLS
Negotiating

A **Which of these negotiating tips do you agree with? Why? / Why not?**

1. In the early stages, you need to ask the other side a lot of questions.
2. Always interrupt if you don't understand something.
3. Never make a concession for free. Always get something in return.
4. Use simple, direct language and be open about your aims.
5. Signal what you are going to do. For example, say, 'I'd just like to clarify that.'
6. Summarise often so that everyone is clear when you reach agreement.
7. Adapt your language so that you don't appear aggressive.
8. Talk about your emotions and how you are feeling.

B **Research shows that skilled negotiators often use the techniques listed below to achieve their negotiating objective. Match the techniques (1–5) to their definitions (a–e).**

1 Open questions
2 Closed questions
3 Softening phrases
4 Signalling phrases
5 Summarising

a) say what you are going to do before you do it.
b) modify language so that it does not appear too aggressive.
c) go over the points covered to highlight when agreement is reached.
d) gather information and explore the opposite number's views.
e) check understanding and ask for precise information.

C CD3.4 **Listen to five expressions and match each one to the correct technique in Exercise B.**

D CD3.5 **Listen to the dialogue and complete these expressions. Then place each expression under the correct heading in the Useful language box below.**

1 Could I ask you, what other people are .... for you?
2 Have you .... any other bank, if I may ask?
3 I'd like to make a .... Why don't you revise your business plan?
4 Good. Could I ask what sort of .... you have in mind?
5 .... what the money's for. The 250,000 would be for working capital ...
6 We seem to be getting somewhere now. Let me .... what we've agreed so far ...

E **Work in pairs. Role-play this situation.**

The manufacturer of a range of high-quality herbal tea products, sold under the brand name Quality Leaf, meets a business angel to get additional investment to develop its business. The business owner has already borrowed $100,000 from a family member, and in return has given that person a 5% stake in the business.

Student A: Turn to page 137.
Student B: Turn to page 139.

USEFUL LANGUAGE

OPEN QUESTIONS
Why do you need a loan?
What other sources of finance do you have?
What did you have in mind?

CLOSED QUESTIONS
Do you have any other backers?
Can you transfer the money by next week?
Could you improve your credit terms?

SOFTENING PHRASES
I'm sorry, we can't go that high.
We were hoping to pay a little less.
That seems very expensive

SIGNALLING PHRASES
I'd like to make a proposal. I think we should ...
Could I make a suggestion: why don't we ... ?
Let's look at this another way.

SUMMARISING
Let's see what we've got so far.
Let's recap before we go on to ...
So, to sum up, ...

Case study 9

Last throw of the dice

A talented team of filmmakers needs finance for their first feature film. Can they negotiate the right terms from an established distributor?

Background

Charles Williams and Gunnar Larsson met on a film-studies course in Paris. After graduating, they formed a company and produced short films for television which won awards at international film festivals. They then decided to make a feature film. They produced a business plan for their project, then looked for an independent distributor to finance their low-budget film.

Read this extract from their business plan summarising the concept of their film. What sources do you think they will use to get the finance?

Executive summary

This proposal is for a feature film shot on digital video. Its running time will be 110 minutes. There will be a four-month shooting schedule and six weeks of editing. The budget for the film is 1.2 million euros. A total of 200,000 euros has already been raised from family and friends.

All for one is the story of three women in Paris. They are in their late twenties and of different nationalities. They become great friends, go out together, talk about their experiences and get advice from each other. The film focuses on their difficulties adapting to French culture and on their complex relationships with the men in their lives. There will be a bitter-sweet ending to the film, but the final scene will highlight the strength of their friendship, which helps them to overcome their problems.

Financing the film

Getting finance for the film has been very difficult. However, at the last moment, an independent film distributor, Concordia, expressed interest in their concept. Charles and Gunnar sent their business plan to Concordia and arranged to have a meeting with them. At the same time, Charles's father e-mailed them to say that he had sent their business plan to a well-known distributor in the US.

If Concordia agree to finance the project, what do you think will be the financial terms they offer? What will they expect to get in return for their investment?

Here are some extracts from the business plan.

Target audience
20–40-year-olds. Frequent film-goers who enjoy sophisticated films, witty dialogue and the complexities of human relationships. Older people should also enjoy the film.

Target market
Initially European countries, but eventually worldwide distribution

Promotion
The film will be shown at European film festivals (Cannes, Berlin) and also at the prestigious Sundance Festival in the US. There will be other marketing initiatives at the launch and during the distribution of the film.

Production schedule
- Pre-production: one month
- Production: four months
- Post-production: six weeks
- Release of the film *All for one* in Europe: in nine months' time

Three-year income projection summary (gross revenues)
- Low: 15 million euros
- Medium: 20 million euros
- High: 40–60 million euros*

* Depends on US distribution

Reasons why *All for one* will appeal to audiences
- Outstanding script (Gunnar Larsson) and brilliant director (Charles Williams)
- Fascinating storyline
- Original film score by Gunnar Larsson
- Cross-cultural appeal of the main characters and situations
- Dramatic tension
- High-quality photography
- Paris location

Task

Work in two groups. The filmmakers are going to negotiate with the distributors.

Group A (the two filmmakers):
Turn to page 137.
Group B (Directors of Concordia):
Turn to page 144.

1 Read your role cards and prepare for the negotiation.

2 Hold a meeting and negotiate a draft agreement.

3 **CD3.6** At the end of the meeting, Charles's father phones from the United States. He has some interesting news for the filmmakers and Concordia. His call is heard by both sides in Concordia's office. Decide whether you want to revise the terms of your draft agreement in the light of the news you've just heard.

Watch the Case study commentary on the ***DVD-ROM.***

Writing

As Director of the film or as Chief Executive of Concordia, write a summary of the points you agreed during the negotiation and indicating how the project will proceed.

→ *Writing file* page 129

3 Managing international teams

A Discuss these questions.

1 Think about a team you have been a member of. Was it successful? Why? / Why not?

2 What do you understand by an 'international' team?

3 Have you ever been a member of an international team, or do you know of one? If so, how well did the team work together?

B Which of these descriptions of the role of a team leader do you most agree with? Explain your ideas.

The team leader is someone who:

1 has a charismatic personality. They are not only able to do their job well, but can get other team members to follow them. Their skills enable them to get the best from the rest of the team.

2 is an older person and is therefore greatly respected. Their role is to collect information from the other team members and from outside, to consider options and then to make decisions.

3 is simply the boss. They will provide clear instructions and directions for team members. They are there to make decisions, which could be right or wrong but which they must make. It's what they are paid for.

4 is the most competent person, but no more important than the others. They will make proposals, which the other team members are expected to analyse and question. This will help the decision-making process.

C Ideas about the role of a team leader vary from culture to culture. What other cultural differences do you think international teams may have? Think about these points.

- methods of communication
- motivation and rewards
- ways of problem-solving
- sharing knowledge
- the role or use of humour
- the purpose/role of meetings
- job titles / position
- social behaviour

D CD3.7, 3.8, 3.9 **Listen to all three parts of a radio programme and answer these questions.**

1 Which of the topics in Exercise C do the experts talk about?

2 Which do they think is the most interesting?

E CD3.7 **Listen to the first part again and answer these questions.**

1 What types of international team are identified?

2 What expectations of a team leader are discussed?

3 Why is praising an individual team member not always a good idea?

F CD3.8 **Listen to the second part again and take notes to answer this question.**

How are attitudes to sharing knowledge different for:

a) individual cultures?
b) collective cultures?
c) mutual debt cultures?

G CD3.9 **Listen to the final part again and answer these questions.**

1 In what ways can meetings cause problems?

2 What social factors are mentioned?

3 Why is a handshake important?

What is the most interesting or surprising piece of information for you?

Task

You work for a leading mobile phone company based in Amsterdam in the Netherlands. The working language of the company is English. You are managers in charge of setting up an international team of 12 people who are based all over the world. The team will be working on a major project lasting three years, building and testing a new network for the company's next generation of products. In the past, there have been both cultural and teamworking problems in project teams set up by the company. A meeting has been called with fellow managers to agree the way the team will work.

Work in groups of four. Turn to the correct page and study your role card. Look at the agenda below and prepare for the meeting.

Manager A: Turn to page 139. Manager C: Turn to page 143.
Manager B: Turn to page 137. Manager D: Turn to page 135.

Hold the meeting. Discuss the items on the agenda below and come up with recommendations.

Write a list of tips for managing or working in international teams.

AGENDA

1. The team leader and his/her role
2. The role of meetings
3. Communication between team members
4. Rewards and bonuses
5. Cultural training programmes
6. AOB

7 Management styles

VOCABULARY

1 Complete this table.

adjective	negative adjective	noun
considerate	...........[1]	...........[2]
...........[3]	incompetent	...........[4]
...........[5]	...........[6]	creativity
diplomatic	...........[7]	...........[8]
...........[9]	indecisive	...........[10]
...........[11]	...........[12]	flexibility
inspiring	...........[13]	...........[14]
...........[15]	illogical	...........[16]
...........[17]	...........[18]	loyalty
organised	...........[19]	...........[20]
...........[21]	inefficient	...........[22]
...........[23]	...........[24]	responsibility
sociable	...........[25]	...........[26]
...........[27]	unsupportive	...........[28]

2 Choose the best word to complete each sentence.

1. Byron makes all the decisions himself. He's not at all *autocratic / collaborative.*
2. Melanie is really *people-orientated / controlling*. She's a very good listener, and I think she really enjoys the social side of work.
3. Pete has a *centralising / laissez-faire* management style. He doesn't make all of the decisions, but everything that happens in the office crosses his desk.
4. Alberto's real strength is that he's *directive / task-orientated*. He loves scheduling, organising and completing a job.
5. Leyla's a *hands-on / empowering* manager. She doesn't just tell people what to do, she really gets involved in the work.
6. Andre's *delegating / democratic* style means that when we have meetings, he really listens to everyone's opinion. Consensus is very important to him.

TEXT REFERENCE

Complete the e-mail below with the pronouns in the box.

he it the one them they we

Dear Mika,

...........'s[1] 10 p.m., but I'm still in the office. Mr Chang is in New York today, and ....[2] asked me to help him finish his two PowerPoint presentations. He wants to show ....[3] to the New York team first thing tomorrow morning when ....[4] start work.

Do you remember Dr Jarvis? He was ....[5] who invited Mr Chang to come to New York. He's there, and he said if the project goes well, ...[6] can all expect a rise! I'd better get back to work.

Irving

SKILLS

Match the sentence halves.

1 Let me give
2 OK, now I'll talk
3 It will give
4 The consequence
5 Let's look
6 Let me draw your attention
7 The purpose of my talk today
8 I'd just like

a) us an edge over the competition.
b) you an example.
c) to highlight last year's figures.
d) to the slide.
e) about the budget.
f) of this is an increase in price.
g) at the chart.
h) is to explain our new sales campaign.

8 Team building

VOCABULARY

Complete the sentences below using the prefixes in the box.

bi dis hyper mis multi post- pre- pro-

1 The electricity was off yesterday morning. Workers ....connected it to make some repairs.
2 Before the conference, we had a ....event party with a light meal and drinks.
3 Malcolm's company has offices in Luxembourg, Madrid and Paris, so he's very ....European in his thinking.
4 I'm afraid there's a real ....match between your salary expectations and what we can afford to pay you.
5 After we did the role play, we had a ....activity discussion to talk about what we'd learned.
6 We're very happy that both sides feel the same way. This ....lateral agreement will make it easy to move ahead.
7 With workers from 27 different nations, our company is truly ....cultural.
8 If you go to our website, you'll see that our list of distributors is ....linked to each company's website.

SKILLS

a) What's really bothering you?
b) Well, one thing you could do is offer to help him.
c) I know how you feel. We've put a lot of work into it.
d) OK, good. You talk to Anita, and let's meet tomorrow and see how things are going.
e) It might be worth asking Anita, then.
f) What's the best approach, do you think?

Complete this conversation with the sentences on the left.

Brad I'm worried about the sales conference next week.
Ana ....[1]
Brad Yes, we have. But we're used to hard work. That's not really what I'm worried about.
Ana ....[2]
Brad My main concern is Nick. What really worries me is that he still hasn't prepared his presentation. Everyone else has shared their PowerPoint shows and done a practice presentation, but we have nothing from Nick.
Ana ....[3]
Brad That's the problem. I really don't know what to do.
Ana ....[4]
Brad I don't think that would do much good. I'm afraid Nick is still upset that I was promoted and he wasn't.
Ana ....[5]
Brad Mmm. I think that's the right approach to take. Nick really trusts Anita.
Ana ....[6]

WRITING

Write a positive, encouraging e-mail of 100–120 words from Ana to Nick based on the conversation in Skills on page 93.

- Remind him about the conference.
- Remind him of the work his colleagues have already done.
- Offer encouragement and specific help.

9 Raising finance

VOCABULARY

1 Match the sentence halves.

1 A major client is late paying, so we have
2 Every month, we pay
3 We're trying to raise
4 Our main shop has a €200,000
5 We're paying a 4%
6 We'll declare
7 If the business fails, it will go into
8 Our town-centre location is a real

a) administration.
b) mortgage on it.
c) an instalment of our loan.
d) asset.
e) interest rate on our loan.
f) some venture capital to start our new business.
g) bankruptcy if we run out of money.
h) a cashflow problem.

2 Circle the odd expression out in each group.

1 in the red in the black in credit assets
2 a loan a debtor a grant an overdraft
3 liabilities debts costs collateral
4 a creditor an interest payment a dividend payment a deposit

DEPENDENT PREPOSITIONS

Complete these sentences with *to, for, of, about* or *in*.

1 We have a lot of overseas sales, so we're vulnerable .... exchange-rate fluctuations.
2 Do you have access .... the online database?
3 If there's a safety problem, we'll take responsibility .... it.
4 Times are hard now, but I'm optimistic .... the future.
5 We're capable .... filling large orders in a short period of time.
6 Mr Iqbal was the founder .... the company back in 1889.
7 Rising oil prices pose a threat .... low-cost transport.
8 We need to complain .... the quality-control problem. The stuff they've been sending us isn't good enough.
9 If we pitch .... serious athletes, the product will also appeal to people who wear athletic clothes for fashion.
10 We invest .... our employees because we believe that people are our greatest asset.

SKILLS

Complete the text below with the words in the box.

aggressive closed open signalling softening summarising

Skilled negotiators often use several techniques to achieve their negotiating objectives. They use ....[1] phrases such as *I'm sorry, but* ... and *we were hoping* ... to modify language so that it doesn't sound too ....[2]. They also use two types of question. ....[3] questions gather information and explore the opposite number's views, while ....[4] questions check understanding and ask for precise information. Phrases such as *I'd like to make a proposal* are called ....[5] phrases. Skilled negotiators use them to say what they're going to do before they do it. Finally, skilled negotiators usually use ....[6] phrases to highlight when agreement is reached, for example: *Let's recap before we go on.*

Cultures 3: Managing international teams

1 Read these opinions about managing team dynamics. Tick the culture type(s) in which you would expect to see the dyamnic operating. Some dynamics appear in more than one culture type.

team dynamics	general culture type		
	individual	collective	mutual debt
1 Praising a member of my team is the best way to motivate them.			
2 I often ask a colleague for help, even if I don't need it. It helps build team spirit.			
3 I share knowledge and information only on a 'need-to-know' basis.			
4 I prefer to ask a colleague for help rather than go to the boss.			
5 If someone helps me, I try to find a way to help them in return.			
6 Knowledge confirms status, it's as simple as that.			
7 I praise my whole team for successes and equally, we all share any blame for failures.			
8 In my team, we share knowledge because that's good for everyone.			

2 Choose the best word to complete each sentence.

1 Some team members may expect tasks to be very clearly set out by the manager or team leader, while others expect to use their own *initiative / empowerment.*

2 Team members from different cultures will have *expectations / plans* about the number and purpose of meetings.

3 Because of time-zone differences, *scheduling / writing minutes of* virtual meetings can be difficult.

4 When teams meet *virtually / face to face*, body language, dress and manners become very important.

5 A firm handshake can have different *connotations / challenges* in different cultures.

6 In some *cultures / people*, team meetings are simply for planning.

3.1 Presentations

Objectives

Speaking
Can give clear presentations highlighting significant points with relevant supporting detail.

Listening
Can understand the main points of complex academic/ professional presentations.

Lesson deliverable
To plan, prepare and give a presentation on life skills including main points with supporting detail.

Performance review
To review your own progress and performance against the lesson objectives at the end of the lesson.

A SPEAKING 1

1 Work in pairs. Which items 1–10 represent confident body language in presentations? Add more examples.

1 Cross your arms or legs.
2 Stand up straight with your arms open.
3 Put your hand over your mouth.
4 Face the audience.
5 Speak in a monotone voice.
6 Make eye contact with the audience.
7 Turn your back to the audience to read your slides.
8 Constantly touch your hair or face.
9 Nod your head to emphasise your points.
10 Use vocal variety.

2 Work in pairs. Discuss these questions.

1 Have you ever stood in front of a mirror to rehearse a presentation?
2 Have you ever recorded or made a video of yourself rehearsing or giving a presentation (on a smartphone or video camera)?
3 What did you notice about your voice and body language that you wanted to change?
4 How can we use body language to highlight significant points in a presentation?

3 Work in small groups. Take turns to stand up and talk for one minute about a topic you know well (your work, a hobby ...). Use confident body language.

B LISTENING 1

1 BSA3.1.9 Listen to part of a presentation by a communications expert.

1 How does she start her presentation?
2 What is her main point?
3 When does she make it?

2 BSA3.1.10 Listen to the next part of the presentation. Match the four significant points the speaker makes to slides A–D below.

1 Point 1 – slide ________
2 Point 2 – slide ________
3 Point 3 – slide ________
4 Point 4 – slide ________

A
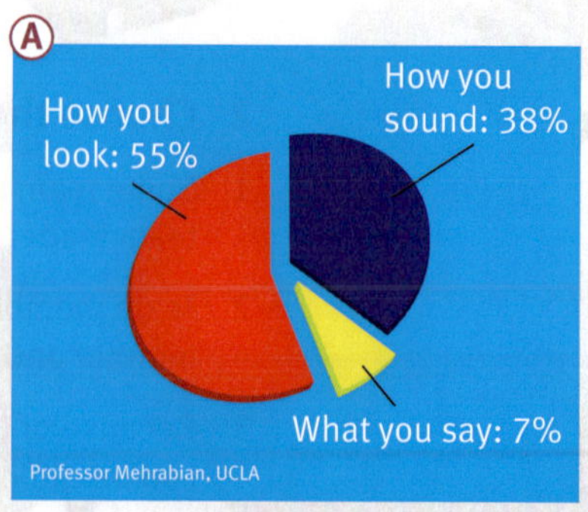

B

C Body language
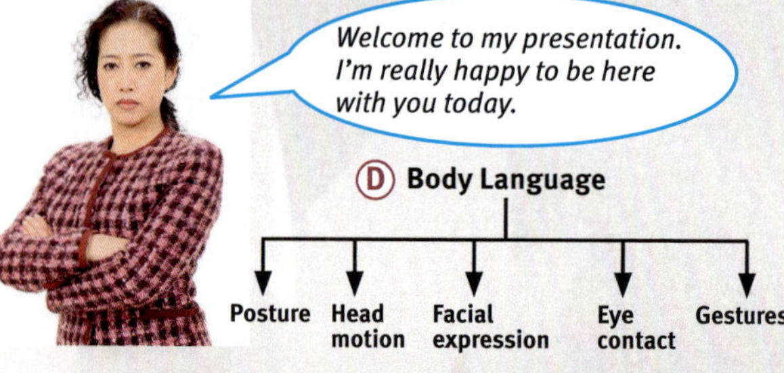

C LISTENING 2

1 BSA3.1.9–BSA3.1.10 **The presenter uses different techniques to support her points. Listen to the whole presentation again. Tick (✓) the techniques she uses.**

Techniques	Main point	Point 1	Point 2	Point 3	Point 4
Quote a famous person	✓				
Show an image or graphic					
Refer to evidence from research					
Quote a statistic					
Give a demonstration					

2 BSA3.1.9–BSA3.1.10 **What did the presenter say? Choose the correct option. Listen again and check.**

1 *In the words of Mark Twain ... / The writer Mark Twain once said* there are only two types of speaker ...

2 *I'd like to show you ... / Let's take a look at* this photo here ...

3 *This brings me to ... / This leads me to* Professor Albert Mehrabian's communications model ...

4 *You may have seen ... / You might be familiar with* this pie chart ...

5 Mehrabian's *findings were ... / research was* not related to all communication ...

6 *This next slide shows that ... / So, as you can see on this next slide,* there are many aspects of body language ...

7 *That brings me to my final thought ... / Moving on to my final point* for today ...

8 *This was demonstrated by ... / This was shown by* American psychologist Amy Cuddy ...

D SPEAKING 2

Student A turns to page x. Student B turns to page xi. Practise making statements and giving supporting detail.

Task

Pre-task: Discussion

1 Work in pairs and brainstorm the following topics.

Student A and B: Time management tips.
Student C and D: Stress and relaxation tips.

2 Work with another pair and share your ideas. Go online to do further research or refer to the texts on pages xii and xiv. Note down any new ideas.

Part 1: Preparation

You work for a multinational company. You need to prepare a 3–5 minute presentation about life skills for new recruits to your company. Focus on your Pre-task topic.

Work in your pairs from Pre-task Exercise 1. Prepare your presentation. Think about the following.

Structure:
- Decide on an overall statement to introduce your talk and get the audience's attention.
- Agree on three or four significant points for your presentation, choosing ideas from the Pre-task.

Techniques and language:
- Remember to use confident body language.
- Give relevant supporting detail for each significant point, using a range of techniques.
- Use signalling language to highlight your points.

Part 2: Presentation

Presenters:
Use the guidance in Task Part 1. Give your presentation.

Audience:
Make notes. What examples of supporting detail did the presenters use? Think of one question to ask.

Extra Practice: DVD clip and Worksheet 15

E PEER REVIEW

Complete the sentences about another presentation. Give feedback.

- The significant points you highlighted were ....
- The types of supporting detail you used were ....
- What I liked about your presentation was ....
- One suggestion to improve the presentation is ....

F SELF-ASSESSMENT

Look back at the lesson objectives. Write 50–80 words to assess your presentation. Think about:

- What techniques and language did you use to highlight significant points with relevant supporting detail?
- What do you think you did well?
- What would you like to do better next time?

G PROFESSIONAL DEVELOPMENT AND PERFORMANCE GOALS

Write three sentences about ways you will improve how you present main points in future.

3.2 Meetings

Business skills

Objectives

Speaking

- Can give detailed opinions during work-related meetings if provided with sufficient background information.
- Can lead a meeting about a product or service offered by a company or institution.

Listening

Can understand main points and check comprehension by using contextual clues.

Lesson deliverable

To plan, prepare and participate in a meeting.

Performance review

To review your own progress and performance against the lesson objectives by the end of the lesson.

A SPEAKING 1

Discuss the following points with a partner. Then compare your ideas with the rest of the group.

1 Should a meeting always have a leader?

2 What can happen if it does not have one?

3 Think of the different tasks a meeting leader has to perform. How does he or she do this effectively?

B LISTENING 1

1 BSA3.2.11 **Amita is the director of Bright Ideas, an advertising agency. She has called a meeting to kick off a new project. Listen to the opening of the meeting. What is the aim of the meeting?**

2 BSA3.2.11 **Listen again and put Amita's actions in the order you hear them.**

.... States the meeting aim.

.... Refers to the agenda.

.... Gives timings.

.... Runs through the agenda points.

.... Starts the meeting.

.... Greets the participants.

3 BSA3.2.12 **Listen to the main part of the meeting. Take notes on the agenda.**

Meeting, September 15th

Agenda

1 Service

2 Target market

3 Production budget

4 Filming schedule

5 Storyline

6 Location

4 BSA3.2.12 **Listen to the main part of the meeting again. Amita uses a number of expressions to lead the meeting. Note them down next to the headings.**

1 Asking a participant to talk: *Right, I'll hand over to Vijay.*

2 Dealing with an interruption: Isabella ....

3 Asking for an opinion: Isabella, ...?

4 Asking a different participant to speak: Over ....

5 Setting the group a task: So ....

6 Assigning a responsibility to one participant: Isabella, ...

C LISTENING AND SPEAKING 2

BSA3.2.13 **Listen to Amita close the meeting. Which expressions does she use to:**

1 Give feedback to the participants

2 Sum up the situation

3 Allocate tasks

4 Plan

Task

Pre-task: Preparation

Context: You are a group of advertising agency creatives. A client has asked you to make a series of 40 second adverts for four different products and services. The adverts will be shown in cinemas around the world. You have a budget of £1 million.

Work in small groups. You are going to hold a series of brainstorming meetings to decide on a storyline for each of the four adverts. In each meeting you will plan a storyline for a different product or service. Look at the list of products and services below and choose one to discuss in your first meeting.

a budget airline	an eco-friendly holiday resort
a smart watch	a luxury skin care range

Part 1: Brainstorming meeting

1 **Choose a meeting leader and an observer. Turn to page xiii for the meeting leader role card and observer worksheet.**

2 **Hold the first meeting and brainstorm ideas for a storyline. The observer should pay attention to the meeting leader and one of the participants. The meeting should last for 5–10 minutes.**

3 **Hold the next meeting for a different product. Elect a new meeting leader and an observer who pays attention to a different participant.**

4 **Repeat and change roles in each meeting.**

Part 2: Collaborative writing

In small groups, write up the storyline for one of your adverts.

Extra Practice: DVD clip and Worksheet 16

D PEER REVIEW

Use the completed observer sheets to give feedback to the classmates you observed. Consider the following questions in your discussion, be specific and give examples:

1 What was good about the way in which they led the meeting?

2 What was good about the way in which they participated in the meeting?

3 What point would you suggest that they develop next time they take part in a meeting

E SELF-ASSESSMENT

Think about your performance and write a 150-word report. Look back at the learning objectives. How successfully have you achieved them? What do you need to improve further? How might you achieve this?

F PROFESSIONAL DEVELOPMENT AND PERFORMANCE GOALS

Identify an opportunity in work or a study situation where you would be able to practise leading meetings using the language you have learnt.

UNIT **10**

Customer service

'The customer is never wrong.'
César Ritz (1850–1918), Swiss hotelier

OVERVIEW

VOCABULARY
Complaints

LISTENING
Customer service

READING
Changing customer service

LANGUAGE REVIEW
Gerunds

SKILLS
Active listening

CASE STUDY
Hurrah Airlines

STARTING UP

A **Which of the following irritate you the most when dealing with customer service departments? Choose the top three and compare with a partner.**

on the phone	face to face	repairs and refunds
• Being put on hold • Speaking to a disinterested person • Choosing a series of options during your call • Finding the customer service number is continuously engaged • Being cut off	• Unhelpful customer service personnel • Stressed or indifferent staff • Salespeople with poor product knowledge • Too few staff at peak times • No company policy on customer service or complaints	• Delays on repairs • Delays in getting money back • No replacement equipment while repairs are carried out • Poor-quality repairs • Disputes over credit notes, 'proof of purchase', etc.

B **Discuss these questions.**

1 How important to a company's success is customer care?

2 Is it possible to have too much customer care?

3 In what situations can too much customer service become a problem? Have you ever experienced this?

vocabulary
Complaints

A **Complete the beginnings of the sentences (1–7) with words from the box. Then complete each sentence with an ending (a–g).**

compensation complaints guarantee payment rapport refunds standards

1 When you handle ...., it is important
2 You can establish a .... with a customer if
3 A money-back .... if not completely satisfied is often
4 Companies which do not meet their .... of service
5 Giving .... promptly and without fuss to dissatisfied customers is one indicator
6 When a company is at fault, a one-off goodwill .... is a useful way
7 Financial .... for poor customer service is not the

a) only way to meet customer expectations.
b) will lose customers.
c) you know about their buying habits.
d) to be diplomatic.
e) to retain customer loyalty.
f) of high-quality customer service.
g) a minimum expectation these days.

B **Match the idiomatic expressions (1–7) to their meanings (a–g).**

1 pass the buck
2 get to the bottom of the problem
3 the last straw
4 slip my mind
5 ripped off
6 talk at cross purposes
7 go the extra mile

a) forget to do something
b) paid far too much for something
c) avoid responsibility
d) find the real cause of something
e) the last in a series of irritating events
f) try harder in order to achieve something
g) misunderstand what someone else is referring to

C **Use the expressions from Exercise B in the correct form to complete these sentences appropriately.**

1 The helpline person was very good and spent time with me. She started at the beginning in order to .... and find a solution.
2 He's the person responsible. He shouldn't try to .... and blame others for his mistakes.
3 Several customers have complained about our service contract. They say they're paying far too much and feel they have been ....
4 I meant to send him a brochure, but we were very busy. I got distracted and it ....
5 They wanted to place a larger order. I thought they wanted a bigger discount. We were ....
6 They ignored my complaints, but what made me really angry was when they refused to refund my money. Really, it was ....
7 She was extremely helpful and was prepared to .... to solve the problem, so I'll definitely use the company again.

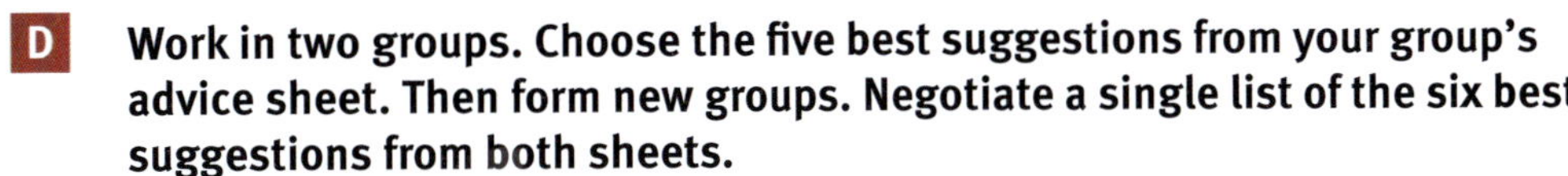
D **Work in two groups. Choose the five best suggestions from your group's advice sheet. Then form new groups. Negotiate a single list of the six best suggestions from both sheets.**

Group A: Turn to page 144. Group B: Turn to page 138.

LISTENING
Customer service

A **You are going to hear an interview with Philip Newman-Hall, Director and General Manager of Raymond Blanc's restaurant Le Manoir aux Quat'Saisons in Oxfordshire, England. In groups, discuss the best and worst customer service you have had in a restaurant.**

Philip Newman-Hall

B CD3.10 **Listen to the first part of the interview. Would you like to go to Le Manoir? Why? / Why not?**

C CD3.11 **Listen to the second part and complete these extracts.**

I would say that we try to exceed ....[1], [...] we have to have ....[2] with the ....[3] and we have to try and judge each client ....[4], so that we sense what they are ....[5] for and try and ....[6] that service all the time.

We also must provide ....[7] of service.

... 'the standards you set are the ....[8] you ....[9]'.

D CD3.12 **Listen to the third part and answer these questions.**

1 What do all the staff at Le Manoir do, and why is this useful when dealing with demanding customers?

2 What does Philip say about expectations?

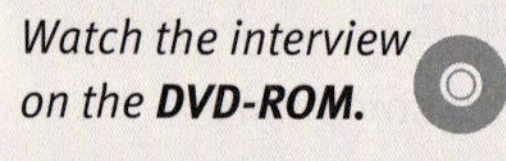

E CD3.13 **Listen to the final part. How are customers changing, what are they doing, and how can this be useful?**

READING
Changing customer service

A **Read the article on the opposite page quickly and say if the writer agrees with these statements. Ignore the words in bold for the moment.**

1 Customer service is very important.

2 Good customer service means always being able to speak to a person.

B **Read the article again and answer these questions.**

1 How has customer service changed?

2 What did some customers not like at first?

3 What can companies do with customer data?

4 Why do a lot of customers have bad experiences?

C **Summarise paragraph 5 in one sentence. Then compare your summary with a partner. Finally, discuss whether you agree with the position taken by the author of the article.**

D **Find idioms in the first and last paragraphs that mean the following.**

1 to say that you support or agree with something without doing anything to prove it

2 while physically close to someone

3 information you get by someone telling you

E **Complete these sentences using the idioms in Exercise D.**

1 I'd rather explain ...., not on the phone.

2 .... is one of the best ways of getting business.

3 Some companies don't really care about career development, they just .... to it.

FT

Customer service is changing the world: Up close and global

by Mike Betzer, President of Relationship Technology Management at Convergys

Customer service has changed. Thirty years ago, for example, service was personal and familiar and when issues arose, they were typically handled face to face with a local manager.

Now, global corporations have millions of customers. **By using** customer service experts and the latest technology, these companies were able to focus on **dealing** with their bread-and-butter business. The thinking was that **by refocusing** in this way, productivity and innovation would increase, enabling organisations to bring new products to market more quickly.

This approach generated its share of bad press. It took many customers a long time to get used to **speaking** to customer service representatives based in other parts of the world or mechanical systems that didn't offer the right choices.

A new approach was called for. Businesses needed to adapt locally in order to capitalise globally. They needed to take the traditional, personal approach and apply it to their customer service strategy across the world. They needed to get personal while operating on a global scale. For example, confectioner Thornton's listened to customer feedback and developed a more personal service, using a new gift service to drive sales of its high-end products.

Companies need to use all their resources effectively. The familiarity of technology today means customers no longer recoil from voice and touch automated services, as long as they meet their requirements, whether they are requesting account statements or need to replace a broken phone. The response also has to be personal. This means **pre-empting** the customer's needs and **acting** intuitively to minimise the time they spend on the phone. This is where the customer insight, mentioned above, coupled with the means to deploy this with the front line, comes in.

Companies need to collate and analyse the huge amounts of customer data they store, creating a central repository that can build profiles of customers. Using insights into their location, previous purchases, personal data and other information, customer management systems can react as soon as a customer contacts the business. A bank customer rings an automated number and is prompted to enter an account number. Triggered by the unique number, the technology 'knows' what services the caller already has, what issues they may have inquired about in the past, and then builds a profile of the customer and offers choices or remedies to suit their individual needs. Behind all this waits an agent, monitoring several calls. Should a customer become irate or frustrated, the agent can intercede and provide a valuable human contact, knowing exactly what the customer is trying to achieve.

Using analytics can be the difference between a positive and a negative experience for the customer. Yet businesses often don't make the best use of these insights. Companies seem happy to rely on canned, scripted responses, poorly trained agents and clunky systems to deliver customer services. It's therefore no surprise that so many people have horror stories. While 30 years ago, word may never have leaked out about a poor customer service incident, now it can be found as easily as **searching** on Google.

What companies need to remember is that **maintaining**, or perhaps even **acquiring**, an outsourced customer service infrastructure could be the difference between **maintaining** a cadre of loyal customers during the downturn and **being** first off the line when the race restarts, and being left behind. **Outsourcing** like this is not an indulgence; it is a crucial part of business.

If companies pay lip service to customers, whether consumer or business, they run the risk of **missing** out on valuable profits; those that value their customers and view them not only a source of revenue but also a means to improve as a business can reap the rewards. They can secure continuous business as well as positive word of mouth **by keeping** things personal when working globally.

F **Which changes in customer service mentioned in the article have you noticed, and in which industries?**

LANGUAGE REVIEW
Gerunds

- A gerund is formed from a verb but can behave like a noun.
  - It can be the subject of a sentence or clause.
    Satisfying *the customer is the aim of every business.*
  - It can be the object of a sentence or clause.
    I hate ***listening*** *to computerised voicemail mazes.*
  - It often follows a preposition.
    They became successful ***by listening*** *to their customers.*

  A useful way to use gerunds is in lists. (See page 96, Exercise A, 'on the phone'.)
- Gerunds are formed by adding *-ing* to the base form of the verb:
  launch → launching; involve → involving; get → getting
- *Begin, start, continue* and *intend* can be followed by the gerund or *to* with little or no difference in meaning.
- Some verbs can be followed by either a gerund or an infinitive, but the choice can lead to a change in meaning.
  – *She remembered to update the customer database. (She didn't forget.)*
  – *She remembered updating the customer database. (She has a clear memory of this.)*

→ ***Grammar reference*** page 150

A **The article on page 99 has many examples of the gerund (shown in bold). Find:**

1 two examples as the subject of a sentence
2 one example as the object of a sentence or clause
3 three examples following a preposition.

B **Match these sentences (1–6) to their meanings (a–f).**

1 I regret telling you …
2 I regret to tell you …
3 We stopped producing the Alpha model.
4 We stopped to produce the Alpha model
5 I tried speaking to Customer Services.
6 I tried to speak to Customer Services.

a) I am sorry about the bad news I am about to tell you.
b) I told you and I wish I hadn't.
c) We stopped the production of something else in order to produce the Alpha model.
d) We stopped the production of the Alpha model.
e) I couldn't get through to anyone there.
f) It didn't resolve the problem.

C **Complete these guidelines for improving customer service with suitable gerunds. Add some tips of your own.**

Improving customer service

Recommended ways of improving customer service include:

1 returning calls promptly.
2 …………… research to find out what customers need.
3 …………… staff training programmes in customer care.
4 …………… quickly with complaints.
5 …………… the customer is happy with the outcome.
6 …………… from complaints.
7 …………… a rapport with customers.
8 …………… about customers' buying habits.
9 …………… refunds promptly to dissatisfied customers.
10 …………… customers who are worried.

SKILLS

Active listening

A **How do you know if someone is not listening to you? How does it make you feel?**

B **Which of the following do you do to show people that you are listening to them? Can you add any other suggestions?**

- Look people directly in the eye at all times.
- Nod your head often to show interest.
- Repeat what the speaker has said in your own words.
- Be aware of the speaker's body language.
- Interrupt the speaker often to show you are listening.
- Think about what you are going to say while the speaker is talking.
- Use body language to show you are attentive.
- Try to predict what the speaker is going to say next.
- Ask questions if you do not understand.
- Say nothing until you are absolutely sure that the speaker has finished.

C CD3.14, 3.15, 3.16 **Listen to three conversations in which people are talking about customer service and make notes under these headings.**

a) The product or service involved

b) Reasons why the customer thought the service was good or bad

D CD3.14, 3.15, 3.16 **Listen again. Tick the words and phrases in the Useful language box below that you hear. Then add other words and phrases of your own.**

E **Work in pairs. Describe the best thing that you have ever bought and say whether you were influenced by the service you received. When your partner is speaking, make an effort to listen actively. Use some of the language from the Useful language box.**

USEFUL LANGUAGE

SHOWING INTEREST

How can I help?
Really?
That's interesting.
Right/OK/Mmm/Yes/No
Mmm, let's hear the full story ...
OK, go on ...

SHOWING EMPATHY

I know what you mean.
How awful!
I'm not surprised you're upset.
I really understand how you feel.

ASKING FOR DETAILS

So what happened?
What did you do next?
How did you deal with it?
What did you like especially about ... ?
What else impressed you?

CLARIFYING

Yes, that's right.
Are you saying ... ?
What (exactly) do you mean by ... ?
Could you be more specific, please?
Have I got this right?

SUMMARISING

(So) you think ...
(So) you're saying ...
(So) what you're really concerned/unhappy about is ...

REPETITION / QUESTION TAGS

A: We've reduced customer complaints by 30%.
B: 30%? / Have you?

A: Our department gets at least 20 complaints a week.
B: Wow! Twenty complaints a week?

A: We believe the customer's always right.
B: Always right? Do you really believe that?

10

Case Study

A US budget airline receives a lot of communication from its passengers. It needs to prioritise its response and ensure customer satisfaction wherever possible

Background

You are members of the Customer Services Department of Hurrah Airlines, a budget airline company based at JFK Airport, New York. Hurrah Airlines offers low ticket prices for flights to Europe and limited services. It makes up for the low ticket prices by charging for extras like food, priority boarding, seat allocation, excess baggage, etc. You often receive correspondence, telephone calls and voicemail messages from customers who are unhappy with your service. Callers seem to forget that you are a budget airline, so you must keep operating costs low in order to provide passengers with cheap tickets. However, you have to deal diplomatically and effectively with these dissatisfied customers and to come up with solutions to their problems.

Task

1 **CD3.17, 3.18** Work in pairs. One of you is the Customer Service Manager and the other is the Assistant Customer Service Manager. Read the written correspondence on the right and on the opposite page. Then listen to the telephone conversation and the recorded message, and make notes on the key points made by each customer.

2 Because you are so busy, decide which complaints you will handle now as a priority, and which you will leave until later.

3 Discuss how you are going to deal with the complaints that you have prioritised.

4 As one group, discuss how you could improve the service you offer to your customers.

1

To: Customer Services Department
From: Martha Gómez
Subject: Complaint

I'm writing to you because I can't get through to your helpline. I've been trying all week, but I get put on hold and then no one answers me. My problem is, I flew from New York to London last week on your airline, but when I got to the airport, I couldn't find my suitcase at baggage reclaim. I told someone at your desk. They promised to investigate and call me. Since then, nothing. I'm Brazilian, a single woman and on my own in London. I must get my suitcase back. It's got some expensive clothes, some important documents and some jewellery. I've no insurance for the items. And I don't think I've got any bills for the things I brought.

Please help me.

3

To: Customer Services Department
From: Jacques Duperrier
Subject: September 3

I'm a disabled man. At the airport, your company charged me $30 for the hire of a wheelchair to get me on the airplane to Paris. I cannot believe that a company with annual profits of over $300 million refuses to provide disabled people with wheelchairs free of charge. I'm not going to put up with this. I've contacted the Disability Rights Commission, who are willing to take this to court on my behalf. I've also talked to a national newspaper, which is interested in publishing an article about what's happened to me. Does your airline really want to be involved in a court case and to receive unfavourable publicity?

2

To: Customer Services Department
From: Robert MacKenzie
Subject: 27 June

I'm writing to complain about the poor customer service you've given me and my family. I called your airline to change our flights to Indonesia – there was an emergency there and I was advised to delay my visit. I e-mailed you several times and called your service desk, but got no answers. In the end, I had to go to the airport to change the flights – the journey cost me $40. I booked new flights for two months' time, and was amazed when you made me pay a $300 penalty for the new booking. You said the new booking had to be within 14 days of the earlier booking. I'm disgusted with the way you've treated me and my family. What are you going to do about it?

5

I've flown with your airline several times and have never had any problems. You have to pay for your food and extras, but I expect that. You get what you pay for in this world.

However, I didn't expect what happened to me last Sunday. I got to the airport, went through departures and checked the departure board for the flight to Philadelphia. Delayed! One hour later, delayed! Then the flight was cancelled. I stood in line with a lot of other unhappy passengers for about three hours at your desk. When my turn came, you refused to put me on a later flight. The earliest flight you offered me was 7.30 p.m. on Wednesday. That was too late for me. I tore up the ticket and went home.

I've heard nothing from your company about a refund. I should point out that the taxi to the airport cost $38, the hotel room near the airport was $100 and the ticket $220 return.

I look forward to hearing your comments with interest.

Yours sincerely,

Kirk Danson

4

FAX TRANSMISSION

Is this what you call customer service? I pre-booked seats 32B and 32C for me and my ten-year-old daughter. I wanted an aisle seat because I'm pregnant and you often get a little more room in an aisle seat. When we got on board, someone was already sitting in the aisle seat and the seat next to it. I had to sit in a window seat, even though I complained to the stewardess. My daughter was put in a seat far away from me.

My seat had no cushion, just the bare seat base. The stewardess wouldn't let me look for another seat. The flight was turbulent, it was a nightmare for me. On my arrival in Warsaw, I contacted your desk. Your representative wasn't interested in my story – 'What do you expect, we're a budget airline,' she said to me.

Krystyna Kaminski

Watch the Case study commentary on the ***DVD-ROM.***

Writing

Write a short report for the Director of Customer Services summarising the problems that customers have experienced and make recommendations for improving the service to customers.

➡ *Writing file* page 131

UNIT 11

Crisis management

'In a crisis, be aware of the danger – but recognise the opportunity.'
John F. Kennedy (1917–1963), 35th US President

OVERVIEW

VOCABULARY
Handling crises

LISTENING
Dealing with crises

READING
Dealing with crises

LANGUAGE REVIEW
Conditionals

SKILLS
Asking and answering difficult questions

CASE STUDY
In Range

STARTING UP

A **Work in groups. Think of a crisis you have / your country has experienced. Say what happened and how it was handled.**

B **Crisis-management experts have identified 10 key steps for companies in a crisis. Complete steps 5–10 below using the verbs in the box.**

analyse	disclose	inform	practise	predict	set up

1. Work out an action plan to ensure the crisis does not happen again.
2. Role-play a potential crisis.
3. Find out what happened and how it happened.
4. Write down and circulate your crisis-management programme.
5. Try to .... what crises could occur.
6. .... a crisis-management team.
7. .... the directors.
8. .... as much information as you can.
9. .... the actions you took to deal with the situation.
10. .... making decisions under stress.

C **Complete this table with the steps in Exercise B. Discuss your answers.**

before the crisis	during the crisis	after the crisis

D **Answer these questions.**

1. What sort of crises do business managers have to face?
2. How is a business crisis different from a business problem?
3. Can you think of any examples of recent business crises? Which do you think have been the worst in recent years?

VOCABULARY

Handling crises

A **Match words from Box A with words from Box B to make word partnerships, adding *of* if necessary.**

examples: *action plan, admission of liability*

A

~~action~~ ~~admission~~ contingency damage
flow legal loss press press speed

B

action conference confidence information ~~liability~~
limitation ~~plan~~ plan release response

B **Complete these sentences with the word partnerships from Exercise A.**

1 How quickly management react to a crisis is known as the ....

2 In a breaking crisis, a manager may speak to the media at a(n) ....

3 Alternatively, there may be a written statement, which is given to the media in the form of a(n) ....

4 During the crisis, management may choose to keep customers, employees and shareholders up to date with a regular ....

5 A(n) .... is part of a crisis strategy prepared in advance.

6 A backup strategy is a(n) ....

7 The risk of being taken to court is the threat of ....

8 An acceptance of responsibility in a crisis is a(n) ....

9 Following a crisis, a company may suffer a decline in loyalty from its customers, or a(n) .... in its product or service.

10 Minimising the negative effects of a crisis is known as ....

C **Match an expression from Exercises A and B with each of these verbs. Three of the expressions are not used.**

1 implement *an action plan*

2 issue

3 take

4 hold

5 suffer

6 prepare

7 control

D **Answer this question, then discuss your ideas in small groups. Can you give any examples?**

Which of the word partnerships in Exercise C do you think are:

a) essential in a crisis?

b) important to avoid?

c) useful but not essential?

See the **DVD-ROM** for the i-Glossary.

LISTENING

Dealing with crises

A **In groups, tell each other three things you know and three things you would like to know about the Toyota crisis of 2009/2010.**

B CD3.19 **Listen to Craig Smith, Professor of Ethics and Social Responsibility at INSEAD in Paris. Does he make any of your points or answer any of your questions from Exercise A?**

Craig Smith

C CD3.19 **Listen again and complete these extracts using no more than three words in each gap.**

... it's a problem that the company frankly has been very ....[1] and very ....[2] to.

... it was only September 2009 that the company really truly acknowledged there was a ....[3] and said 'we're gonna have a ....[4]'.

... its communication around the causes of the problem has been ....[5], and consumers have been left ....[6] and ...

The classic advice here is ....[7] and ....[8]. And the thing to do is to ....[9] and let people know that you acknowledge that there is a problem, and know that you're ....[10] about it.

D CD3.20 **Listen to the second part of the interview and answer these questions.**

1 What is the three-part model?

2 What are the three critical activities or questions for part one?

E CD3.21 **Listen to the third part. What three things need to be done during a crisis?**

Watch the interview on the ***DVD-ROM.***

F CD3.22 **Listen to the final part. What questions does he ask with regard to:**

1 the recovery? 2 the auditing of the management of the crisis? 3 rebuilding?

READING
Dealing with crises

A **In groups, brainstorm the crises that these companies could have.**

a) a pushchair (buggy) company b) a mobile phone company

1 Expect the unexpected

2 How not to take care of a brand

3 No way back from a crisis

B **Work in pairs. Read your article quickly and choose the best headline on the left.**

Student A: Read Article A on the opposite page.
Student B: Read Article B on the opposite page.

C **Read your articles again and take notes on these questions.**

1 What crises happened?

2 How did the companies mentioned deal with their crises (if this is mentioned)?

3 What lessons can be learned?

D **Using your notes, tell your partner about the content of your article.**

E **In pairs, make as many word partnerships as you can by matching the verbs (1–7) to the nouns (a–g). More than one combination may be possible.**

1 handle	a) a warning
2 issue	b) a problem
3 face	c) a crisis
4 announce	d) an investigation
5 cope with	e) a recall
6 deal with	f) the public
7 reassure	g) an issue

F **Discuss other companies you know who have handled crises well/badly.**

FT

Article A

by John Gapper

Maclaren is a small private company with a big public problem, one that it has not handled well.

On Monday, Maclaren announced that it was issuing repair kits for up to 1 million pushchairs it had sold in the US over the past decade after 12 cases in which children's fingertips were chopped off in the pushchairs' hinges. By that afternoon, its website had frozen and its phone lines were overwhelmed by parents. Meanwhile, the British company told non-Americans they would be treated differently.

Instead of a formal product recall, it was simply issuing warnings to owners not to let children stick their fingers in the folding mechanism as they opened the pushchairs. Repair kits to cover the hinges would not be automatically dispatched to every Maclaren owner, as in the US.

Outrage ensued, with messages on Twitter such as 'WHAT?! Amputations from a stroller?!' By the time Farzad Rastegar, Chief Executive of Maclaren in the US and the brand's controlling shareholder, had lunch with me in New York on Tuesday, he sounded shaken.

'Did I expect this kind of coverage? No, I did not,' he said. It was hard to grasp why. The words 'child' and 'amputation' in a media release from the US safety regulator would surely terrify anyone.

After talking to him, I concluded that Maclaren does not have a bad story to tell – its safety standards are higher than cheaper rivals. But it has done a poor job of telling it.

Therein lie lessons for companies that face similar crises, of which there are a lot. Nokia has announced a recall of 14 million phone batteries, while Toyota is still coping with a recall of 3.8 million cars with floor mats that can make the vehicles accelerate uncontrollably and crash.

Lesson one: be ready. When the announcement of the recall leaked early, Maclaren was left floundering. Lesson two: empathise. Maclaren is the latest of many companies to fall into the trap of being inwardly focused and failing to realise how customers will react. Lesson three: be polite. Lesson four: don't discriminate. Maclaren's biggest mistake was to appear to be treating American children's fingertips as more precious than those of children in the UK and other countries.

Article B

by Morgen Witzel

Crises are an inevitable part of management, and the larger the business grows, the bigger the crises seem to become. However robust a business seems, it is still fallible. Arthur Andersen, the accountancy firm, and Marconi, the telecoms equipment maker, are two once-great businesses that have disappeared in recent years.

Not every crisis can be foreseen. Sometimes managers will know that a threat exists, but will not know when or where it will materialise. The chances of an airliner crashing, for example, are extremely small, but every airline must still live with the possibility.

When an Air France Concorde crashed on take-off from Paris – the first accident involving a Concorde – Air France was prepared to deal with the issue.

Managers moved quickly to withdraw Concorde from service, announce an investigation into the accident and reassure the travelling public that it was still safe to fly Air France. The following day the airline's share price did decline, but not by much and not for very long.

Intel, the world's leading maker of semiconductors, suffered a huge and unforeseen crisis when it emerged that a small proportion of its Pentium microprocessors were faulty. Quickly assessing the options, the company took the brave step of recalling and replacing the entire production run of the series. The move cost more than $1bn (£550m) and probably saved the company. Intel showed that it was committed to its product, whatever the short-term cost, and customers responded positively.

Looking back on the incident, Andy Grove, Intel's Chairman and then Chief Executive, compared managing in a severe crisis to an illness. Strong, healthy companies will survive, although at a cost to themselves. Weak companies will be carried off by the disease and will die. In Mr Grove's view, the key to successful crisis management is preparedness. Forward thinking and planning are essential; understanding the nature of the crisis that might occur can help managers be better prepared, as the Air France example shows.

However, while forward planning is necessary for crisis management, it is not sufficient. Not every crisis can be foreseen or planned for. Good crisis management requires the ability to react to events swiftly and positively, whether or not they have been foreseen.

LANGUAGE REVIEW

Conditionals

There are many different types of conditional sentence.

- 'Zero' conditional
  *If you **operate** the pushchair properly, your child is not at risk.*
- First conditional
  *If we act quickly, we'**ll limit** the damage.*
- Second conditional
  *If we **recalled** the cars, we'**d protect** our reputation.*
- Third conditional
  *If Maclaren **had withdrawn** its pushchairs immediately, there **wouldn't have been** a crisis.*

➡ ***Grammar reference*** page 151

A **Match the sentences below (1–12) to these headings (a–f).**

a) promise
b) bargaining
c) invitation/request
d) reflecting on the past
e) speculating about the future
f) advice/warning/threat

1 It wouldn't have been a problem if they'd told the truth immediately.
2 If I were you, I'd give media interviews as soon as possible.
3 We'll tell the truth if you print the entire statement.
4 We'll be able to limit the damage if we pay up now.
5 If you'd fixed the fault, we'd have placed an order.
6 Your money back if not 100% satisfied.
7 If we recall the products, it will be expensive.
8 If you would like a refund, call Customer Services on 020 7711 3420.
9 If you order by the end of the year, we can give you a discount.
10 I wouldn't ignore the media if I were you.
11 If we'd tested the product properly, we'd have known about this problem.
12 I would be grateful if you would print our apology as soon as possible.

B **Decide whether each of these situations is a) likely or b) unlikely to happen to you. Then tell your partner what you will or would do.**

1 You get a pay rise next year.
2 You win a lot of money.
3 Your computer gets a virus.
4 You travel abroad next year.
5 You have to give a presentation in English.
6 Your company is taken over by a competitor.

C **Discuss what went wrong in this situation. Use the notes from the crisis management advice sheet on the left.**

example: *If they'd issued an apology immediately, they would have limited the damage.*

Hartley Health Group (HHG), the family-owned healthcare products group, faced a crisis when it was discovered that some tubes of its best-selling toothpaste had been laced with poison. The toothpaste contributed to 20% of its profit. Withdrawing the toothpaste would be very expensive. HHG focused inwardly on saving costs, did not give media interviews, did not recall all toothpastes immediately, did not issue an apology, did not have a crisis management plan, and have now lost sales, share price and their reputation. Within a year, it has lost three-quarters of its market share.

- be prepared
- issue an apology immediately
- react to the crisis quickly
- protect your reputation
- have a crisis management plan
- recall damaged products
- act decisively
- give media interviews

SKILLS

Asking and answering difficult questions

A CD3.23 **Michael Goodrich is a presenter of a television consumer protection programme. Tonight he is questioning Tim Bradshaw, the Marketing Director of TG Products, a large chain of stores which sells imported toys. Listen to the interview and answer these questions.**

1 What kind of toys are popular with children, according to Tim Bradshaw?

2 How many of the toys does his company have in stock?

3 How serious is the problem with the toys? Explain your answer.

B CD3.24 **Listen again to these questions from the interviewer. In each case, decide whether the question is a) neutral/polite or b) aggressive.**

1 Could you please tell me how many of these items you import each month?

2 Could you be a little more precise?

3 Roughly how many complaints about the toys do you receive each week ... ?

4 Isn't it true you've been receiving dozens of complaints from customers every week?

5 Do you deny people have been phoning you and e-mailing you constantly to complain about the toys?

6 Why are you still selling them?

7 Isn't your real reason for not recalling the toys very obvious, Mr Bradshaw?

8 But what are you going to do about these defective toys?

9 When exactly will you get back to us?

10 Would you answer my question, please?

C **Role-play this situation.**

A furniture company has been attacked by a consumer website for selling a lamp which is dangerous to use and could cause a fire. The Sales Manager agrees to appear on a consumer TV programme to defend the company's reputation and answer questions.

Student A: Turn to page 138.
Student B: Turn to page 144.

USEFUL LANGUAGE

INTERVIEWERS

Asking questions politely

Could you please tell me ... ?

I'm interested to know why ...

Asking probing questions

Could you be more specific, please?

Could you be a little more precise?

Asking questions aggressively

Are you saying that ... ?

Do you deny that ... ?

INTERVIEWEES

Dealing diplomatically with questions

I'm happy to answer that.

That's an interesting question. Let me answer it this way ...

Checking if you understand

Have I got this right? Are you saying/suggesting ... ?

I'm not sure I understood you. Could you rephrase that, please?

Avoiding a straight/precise answer

Sorry, I'm not sure I know the answer to that one.

I'll have to think about it.

I can't give you an answer off the top of my head.

Playing for time

Sorry, I can't give you an answer straight away.

I'll have to get back to you on that one.

11

Case study

In Range

A video-games company faces a crisis on the eve of a major product launch

Background

The article below appeared in *Business Today,* a weekly newspaper published in Los Angeles, California.

Read the article and discuss the opinion of the psychologist Carl Davis. Do you agree with him that violent video games like *In Range* should be banned for sale to people under 21?

LAUNCH PLANS OF "IN RANGE" HIT BY PSYCHOLOGY REPORT

Plans to launch the blockbuster video game *In Range* on October 30 have been upset by a new report on violence in computer games and its effect on young people.

Professor Carl Davis, a psychologist specializing in teenagers' behavior, has just brought out a shock report based on a three-year study of young people's reactions to violent video games. His main findings are that violent video games do increase the levels of aggression in young people and they also desensitize youngsters to death and destruction.

Commenting on *In Range*, Carl Davis says, "As founder of the Institute of Media Studies, I cannot approve the level of violence and violations of human-rights law that are apparent in *In Range*. I think it should be banned or, at the very least, only available to adults over the age of 21."

This is a further blow for the creator and developer of the video game, ExtremAction. This Japanese-owned company has its head office here in Los Angeles. *In Range* features a team of mercenaries who are hired by the government of a fictitious country, The Republic, to completely destroy a drugs baron and his private army of bodyguards. There are scenes of extreme violence, including brutal interrogations and summary executions.

It is expected that there will be record-breaking sales of the game in the U.S. and U.K.

Pre-orders from retailers in both countries have been enormous. There's little doubt that *In Range* will be the top-selling computer game of the year. However, there is severe criticism of the company and its new game from politicians, academics, community leaders, the police force, and the media. This threatens the success of the celebrity launch at the end of the month.

CD3.25 Listen to part of a conversation between Linda Thomson, Chief Executive of ExtremAction (US), and Bob Morgan, Director of Public Relations. Discuss what information they give about the following:

- the plans for the launch
- the sales projections for the US and UK
- why the Chief Executive is worried

Sample of reactions to *In Range* before the launch on October 30.

Negative comments

U.S. Senator
We need a bill to ban sales of ultra-violent video games to youngsters under 21. I intend to introduce a bill in Congress as soon as possible.

State Governor
I'd like to ban sales of *In Range* in our state. The publishers of the game have gone beyond the limit. It's a disgusting, depraved game which will corrupt our children and desensitize them to violence and death.

Principal of a large international school
It's wrong to advertise the game in bus shelters and movie theaters near our schools. There should be no adverts or commercials within the radius of any school or on TV for that matter.

Police-financed advert in a local newspaper
In Range will make young people more aggressive, more rebellious, and increase crime in our city. Shouldn't ExtremAction be showing a sense of social responsibility?

Children's charity spokesperson
In Range is typical of the harmful products of the U.S. entertainment industry which reflect the increasing violence in their society.

Positive comments

Spokesperson for the computer games industry
In Range will be an all-time winner. It'll invigorate our industry, create a lot of jobs, and help us to make more money than the fat cats in the movie industry.

***Game On* magazine**
What more can you say about *In Range*? It's exciting, easy to complete, and can be replayed many times. Great graphics and sound effects, fantastic action, and a credible storyline. No wonder people can't wait to get their hands on a copy.

A champion gamer
What an awesome game! This takes video games into a new dimension. I hope they'll do a follow-up as soon as possible.

A teenage gamer
Really thrilling and scary. Best game I've ever played. Took me ten hours to finish. Killing that drugs baron and his bodyguards gave me a real buzz.

Task

Because of the severe criticisms that they are receiving from politicians, academics, community leaders and the media, ExtremAction decide to hold a press conference. This will enable them to defend the company, explain how they are dealing with the crisis and answer the questions from journalists. Work in two groups.

Group A: Turn to page 138. Group B: Turn to page 145.

1 Read your role card and prepare for the press conference.

2 Hold the press conference.

Watch the Case study commentary on the ***DVD-ROM.***

Writing

Journalists
Write a powerful article for your newspaper, reporting on the press conference you have just attended. You can either strongly criticise or praise ExtremAction for the way their company is handling the crisis.

ExtremAction Directors
An influential charity called Media Watch has asked you to send them a report on the recent crisis regarding the launch of *In Range*. The report should include the following information:

- **the background to the crisis**
- **an explanation of the actions you have taken to deal with it**
- **a conclusion, in which you justify your actions.**

When you have completed your writing task, exchange your article or report with a partner. Make suggestions, if necessary, to improve the document you have received.

➡ *Writing file* page 131

UNIT 12 Mergers and acquisitions

'Forty for you, sixty for me. And equal partners we will be.'
Joan Rivers, American comedian and businesswoman

OVERVIEW

STARTING UP

A **What do you understand by these terms?**

1 a takeover/acquisition
2 a merger
3 a joint venture

B CD3.26 **Listen to a business expert talking about the terms in Exercise A. Compare your ideas.**

C **Think of three reasons why one company might wish to take over another company.**

D **What do you think the advantages and disadvantages of acquisitions may be for a company's:**

1 employees?
2 customers?
3 suppliers?
4 shareholders?
5 products and services?

VOCABULARY

Describing mergers and acquisitions

A **Match the terms (1–6) to the definitions (a–f).**

1 joint venture
2 MBO (management buyout)
3 merger
4 takeover/acquisition
5 bid
6 stake

a) money risked or invested in a company
b) two or more companies joining to form a larger company
c) offer money for shares in a company
d) when a company's top executives buy the company they work for
e) a business activity in which two or more companies have invested together
f) getting control of a company by buying over 50% of its shares

B **Circle the noun which forms a word partnership with each verb.**

1 **take** a stake / a bid / an acquisition
2 **make** a merger / a stake / a bid
3 **launch** a bid / a share / a stake
4 **target** a company / a bid / a takeover
5 **set up** a share / a joint venture / a stake
6 **make** a merger / a joint venture / an acquisition
7 **reject** a bid / a stake / a share
8 **sell** a merger / a bid / a stake

C **Choose the correct words or phrases to complete these extracts.**

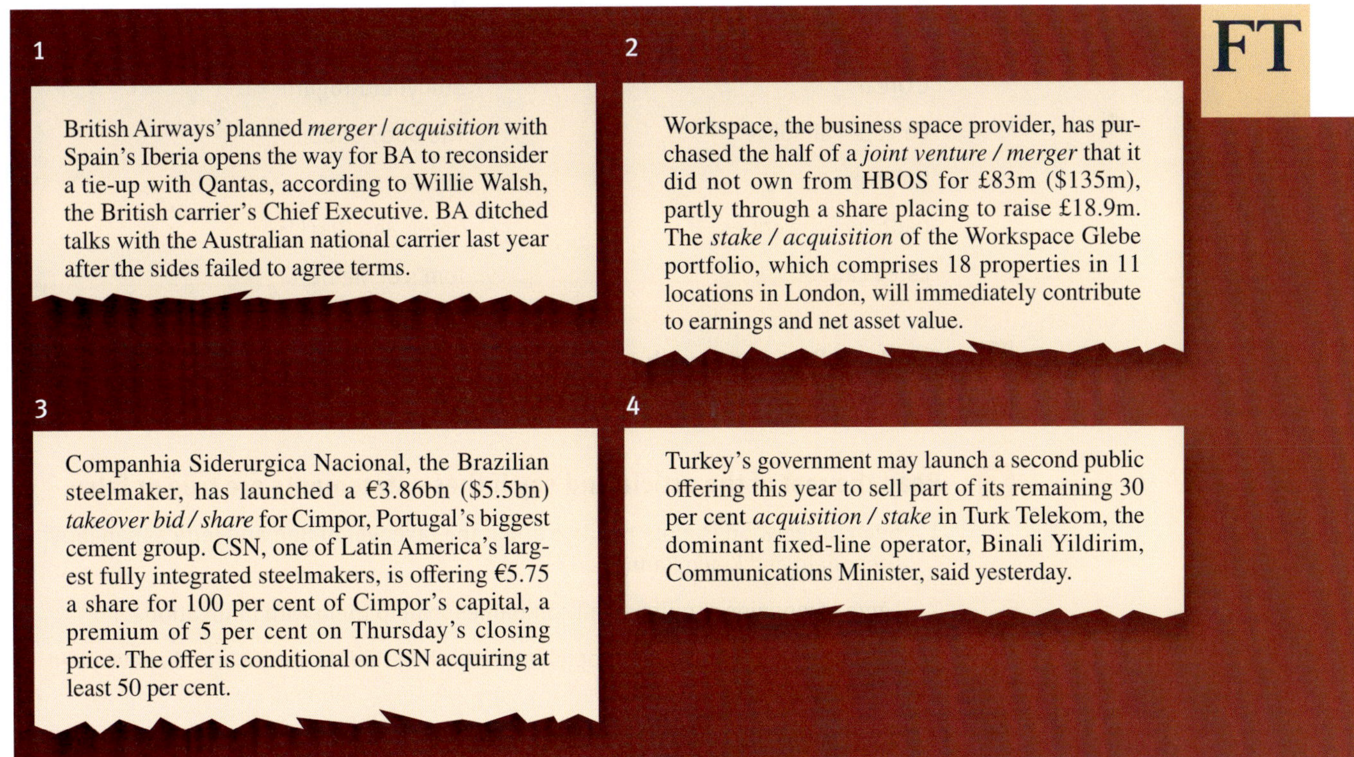
FT

1

British Airways' planned *merger / acquisition* with Spain's Iberia opens the way for BA to reconsider a tie-up with Qantas, according to Willie Walsh, the British carrier's Chief Executive. BA ditched talks with the Australian national carrier last year after the sides failed to agree terms.

2

Workspace, the business space provider, has purchased the half of a *joint venture / merger* that it did not own from HBOS for £83m ($135m), partly through a share placing to raise £18.9m. The *stake / acquisition* of the Workspace Glebe portfolio, which comprises 18 properties in 11 locations in London, will immediately contribute to earnings and net asset value.

3

Companhia Siderurgica Nacional, the Brazilian steelmaker, has launched a €3.86bn ($5.5bn) *takeover bid / share* for Cimpor, Portugal's biggest cement group. CSN, one of Latin America's largest fully integrated steelmakers, is offering €5.75 a share for 100 per cent of Cimpor's capital, a premium of 5 per cent on Thursday's closing price. The offer is conditional on CSN acquiring at least 50 per cent.

4

Turkey's government may launch a second public offering this year to sell part of its remaining 30 per cent *acquisition / stake* in Turk Telekom, the dominant fixed-line operator, Binali Yildirim, Communications Minister, said yesterday.

See the **DVD-ROM** *for the i-Glossary.*

D **Think of a merger or acquisition you know about. What kinds of businesses were involved? Were both companies successful before it happened? What about now?**

LISTENING
Making acquisitions

A CD3.27 **Listen to Professor Scott Moeller, Director of the Mergers & Acquisitions Research Centre at Cass Business School. What three reasons does Scott give for the lack of success of some mergers and acquisitions?**

Scott Moeller

B CD3.28 **Listen to the second part of the interview and answer these questions.**

1 Why is it sometimes better for the newly acquired company to be:

a) kept separate for a period of time?

b) integrated very quickly?

2 What do you need to determine in addition to the speed of the merger?

3 What other questions does Scott say you need to ask?

C CD3.29 **Listen to the final part and take notes on why the merger between Bank of New York and Mellon Bank was eventually successful.**

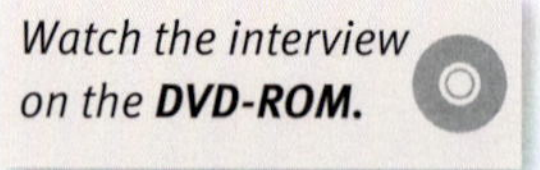

Watch the interview on the ***DVD-ROM.***

D **How would you go about making sure that the staff of a company that you have just acquired feel valued and welcomed?**

READING
Acquiring a green business

A **In groups, look at the table below and answer these questions.**

1 What do the companies in column A do?

2 Match the company in column A to the company that it acquired in column B. Feel free to guess.

3 What do you think all the companies in column B have in common?

A	B
Danone	Ben and Jerry's
L'Oréal	Stonyfield Yogurt
Colgate-Palmolive	The Body Shop
Unilever	Aveda
Cadbury Schweppes	Green and Black's
Estée Lauder	Tom's of Maine

B **Read the first paragraph of the article on the opposite page and check your answers to Exercise A.**

C **Read the rest of the article and say if these statements are true or false.**

1 Sean Greenwood is more positive about the takeover of Ben and Jerry's than Jerry Greenfield and Kevin Ranney.

2 Large companies acquire small companies to help them with innovation.

3 The majority of customers shop elsewhere when their favourite brands have been taken over.

4 Ben and Jerry's shares were doing well just before Unilever bought them.

5 Ben and Jerry's are using more freetrade ingredients than before the acquisition.

D **Answer these questions.**

1 What do large companies have that smaller companies don't?

2 What problems did Ben and Jerry's have just after the acquisition?

E **Find the three expressions in the first paragraph that describe one company being taken over by another company.**

F **Complete the paragraph below with the words in the box.**

conglomerate	corporations	multinational	partnership	subsidiary

Toshiba is a large ....[1] that has acquired several ....[2] engaged in different industries. It is also a ....[3], as it has offices in many different countries. Toshiba recently formed a ....[4] with United Parcel Services to design a more efficient repair process for laptop computers. In 1987, Toshiba Machine, a ....[5] of Toshiba, was accused of selling parts used to produce submarine propellers to the Soviet Union.

G **Discuss this statement.**

The transport of values from a smaller green company to a large multinational that has taken it over is impossible.

Green targets

by Melissa Shin

It ain't easy being green these days – especially if you're an independent green business.

The list of smaller, green companies being swallowed up by global conglomerates is growing in both prestige and numbers: responsible ice-cream producer Ben and Jerry's, now owned by Unilever; organic yogurt maker Stonyfield Yogurt, now in partnership with Danone; alternative beauty companies The Body Shop and Aveda, now owned by L'Oréal and Estée Lauder respectively; organic chocolatier Green and Black's, now owned by Cadbury Schweppes; Tom's of Maine toothpaste, now owned by Colgate-Palmolive; personal-care company Burt's Bees, acquired by Clorox in November 2007; and Husky Injection Molding Systems, acquired in December 2007 by Onex Corporation for $960 million.

It's not hard to see why small companies are vulnerable – multinationals can offer increased distribution, access to more markets, and most of all, cold, hard cash. And large corporations often find it easier to acquire than to innovate.

Consumers are at the very least surprised to discover that their favourite brands have become mere subsidiaries within a large multinational.

A recent poll by the website Treehugger.com (ironically, this once-independent site is now owned by the Discovery Channel) found that 35 per cent of consumers take their business elsewhere when corporations acquire their once-revered brands.

Skeptics of responsible retailing can easily suggest that small companies have simply reached their expiration date – unfortunate hippie victims of corporate Darwinism. But these partnerships can help bring ethical activities into the mainstream.

"We're fortunate," says Sean Greenwood, spokesperson for Ben and Jerry's. "We could have had a lot of businesses that could have bought us and [closed us down]. But they didn't do that. And I applaud them for that and for recognizing and understanding that that there's a value in keeping the folks who are trying to hold on to what's really important: the essence of Ben and Jerry's."

In April 2000, the Anglo-Dutch Unilever NV announced it would buy flagging Ben and Jerry's stocks for $43.50 a share, a large premium over the previous day's closing price of $34.93.

Even though the initial takeover caused factory closings, job losses, and management changes, Greenwood says that his company has helped change Unilever.

"There's been a good give and take, back and forth with the organizations," he says. "It feels like this is a good fit."

But co-founder Jerry Greenfield told the UK's *Green Futures* magazine in 2006 that he doesn't feel that fit with Ben and Jerry's any more.

"I have no responsibility and no authority in the company," he said. "I have my good name. I have an ability to influence things I want to, and to not be interested in things I'm not interested in. That's the extent of my role."

He went on to add, though, that influence does exist.

"I was skeptical about this supposed 'transport of values' from Ben and Jerry's to Unilever, but it has happened to some degree," Greenfield observed.

Kevin Ranney, Managing Partner and Director of Research at Jantzi Research, says that positive transfers from the acquired company to the acquirer are difficult to quantify.

"That's one of the reasons why we're not really excited to see these acquisitions occur," he says. "The reality is that what Ben and Jerry's was all about is now buried deeply within a massive corporate structure, and it has relatively little impact on anyone's assessment of Unilever."

Sean Greenwood says that while customers understand there has been a management change, they still support the ice cream.

"I don't think people say, 'Wow, this pint today in January 2003 is different than the December pint of 2002.' I think they are saying Ben and Jerry's has continued to be a Ben and Jerry's organization and product throughout our years."

The proof is in the pudding – or ice cream, as it were. Ben and Jerry's announced in 2006 that it would be expanding its fairtrade ingredients to include Fair Trade Certified coffee, vanilla, and cocoa, and it was also the first national American food manufacturer to move towards a total transition of its products to "Certified-Humane" cage-free eggs.

Nevertheless, the Ben and Jerry's experience has served as a warning sign **to other firms.**

from *Corporate Knight, The Canadian Magazine for Responsible Business*

language review

Prediction and probability

There are many ways to talk about prediction and probability.

- We can use ***will*** or ***going to.***
  Buying Kraft's pizza business ***will*** *boost Nestlé's presence in North America.*
  After the acquisition, the returns to investors ***are going to*** *be extraordinary.*
- We can use **the future continuous** and **the future perfect** to predict what will be in progress or will have been accomplished in the future.
  Orange ***will be selling*** *the iPhone from November 10.*
  The Bank of England ***will have bought*** *£125bn in bonds by the end of July.*
- We can use **modals.**
  More European mergers ***may*** *be on the way in the airline industry.*
- We can use lexical phrases.
  certain: *There's* ***certain*** *to be more acquisitions of green companies in the next two years.*
  probable: *It's* ***highly likely*** *that Unilever will acquire them.*
  possible: ***Perhaps*** *the share price will rise next month.*
  unlikely: ***I doubt whether*** *L'Oréal will make a bid.*
  impossible: ***There's no chance of*** *the merger taking place.*

➔ ***Grammar reference*** page 151

A Choose the correct verb forms.

1 We *will have paid / will be paying* back the loan by December.
2 I *will be / will have been* here for three years next May.
3 Next year, she *will be working / will have worked* in our Tokyo office.
4 We *will be holding / will have held* a meeting soon.
5 Don't phone me tomorrow because I'll *be working / work* on the bid all morning.
6 We *will be offering / will have offered* a special discount from January 1st.
7 By the end of next year, we *will be launching / will have launched* six new products in three years.
8 This time next year, we *will be enjoying / will have enjoyed* the results of the merger.

B Work in pairs. Say what you really think about the likelihood of these things happening.

- a stock-market crash next year
- Microsoft merging with Apple
- the majority of managers being women
- Brazil, Russia, China and India becoming the major world economies
- the World Wide Web having serious problems

C Work in pairs. Make predictions about your company, your country or yourself. Use as many forms from the Language review box above as possible. You may also find these phrases useful.

In my lifetime, ...	Over the next decade, ...
Before long, ...	By this time next year, ...
In the near future, ...	By the end of this century, ...
In the next ... years, ...	Sometime in the next decade/century, ...

skills

Making a presentation

A CD3.30 **Susan Drake, Chief Executive of Eastman Property, an American hotel group, is giving a presentation to a group of investment fund managers in the United Kingdom. Her company has recently bought Highview, a property company which owns 15 budget hotels in the UK. She explains**
why they bought the company and their plans for the future development of Highview. Listen and answer these questions.

1 For what reasons did Eastman Property buy the Highview group of hotels?

2 What are Susan Drake's plans for Highview in the future?

B CD3.30 **Study the Useful language box below. Then listen again and tick the phrases that you hear.**

C **Read the audio script of the presentation on page 167. Add expressions to the headings in the Useful Language box. Then, in pairs, practise delivering the presentation.**

D **You are the Managing Director of Eastman Property. Your company intends to buy one of these businesses located in your country:**

- a travel agency
- a shopping mall
- a business equipment store
- a cinema complex
- a sports and leisure centre.

Choose one of the businesses. Make a presentation to a group of investors explaining why you wish to buy the business, and what plans you have for its future development.

USEFUL LANGUAGE

REFERRING BACK

So, as I said a few minutes ago, ...

Right, as I mentioned earlier, ...

LOOKING FORWARD

I'll talk about this later.

I'll outline these later in my presentation.

ASKING RHETORICAL QUESTIONS

OK, what were our reasons for the acquisition?

Right, why did we choose this hotel group?

MAKING POINTS IN THREES

The gap in the market, the market conditions, the opportunity for growth.

We have a clear, realistic and ambitious strategy for the Highview brand.

SUMMARISING

Right, I've told you why we've acquired Highview ...

OK, I've talked about our reasons for acquiring the company ...

USING EMOTIVE LANGUAGE

We're absolutely delighted ...

This is a fantastic opportunity ...

TALKING ABOUT THE FUTURE

By that time, we'll have developed a portfolio of budget hotels ...

By 2020, we'll have become market leader in the budget hotel sector ...

REPETITION

Highview will be the future ...
Highview will lead the way ...
Highview will set a new standard ...

The company has a strong brand, strong management and strong cashflow.

ASKING FOR FEEDBACK

And now, any questions?

Would anyone like to ask any questions?

12

Case study

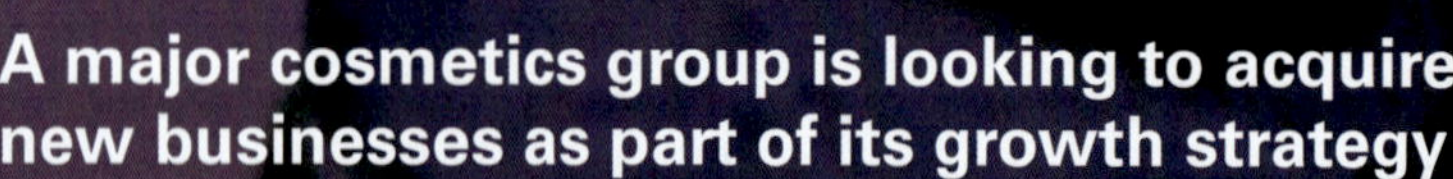

Background

Rinnovar International Inc. (RI), with annual revenues of $14 billion, has a 6% share of the cosmetics, fragrance and skincare market. It is currently seeking to buy established companies which will add new lines to its range of products. RI has a strategy of expanding both in its domestic market, the United States, and overseas by buying companies rather than expanding through organic growth. Its mission is to be able to compete strongly within five years in the prestige and mass-market cosmetics and skincare segments with major companies such as Revlon, L'Oréal and Procter & Gamble.

A recent internal marketing survey revealed the following:

- products: Rinnovar needs to produce more innovative cosmetic products and to have a wider product range, for example, for health and haircare.
- markets: It currently has low sales in South Asia and South America.
- distribution networks: It uses only exclusive agents in its overseas markets.
- production centres: All its products are made in high-cost US factories.

What are the advantages of companies expanding in domestic and foreign markets by buying existing businesses rather than by organic growth (setting up their own branches and subsidiaries)? Are there any disadvantages?

Look at the criteria below that Rinnovar International use to select companies that they are thinking of acquiring. If you were Chief Executive of RI, which three criteria in the list would you consider to be particularly important and give priority to?

Type of business
We seek a company that has:
- a leading or well-established position in its field
- growth potential driven by steady demand
- a diverse range of customers and suppliers
- a reputation for high quality
- excellent customer relations
- a desire to expand internationally or has already done so.

Financial
The company should have:
- a record of increasing profits over the previous three years
- strong cashflow
- turnover between $20 million and $100 million
- high profit margins on its products.

Management
We look for a strong, motivated, experienced, entrepreneurial team.

Ownership
We prefer 100%, but would consider a majority shareholding.

Location
Preferably in a fast-growing, developing country, but all locations considered.

CD3.31 Listen to the news programme, *Business Focus*. Make notes on each company's financial performance a) last year and b) in the three previous years.

Task

1 You work in the Corporate Strategy Department of Rinnovar International. Work in small groups. Analyse the information you have gained from the Listening (see audio script page 167) and from reading the company profiles below. Discuss the advantages and disadvantages of buying each company and note down your ideas.

2 Prepare a presentation of your ideas. Rank the companies in order of suitability and indicate which company you think is the best choice for an acquisition.

3 Listen to each other's presentations. Note down any key points.

4 Meet as one group. Decide which company, at this stage, seems to be the most suitable as an acquisition.

COMPANIES FOR ACQUISITION PROFILES

Mumbai Herbal Products

Location: Mumbai, India

Type of business

Established: 2004, by two Indian women, a famous model and a film star.

Products: Hair- and skincare. Strong position in bath and shower products. Very dynamic R&D department creating high-quality, reliable products for the competitive world market.

Customers: High-profile clients, e.g. airlines, hotel groups, embassies, top department stores.

Financial

Good record of profits in previous three years, but international sales have slowed down.

Management

Team needs to be strengthened. Its board of directors is dominated by the two founder members; other members are relatives with little business experience. Company needs more exporting, marketing and financial expertise from outside the company to expand.

Ownership

Owners may not permit 100% ownership by Rinnovar. They will probably want 50/50 share of equity and profits.

Additional information

The market for hair- and skincare products is growing fast in India, but the company faces strong competition in world markets.

Hondo Beauty Products

Location: **Seoul, Korea**

Type of business

Established: **1982**

Products: A range of cosmetics, bath and shower products supplied to major cosmetic companies in Korea and to buyers in Asia, the US and Europe.

Ultra-modern factory in Korea. Exceptionally good quality control. Very flexible. Has many partnerships with foreign companies.

Financial

Fast profit growth in the previous three years, but increasing competition from China and India could reduce its profit margins.

Management

The members of the board of directors are all Korean. The management style is very consensual and decision-making is slow.

Ownership

60% owned by the Kim family. 40% private shareholders.
The family would consider 100% ownership by Rinnovar International, but are likely to negotiate hard to get the right price.

Additional information

In the future, Hondo is certain to experience strong competition from low-cost producers in developing countries.

Good Earth

Location: Belo Horizonte, Brazil

Type of business

Established: 1992

Products: A wide range of mass-market products in the hair-, skin- and bodycare segments of the market.

Strong position in cosmetics and fragrances market.

Uses direct selling. Has over 480 sales reps in Latin America, including 265 in Brazil. Is considered a highly ethical company using natural ingredients. Does not test products on animals.

Financial

Expansion seems already to be slowing down. Slow growth in profits in previous three years. Heavy investment in overseas plants will affect future profits in the short term.

Management

The company is run by Gustavo Lopez and his family. Lopez is a strong, autocratic CEO, while the younger members are much more entrepreneurial. This is creating great tension in their team. The younger members would like a more decentralised structure for the company.

Ownership

Probably the family would want to retain a majority shareholding in the company unless Rinnovar made an offer they couldn't turn down.

Additional information

The market for cosmetics is growing fast in Brazil.

Sheen Hair Products

Location: *Palm Beach, Florida*

Type of business

Established: 1978

Products: Shampoos, hair colours and other haircare products sold exclusively to beauty salons. Its products include many well-known brand names.

All its production is located in low-cost developing countries.

Financial

Steady but unspectacular profits growth in the last three years. Profit margins have declined due to strong competition.

Management

An experienced team.
All members are American. They have little experience of selling in global markets.

Ownership

Publicly owned company. 100% ownership possible if the right price was offered.

Additional information

Because of its strong brands, the company has maintained its share of the US market in spite of strong competition.
Has received a bad press recently for locating its production overseas and for paying local employees very low wages.

*Watch the Case study commentary on the **DVD-ROM.***

Writing

Write a report to the Chief Executive of Rinnovar International on the four possible acquisitions. Give your recommendation for acquisition.

Writing file page 131

4 International negotiations

A Discuss these questions.

1 What sort of negotiations have you taken part in (at work or outside work)?

2 How many people were involved? Were you alone or part of a team?

3 Was the atmosphere formal or informal?

4 Was the negotiation successful or unsuccessful? Why do you think this was?

B Choose the correct option to complete each sentence.

1 At the start of a negotiation, it can be important to establish a .... with the other side.

a) rapport b) stalemate c) guarantee

2 When both sides give something away in order to make a deal, they reach a ....

a) concession b) compromise c) guarantee

3 When one side gives something away, they make a ....

a) compromise b) breakthrough c) concession

4 Something which stops a negotiation going smoothly is a ....

a) limit b) sticking point c) lock

5 A situation in a negotiation where no progress can be made is a ....

a) deadweight b) deadline c) deadlock

6 A .... is a creative solution which allows the negotiation to progress.

a) breakthrough b) breakout c) breakpoint

7 If both sides in a negotiation leave the table without a deal (empty-handed), the negotiation process ....

a) breaks down b) breaks off c) breaks out

8 The minimum offer you are willing to accept is known as your ....

a) opening position b) fallback position c) bottom-line position

9 Some negotiations may involve a time restriction or ....

a) deadlock b) deadline c) dead end

C Which of the ideas in Exercise B could contribute to the success or failure of an international negotiation?

D Read about the experiences of negotiating internationally below and answer these questions.

1 What are your personal reactions to the experiences described and views expressed?

2 Would the experiences described be a) normal, b) a little unusual, or c) very unusual in your country?

1 It was very different to what I am used to. They didn't seem to want to write anything down. There was a real emphasis on getting to know you – lots of small talk. I felt it was all rather slow. No one seemed to be in a hurry to get anything done.

2 Our negotiation was interrupted by new people coming in all the time. There was also a lot of attention paid to the business cards, which was new for me. We had three meetings before we talked about any business at all. We were kept waiting for a long time.

3 There were too many jokes and first names. It wasn't clear who was in charge and making the decisions. It was too casual and relaxed for me. I think people should behave more formally, use surnames and behave like businesspeople.

4 We thought we had a deal and made an agreement. Then they asked for some new concessions.

5 There was no compromise. It was a real fight. In the end, we reached deadlock and they walked out. There was a lot of emotion and shouting – I wasn't sure if it was normal or not. It upset me a bit, if I'm honest.

6 There was a lot of eating and drinking during the negotiation, having lunch at the same time as working.

7 They seemed to want to discuss everything at the same time. It felt disorganised and without structure. I prefer some kind of agenda – you know, more logical.

8 It was all quite hard line. It was more like some kind of competition. They seemed to just want to win – to get something for nothing.

E CD3.32 **Listen to a business expert talking about international negotiations and answer these questions.**

1 What are some of the common misconceptions she mentions?
2 What are the three areas she focuses on?

E CD3.32 **Decide if these statements are true (T) or false (F). Then listen again and check your answers.**

1 It's vital to know about regional differences.
2 Getting a deal is always the main objective.
3 Personal relationships in business are important all over the world.
4 Signing a contract can be the start of the negotiating process.
5 It is not always a good idea to offer gifts.
6 The number and roles of people in a negotiation is not important.

Task

Work in groups of four made up of two pairs.

Pair A: Read your instructions below.
Pair B: Turn to page 140.

Pair A

1 Look individually at the points to consider in an international negotiation listed below and add two more.
2 Choose the five most important points from your list.
3 Talk to your partner and agree the five most important points.
4 Join up with Pair B and try to agree the five most important points from your two lists.

1 Keep an open mind and be flexible.
2 Propose a strict agenda and keep to it.
3 Anticipate the interests of the other side.
4 Let the other side make the first offer.
5 Be very clear and direct about what you want from the other side.
6 Pay careful attention to building a rapport.
7 Put pressure on the other side to make an agreement.
8 Have a deadline for getting a deal.

Write some tips for negotiating successfully with your culture.

UNIT **D** # Revision

10 Customer service

VOCABULARY

Complete the text below with the words in the box.

clients compensation complaints guarantee mile payment products purposes rapport refunds service the bottom the buck the point

When I handle ....[1], I try to establish a ....[2] with the customer. They're almost always a little bit annoyed because they're not happy with something they've bought, so they want to get straight to ....[3]. I always try to reassure ....[4] that we have high standards of ....[5], but if they're feeling that they've been ripped off, it can be hard to get them to listen, and sometimes we end up talking at cross ....[6] because they're really expecting to have to fight with me! But all of our products have a money-back ....[7], and our policy is to replace ....[8] or give ....[9] if that's what people want. If that's still not good enough, I'm authorised to go the extra ....[10] in extreme cases and offer a goodwill ....[11]. An offer of financial ....[12] shows that we're serious about keeping customers satisfied. One thing I never do is pass ....[13]. If a customer comes to me, I think it's my responsibility to get to ....[14] of the problem and sort it out. And I'm happy to say that, in the end, I think almost all of my customers have left feeling happy, or at least happy enough.

GERUNDS

Choose the correct verb form to complete each sentence.

1 I regret *to tell / telling* you that we're cancelling our contract immediately.

2 Luckily, Sharon remembered *to tell / telling* us all to arrive a little early, so we had time to discuss the revised budget before the meeting started.

3 We stopped trying *to break / breaking* into the US market last year because of the recession.

4 Shazia started her presentation at two o'clock and didn't stop *to talk / talking* until after six o'clock!

5 *To work / Working* overtime is something we all have to do sometimes.

6 We need to focus on *to deal / dealing* with our cashflow problem.

7 When I tried *to speak / speaking* to Alphonse about the problem, he listened politely, but he didn't do anything about it.

8 Yanick asked me *to tell / telling* you he's going to be late to the meeting.

9 Jürgen admitted *stealing / to steal* company information from the database.

10 I forgot *to send / sending* an e-mail to my client to cancel our meeting, so she wasn't very pleased.

11 Melanie is not very good *to make / at making* presentations – I think she should go on a course to improve her skills.

12 *Writing / To write* reports is the most boring part of my job.

13 Have you considered *to apply / applying* for promotion?

14 Florence tried *to send / sending* the details from her smartphone, but she couldn't get a signal, so she had to e-mail them instead.

SKILLS

Complete the conversation below using these sentences.

a) So what happened?

b) So what you're saying is that Didier was promoted because he handled this 'spy' complaint really well?

c) Congratulate him?

d) I'm not surprised you're upset.

e) Really? Let's hear the full story.

f) What exactly do you mean by *customer service spy*?

A: Did you hear? Didier's been promoted!

B: ....[1]

A: Well, Didier's been made head of the Customer Service Department. I was supposed to get that job!

B: ....[2]

A: Yeah, I am. I just heard this morning.

B: ....[3]

A: Well, Didier was working on the customer service desk when a really angry customer came in. Didier managed to calm the guy down and solve the problem, and he left happy. It turns out the guy was one of those customer service spies.

B: ....[4]

A: I mean that the guy was only pretending to be a customer. He was sent by the management to test Didier. And as a result, Didier's been made Head of the Customer Services Department.

B: ....[5]

A: Yes, that's it. Well, I'd better get used to it. I guess I'll go and congratulate Didier.

B: ....[6]

A: Well, yeah. He's my boss now.

11 Crisis management

VOCABULARY

Match the sentence halves.

1 An environmental group took legal

2 We suffered

3 We're going to hold a

4 We need to issue a

5 We have to control the flow of

6 Our speed of

7 We have to prepare

8 If we make an admission

9 We've implemented

10 The best we can do now is damage

a) information, because everyone's saying something different about what's going on.

b) press release as soon as possible, so they don't think we're hiding anything.

c) response was pretty good. We started the recall as soon as we found out about the problem.

d) a loss of confidence after the news report about the product's safety.

e) press conference to explain exactly what's going on.

f) limitation. The situation is very bad.

g) of liability, the legal costs could run into the millions.

h) a contingency plan in case the meeting with their legal team goes badly.

i) the action plan, which was to start by making a public apology.

j) action after the accident.

CONDITIONALS

Complete this e-mail with the correct form of the verbs in brackets.

Dear colleagues,

As you know, there was an item in the news this morning about a man reporting being injured by one of our blenders (model WB-110). The injury was not serious; the man has been treated and has not been hospitalised, but we're worried about the fact that it's been in the news. If we ....[1] (*act*) quickly, we'll avert a crisis. Here's the plan of action:

1) We're going to issue a recall. If we ....[2] (*do*) this when we had a similar problem two years ago, there wouldn't have been a crisis at that time. Had we acted more decisively then, the media coverage ....[3] (*be*) far better.
2) The message regarding all of our products is this: If you follow the instructions, our products ....[4] (*be*) completely safe.
3) We're going to offer the injured man a settlement, but this is to remain confidential. If we didn't do this, he might take legal action, which ....[5] (*be*) very bad for our reputation. He has agreed to take the settlement on the condition that he won't speak to the media about it.
4) We're going to hold a press conference this afternoon. ....[6] (*ignore*) the media and we'll never be able to control the flow of information. We're also going to update our website (www.whirlblend.com) regularly.
5) We're expecting a lot of phone calls, and we want to answer them. We need to get all of our customer support people here today. Tell us what you need to make that happen and you ....[7] (*have*) it. We'll supply a document saying exactly what they should (and shouldn't) say.

Should you have any questions, please ....[8] (*contact*) my office. ....[9] (*give*) the right resources, our team can stop this becoming a crisis.

Good luck to everyone!

Steven Biggs
direct line: 0554-987-9983

WRITING

Imagine your colleague Steven Biggs has asked you to write a press release of 120–140 words about the situation described in his e-mail above. The name of your company is Whirlblend.

- Think of the best heading for your release.
- Say what's happened and what action the company is taking.
- Say who the press should contact for more information.

12 Mergers and acquisitions

VOCABULARY

Choose the correct verb to complete each sentence.

1 Pharmaceutical company Lonza has *launched / taken* a bid to acquire Patheon.
2 VMware, Cisco and EMC have *targeted / made* an alliance.
3 I've just written a book on how to *sell / make* a successful acquisition.
4 Lions Gate shareholders have *rejected / set up* a bid by Carl Ichan.
5 Sky has been ordered to *reject / sell* part of its stake in ITV.
6 China's Haier Group *set up / took* a joint venture with Taiwan's AUO.
7 AVG has *taken / launched* a 20% stake in Zbang.
8 There are reports that Vodafone plans to *make / target* an unnamed company for takeover.

PREDICTION AND PROBABILITY

Match each type of probability (1–5) to a prediction (a–e).

1 certain
2 probable
3 possible
4 unlikely
5 impossible

a) I doubt whether Reliance Communications will launch a bid.
b) It's very likely that shareholders will accept the bid.
c) There's no chance of the bid being accepted.
d) Perhaps the merger will solve our problems.
e) We're bound to be targeted in the next year.

SKILLS

Put the words in the correct order to make presentation expressions.

1 earlier, / As / good / I / outlook / mentioned / is / the
2 acquisition / I'll / about / talk / the / of / details / the / later
3 were / merger / OK, / our / for / reasons / the / what / ?
4 make / merger / will / competitive and / more profitable / The / us stronger, more
5 next / Right, / told / I've / you / we're /what / doing
6 has / delighted / We're / our / accepted / absolutely / that / bid / been
7 become / have / By / we'll / market / 2018, / leader
8 brand, we / We / have a great / we / and / have / great workers / have great managers
9 to / questions / Would / any / anyone / ask / like / ?

Cultures 4: International negotiations

Match the sentence halves.

1 International negotiations are
2 Differences in approach reflect national culture, but also
3 Direct eye contact
4 The handshake or verbal agreement is
5 In some cultures, a contract is
6 Personal relationships in business are
7 Business is
8 Cultural preconceptions and regional generalisations are
9 Flexibility and an open mind are

a) can mean confidence in one culture, but disrespect in another.
b) generally different from negotiations in your own country.
c) often incorrect.
d) expected to be a formal, written, legal document.
e) seen in some cultures as objective and impersonal, focused on business-to-business relationships rather than personal ones.
f) far more important in some cultures that business-to-business ones.
g) company culture, gender or even the level of international negotiating experience.
h) very useful things to bring to any negotiation.
i) more important than the written contract in some cultures.

Interviews

Objectives

Speaking
Can carry out an effective, fluent interview, spontaneously following up on interesting replies.

Listening
Can infer attitude and mood in discussions by using contextual, grammatical and lexical clues.

Lesson deliverable
To prepare and participate in an interview.

Performance review
To review your own progress and performance against the lesson objectives at the end of the lesson.

A SPEAKING AND LISTENING 1

1 In small groups, discuss what the following quotation means in the context of a job interview. Think about your own experience of job interviews and the importance of attitude in creating a positive impression.

'*It is not what you say, it's what people hear.*' **Frank Lutz**

2 BSA4.1.14 Listen and match speakers 1–5 to attitudes a–e.

a disinterested
b confused
c enthusiastic
d professional
e uncomfortable

3 BSA4.1.14 Listen again. What helped you decide? What clues were there? Consdier the following:

1 intonation? 2 word and sentence stress? 3 word choice?

B READING

1 Look at this page from a website that helps people to perform more effectively in job interviews. Do you agree that these are difficult questions?

The top six toughest interview questions

Not all job interview questions are the same. We carried out a poll of our readers and identified these as our top six toughest interview questions.

1 Could you tell me a little about yourself?
2 Why did you leave your last job?
3 Do you think you are overqualified for this position?
4 Why should I hire you and not the other applicants?
5 Where do you hope to be in five years' time?
6 Do you have any questions?

2 Work in pairs. How would you handle the questions in Exercise 1 effectively in an interview? Match the advice below to the questions in Exercise 1. Then decide if you agree with the advice.

a Just focus on demonstrating how motivated you are. Whatever you do, do not speculate about the other applicants.

b The interviewer wants to know that you can set achievable objectives, so make sure you are realistic about the chances of promotion.

c Never say 'No!' Ask about the company culture, about other members of the team, or just ask the interviewer about their experience there.

d Do not moan about your past employer! Be professional and make it clear you are looking for new opportunities.

e This question often comes at the beginning, just to assess your communication skills. So sit up straight and talk clearly.

f Never disagree or you will come across as arrogant. Stress your skills and experience and reassure the interviewer that you are committed to this job.

C LISTENING 2

1 BSA4.1.15 **Listen to two job interviews. Which candidate is more effective? Why? What clues are there?**

2 BSA4.1.16 **Listen to another candidate asking the interviewer a question. What could the candidate say next?**

D SPEAKING 2

Work in pairs. Practise describing yourself in a positive light.

Student A: Turn to page vii.

Student B: Turn to page xii.

Task

Pre-task: Research

You are going to hold interviews for a marketing position with an insurance company. Read the information on page xv about the company and the position. Note down possible interview questions.

Part 1: Preparation

Context: You are to attend an interview with the HR Manager of Insure Now, an insurance company, to work in their marketing department. You need to prepare for the interview.

1 **Work in pairs or small groups. Prepare a list of ideal qualities for the candidate.**

2 **Read the role card your teacher will give you on page xv. What is your role? What are your concerns?**

3 **Think about the following points.**

Candidate

- your tone of voice and communication skills (listening and following up on comments)
- how to handle questions effectively
- how to express a professional attitude and present yourself in a positive light
- opportunities to follow up on interesting replies

Interviewer

- your tone of voice and communication skills (listening and following up on comments)
- the questions you want to ask
- your concerns about the candidate's suitability
- the opportunities to follow up on interesting replies

Part 2: Interview

1 **Hold your interviews using the techniques you have learnt.**

2 **At the end of the interviews, think about the points in the table in E below and make notes.**

E PEER REVIEW

Use your notes from Part 2 of the Task and give feedback to your colleagues.

	Good points	One thing to change
The candidate or interviewer's communicative ability (tone of voice and attitude)		
The candidatee or interviewer's effective management of the conversation (listening, answering appropriately and asking follow-up questions)		
The candidate's fluency and confidence handling difficult questions		

F SELF-ASSESSMENT

Write 80–100 words to assess your performance in the interview. Think about:

- your role in answering the questions
- the feedback from your colleagues
- the lesson objectives – did you do well?
- what you think you need to do to get better

G PROFESSIONAL DEVELOPMENT AND PERFORMANCE GOALS

Think about the job you would like to do next.

What difficult questions might you be asked in a job interview?

Presentations

Objectives

Speaking

- Can give well-structured, detailed presentations on a wide range of familiar subjects.
- Can use appropriate linking expressions to signal transitions within a presentation.

Listening

- Can understand the main points of complex academic/professional presentations.
- Can recognise the use of persuasive language in a simple presentation or lecture.

Lesson deliverable

To plan, prepare and give a well-structured presentation proposing a business plan.

Performance review

To review your own progress and performance against the lesson objectives at the end of the lesson.

A SPEAKING 1

1 What makes a presentation effective? Comment on these points.

1 the opening
2 the message
3 the structure
4 the amount of information
5 the slides
6 the use of logic and emotion

2 Add more ideas on how to create an effective presentation.

B LISTENING

1 BSA4.2.17 The Chief Executive of a retail chain is talking to the shareholders. Look at the slides and listen to the first part of his presentation. Then answer these questions.

1 What is his main proposal for the business?
2 What is the short-term negative issue?

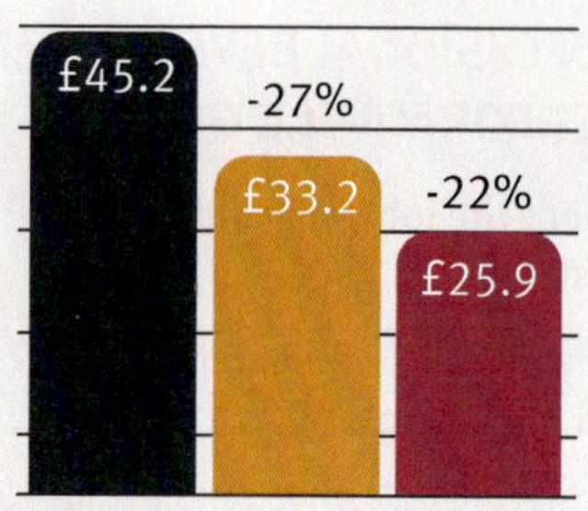

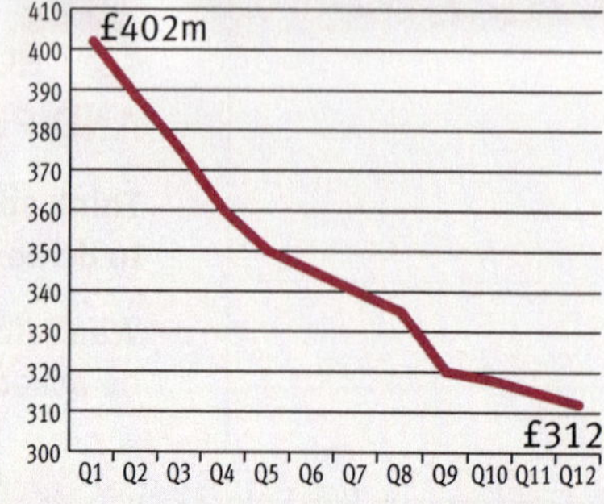

2 BSA4.2.18 Listen to the whole presentation. Which features in Speaking 1 does he use?

3 The CEO organises his argument carefully to make his points clear. Which structure does he use?

1 Start with a proposal. Give reasons and evidence to support it. Make a strong closing statement

2 Describe a problem. Identify possible solutions and compare the advantages and disadvantages of each. Explain why your proposal is the best.

3 Describe the current situation. Say what you want to achieve. Explain specific issues and present your proposals.

4 BSA4.2.19 Listen again to the three main points of his turnaround plan. For each point, identify:

1 the problem
2 his proposal

5 BSA4.2.20 **Look at the list of linking expressions below. Listen to five extracts from the presentation and complete the gaps.**

I would like to begin by ...

Let's ....[1] looking at ...

The first point I want to look at is ...

The next issue to focus on is ...

...........[2] now to ...

Moving on to ...

Let's move on to ...

...........[3] my third point.

Finally, ...

To sum ....[4]

Last, but ....[5]

I'd like to ....[6] that ...

C SPEAKING 2

1 **Work in pairs. Student A turns to page x. Student B turns to page xi. Practise presenting proposals.**

2 **Look at some extracts from the previous presentation. Does the presenter use logic (L), or emotion (E), to persuade the audience?**

1 In total, 150 of our stores need refurbishment to improve the shopping experience. ....

2 A breakdown of investment is included in my report. ....

3 I am asking for your patience and trust so we can transform this company. ....

3 **If you were a shareholder, would you accept the proposal? Explain why or why not.**

Task

Pre-task: Discussion

Context: You work for a bicycle retailer. The company's Senior Management team have been given two targets for the year.

1 To increase sales revenue
2 To raise awareness of the company brand

Work in two teams, A and B, and discuss the ideas below. Decide which three ideas would be the most effective in helping you to achieve the company targets. Use the background information on page ix to help you.

- Manufacture an own-brand high quality bike range.
- Introduce a bike-building service for customers who want to choose their own parts.
- Sponsor family cycling days around the country
- Sponsor a professional team in the *Tour de France*.
- Organise promotional events in gyms to get more women and other age-groups cycling.

Part 1: Preparation

Team A Task: The Senior Management team have asked you to increase revenue from bicycle sales.

Team B Task: The Senior Management team have asked you to create a marketing campaign to promote the company brand.

In your teams, prepare a 3–5-minute presentation outlining your proposals. Think about:

Structure:

- Start and end with a clear main message.
- Choose a logical structure for your presentation.
- Identify the current situation and make proposals.

Techniques and language:

- Use brief examples to make your points.
- Use linking expressions to signal transitions within the presentation.
- Be persuasive by appealing to both logic and emotion.

Part 2: Presentation

Presenters: Use the guidance in Part 1. Give your presentation.

Audience: Make notes about the main points of the proposal. Do you think the Senior Management team would adopt the proposal? Why? / Why not?

Extra Practice: DVD clip and Worksheet 17

D PEER REVIEW

1 **Use the notes you made in Part 2 of the Task. Consider ways in which the other team's presentation was:**

- well-structured
- persuasive

2 **Give feedback and make suggestions.**

1 What I liked about your presentation was: ....

2 One suggestion for improving your presentation is: ....

E SELF-ASSESSMENT

Look at the lesson objectives.

- What techniques and language did you use to create a well-structured and detailed presentation?
- What do you think you did well? What would you like to do better next time?
- Write 50–80 words to assess your presentation.

F PROFESSIONAL DEVELOPMENT AND PERFORMANCE GOALS

Write three sentences about ways you will improve the structure of your presentations in the future.

Writing file

Letters

Salutation

When you don't know the name of the recipient:

Dear Sir/Madam (BrE)
Ladies and Gentlemen (AmE)

When you know the name of the recipient:

Dear Mr/Mrs/Ms/Miss Winch (BrE, AmE)

Note: In the US, the titles *Mr.* and *Mrs.* are followed by a full stop/period, e.g. *Mr. Winch.*

Endings

When you don't know the name of the recipient:

Yours faithfully (BrE)
Sincerely yours (AmE)

When you know the name of the recipient:

Yours sincerely (BrE)
Sincerely (AmE)

Sign the letter, then print your name and position under your signature.

Common abbreviations

Re.	regarding
pp	(on behalf of) when you sign the letter for someone else
encl.	documents are enclosed with the letter (sometimes also *encs.*)
cc	copies: the names of the people who receive a copy of the letter

TM Breweries GmbH

Baubergerstr 17
80991 Munich

Ms Teresa Winch
Vending Machines Inc.
Box 97
New York

19 February

Dear Ms Winch

South-East Asian opportunities

I was very pleased to have met you again at the open day we held in our Munich brewery last week. I hope you enjoyed yourself and felt that your visit was useful.

I found our discussion about the activities of your organisation in Korea very interesting. It seems to me that there are a lot of ways in which our organisations could work together to our mutual advantage in South-East Asia. I have enclosed a brochure with further information about our products. I propose that we get together soon to discuss the matter in more detail.

I hope this suggestion is of interest and look forward to hearing from you.

Yours sincerely

Katherine Sell

Katherine Sell
Sales Manager

Encl. product brochures

E-mails

E-mails have two distinct styles: a semi-formal business style and a more informal personal style.

The semi-formal style is similar to a business letter, but less formal and shorter. A likely ending is *Best wishes* rather than *Yours sincerely*. This style is best used for e-mails to people outside your company or whom you do not know well. The emphasis is on the efficient provision or exchange of information.

To: james.scarfield@tmb.de
From: alison.mcdermott@hasbro.com
Subject: Meeting in Berlin

Dear James

You may remember we met at the Learntech fair in Kuala Lumpur last fall. You were interested in our company's automation equipment.

I am visiting Berlin at the end of next month and would like to visit you, if you are around. I will be there from March 27–31.

Let me know if you have any time.

Best wishes

Alison

Alison McDermott
Product Manager
Has Bro Equipment Inc
Box 28
Chicago

e-mail: alison.mcdermott@hasbro.com

The informal style is suitable for e-mails within your company and for people whom you know well. The greeting is often *Hi*, *Hello* or even *How are you?* The style is much closer to spoken than written English.

To: james.scarfield@tmb.de
From: jennifer.duncan@kingsland.co.uk
Subject: Meeting in Berlin

Hi James

I'm over in Berlin from 6–8 November. Could we meet up some time? It would be great to see you!

Let me know when you're free.

Regards
Jenny

e-mail: jennifer.duncan@kingsland.co.uk

Press releases

The header for a press release should make clear who it comes from, what the subject is and which part of the press it is aimed at.

The subject should be put in bold print so that journalists can see immediately if it is relevant to them.

The main body should have a short introduction with names of people who might be interesting for the press, some description of what is new or interesting for the public and – if possible – a good quote which the newspaper could print.

The style should be formal and concise, with nothing irrelevant to the particular story.

Always include some information as to how journalists can get more information about the subject if they want it.

Press Presse Prensa

Automatix plc
Semi Conductor Division

For the trade press
21 December

Opening of new production facilities in Johor Fahru, Balanesia

At a ceremony attended by Automatix Chairman, Rocco Truffaldino, and the British Ambassador to Balanesia, Sir Edward Faulkner, Automatix plc's new semi-conductor-chip facilities were opened in Johor Fahru on Wednesday.

'The new facilities represent our commitment to expanding our production of advanced memory chips. We aim to be the supplier of choice for the world's leading electronics companies, without damaging the environment,' said Mr Truffaldino.

A special feature of the plant is the clean, no-waste production process, which aims to have zero impact on the environment.

For additional information, visit our website www.pr.automatix.co.uk or contact Jerry Turner +44 (0)1792 536012 (phone), +44 (0)1792 536723 (fax).

Date: 21 December
Title: Opening of new production facilities in Johor Fahru, Balanesia
Addressed to: The trade press
Author: Kylie Dawson

Summaries

Hispanics are more influenced by advertising than other US consumers, suggesting that the growth of the Spanish-speaking population could prove beneficial to big corporate sponsors, according to two studies.

A Nielsen Media Research study released on Wednesday found that Spanish-language television viewers pay more attention to commercials and are more likely to base their purchasing decisions on advertisements than other US consumers. The report was issued after Euro RSCG, the marketing communication agency, released a study that showed Hispanics are more aware of brand names than other US consumers.

Taken together, the reports suggest that growing corporate interest in Hispanic marketing might involve factors that go beyond the mere size of the Spanish-speaking population. The US Hispanic population is estimated at about 39m.

The studies also suggest that Hispanic consumers offer big companies the chance to use the kinds of sales pitches that worked with US consumers in decades past, but which are now less popular with advertising-weary viewers.

Fifty-two per cent of Hispanics say they frequently get information for making purchase decisions from watching TV commercials in Spanish, compared with 7 per cent of non-Hispanics watching English-language television.

When you summarise something, you express the most important facts or points about something in a short and clear form.

Writing a summary involves:

- selecting the most important ideas or facts from a text
- rewriting those ideas/facts in a short, concise form, using your own language
- producing a text which is shorter than the original – usually at least half the number of words.

Here is an example of an original text and a sample summary.

The Spanish-speaking population in the United States (about 39m) is an important group of consumers for large companies.

Recent research has found that Spanish TV viewers are very influenced by television commercials when they buy products, and they also know more about brands than other people in the United States.

Another finding of the research was that conventional methods of advertising appeal to Spanish-speaking people, even though other viewers are tired of them. Some interesting statistics: 52% of Hispanics depend on TV commercials for information about what to buy, whereas only 7% of non-Hispanics do.

(96 words)

This summary is effective because:

- it contains the key ideas from the original text
- the language used to express the key ideas is different from the original
- the new text is much shorter in length.

Guidelines

Guidelines vary enormously from company to company and industry to industry. It is important to distinguish between guidelines and regulations.

- Regulations are required for ensuring the legally correct handling of a contract, or the safe operation of a piece of machinery, for example. The language used in regulations is therefore much more directive.
- Guidelines are also important for ensuring the smooth operation of the company, but they often touch on areas of human behaviour where it is not easy to dictate to people. The language must therefore be more persuasive and less directive, or else staff will object.

Westpak Ltd
Company Guidelines

Welcome to Westpak, the company that cares!

As a new employee, you probably have many questions that you wish to ask about your new position. To help you settle in quickly, here are answers to some of the most frequently asked questions.

1 How does the flexitime system work?

All employees at Westpak are individuals with their own particular circumstances. We believe that it is your responsibility to work out with your supervisor a schedule that is fair to both you and the company. As long as your work is done as efficiently as possible, you can do it when you like. That is why our offices are staffed 24 hours a day.

2 How should I dress?

Most of you will be in regular contact with customers. It is important that they should feel confident about the service they will receive from Westpak. We suggest that you dress in a way which is smart and business-like as a mark of respect to our clients.

3 How are interpersonal problems dealt with?

Teamwork has always been the key to success at Westpak, and anything which is likely to damage co-operation between team members has to be dealt with as quickly as possible. If you feel that efficient …

1

Action minutes

Minutes of the Management Committee Meeting

Date: 7 April
Venue: Building B, Room 10–213
Participants: Jim Scarfield, Andrea Hevitsun, Robbie Gibson, Paul Keown. Apologies: Tony Barton

Point	Discussion	Action
1 Management pay review	We agreed changes to the management pay review. AH will include these when the review is presented at the next meeting of the finance committee.	AH 26 April
2 Sales projections next quarter	We agreed that we need to produce better sales figures for the next quarter after the poor results so far this year. JS and PK will spend the next month personally visiting our top clients to check the reasons for the business downturn.	JS and PK
3 Recruitment and capital expenditure	We decided not to do any recruiting over the next quarter. However, we will buy the new accounting software to increase our efficiency in invoicing customers, if we can get a bigger discount from the software supplier.	RG
4 Company bonus scheme	Because of the present financial situation, a bonus scheme can only work if it is linked to productivity. AH will review different possibilities for discussion with the finance committee and report to us at the next meeting.	AH 3 May

Next meeting: 3 May 14:00
Venue: Building B, Room 10–213

Always put the title, date, time and venue (place) of the meeting, plus the names of the participants.

The minutes can be an important record of what was really discussed at a meeting, so it is important to make sure that the summary of each point is as accurate as possible.

Initials are used to refer to participants.

The 'action' column is important for showing who is supposed to do what by when.

If you are a participant at a meeting, always make sure you check the minutes when they have been written up. If you think something has not been accurately reported, then have it corrected.

Reports

Parry, Parry & Gibson: SITE ACCIDENT REPORT

Executive summary

Damage has been caused to the emergency generator on the Witherby power plant site. It was caused by a fire started by the electrical contractors Mullet & Sons. Although the packing material that caught fire was left by another subcontractor, the personnel from Mullet started work before clearing the waste matter away, in contravention of contract regulation 2.3.8. Mullet & Sons should therefore pay for the replacement of the damaged equipment.

Introduction

This report will look at:

- the sequence of events;
- the subcontractors involved;
- the responsibilities of the subcontractors;
- the financial compensation from the subcontractors;
- recommendations to avoid future incidents of this nature.

Findings

1 Fire broke out at 17:30 on Friday 13 October in the working area around the emergency generator. All personnel were cleared from the site, and the fire service was informed by 17:45. The fire service arrived at 18:00, and the blaze was extinguished by 18:30.

2 The electrical contractors Mullet & Sons started the fire accidentally when carrying out the connection work of the generator to the main power line. Packing material left on the ground by another subcontractor, Harvest Macdougall plc, caught fire, and this quickly spread.

3 Although Harvest Macdougall are obliged to remove any packaging material they bring with them, it seems that the electricians from Mullet told them to just leave it. We assume they wanted to get their own work done as quickly as possible so that they could finish for the weekend. Starting welding work without first making sure there is no inflammable material around is in direct contravention of contract regulation 2.3.8.

Conclusion

Mullet & Sons must pay for the replacement of the generator (€90,000) as they are solely responsible for the damage.

Recommendations

1 Mullet & Sons should not be offered any more work on site if they do not accept these terms.

2 Harvest Macdougall should receive a formal warning.

3 All subcontractors must be reminded of their obligation to follow all fire and safety regulations.

Normal Poole
Site Manager
19 October

1 A report should be well organised, with information presented in a logical order. There is no set layout for a report. The layout will depend on:
- the type of report;
- the company style.

2 The format used for this example is common for many formal reports:
- Title
- Executive summary
- Introduction
- Findings
- Conclusion
- Recommendations

3 Another possible structure would be:
- Title
- Terms of reference
- Procedure
- Findings
- Conclusions
- Recommendations

4 The *Executive summary* is a summary of the main points and conclusions of the report. It gives the reader a very quick overview of the entire situation.

5 The *Introduction* defines the sequence of points that will be looked at.

6 The *Findings* are the facts you discovered.

7 The *Conclusion* is what you think about the facts and how you interpret them.

8 *Recommendations* are practical suggestions to deal with the situation and ideas for making sure future activities run more smoothly.

Activity file

1 Communication, Skills, Exercise F, page 11

Student A

Role play 1

Two colleagues from your company will be visiting company headquarters next month. You need to telephone head office and give the following details about the visit.

Names of visitors: Rachel Buergisser and Ignacio Alfonso Paz
Contact number: 05876 549006
Flight details: BA 3098 arriving at 16:40, not 18:30, on the 13th May
Hotel: Park Crowne Plaza (13th–16th May)
Note: You tend to speak quite fast on the telephone.

Role play 2

You are the overseas agent for an electronics company. The Marketing Manager of the company phones to discuss plans for advertising the company's new range of up-market coffee machines. You and the Marketing Manager have various ideas for promoting the sales of these items. Try to agree on a suitable advertising strategy.
Note: You are on your mobile phone and the battery is low, so check all the details carefully.

You want to:

- spend a lot of money on radio and TV advertising
- hire some models for in-store promotional activities at local department stores (twice a week for eight weeks)
- exhibit the products at a local trade fair
- do some direct mail shots to selected house and apartment owners
- start a viral marketing campaign, but you have no experience in this area.

You want the Marketing Manager to contribute at least 80% of the cost of the advertising, which you expect to be about €100,000 in total. You could contribute 20%, but this would greatly reduce your profits on the products.

While doing the role play, practise some of the expressions you can use for dealing with breakdowns in communication.

3 Building relationships, Starting up, Exercise A, page 22

Key

1	a) 2	b) 1	c) 0
2	a) 2	b) 1	c) 0
3	a) 2	b) 0	c) 1
4	a) 2	b) 1	c) 0
5	a) 1	b) 2	c) 0
6	a) 1	b) 2	c) 0

0–7 Building relationships is not easy for you. Communication is the key. Make the effort to talk to people about problems. Ignoring them won't solve them, and practice makes perfect.

8–9 You are making the effort to build good relationships, but are you trying too hard? It might be better to spend more time developing the relationships you have rather than going out to meet more people.

10–12 Congratulations! You obviously enjoy good relations with many of your business associates. Can you use your skills to help those who work with you improve their business relations, too?

3 Building relationships, Skills, Exercise D, page 27

Student A

Role play 1
You are the US owner of an up-market chain of restaurants. You phone a supplier who was recommended by a friend. You want the supplier to make regular deliveries of lobster and crab to your restaurants in New York.

1 Introduce yourself, and mention your friend's recommendation.
2 Find out if the supplier is interested in doing business with you.

Role play 2
You are a sales manager for a mobile phone company. While having lunch, one of the speakers at the conference sits next to you. You met the speaker briefly at a conference in Vienna (Austria) two years ago.

1 Re-introduce yourself.
2 Find out if the speaker is interested in visiting your company and leading a training session for your sales force.

4 Success, Skills, Exercise E, page 41

Student A

You are the Sales Manager for the Spanish briefcase manufacturer.
You want the retailer to agree the following:

Delivery time:	Four weeks after receiving order
Place of delivery:	The retailer's main warehouses in Zurich and Geneva
Price:	Top-of-the range briefcase: €550
	Medium-priced briefcase: €320
Colours:	Black and brown
Payment:	By bank transfer when goods have been dispatched
Discount:	4% for orders over 100
Returns:	Medium-priced briefcases (easier to resell)

4 Success, Case study, page 43

Kensington United negotiating team
There are two other companies interested in sponsoring the club if the negotiation with Universal Communications (UC) fails. However, UC is an international company, with excellent management and a high profile in the business world. You want:

1 **A four-year contract**
The contract should have a total value of €80m. €40m should be paid within the first year, as you need money to enlarge the stadium's seating capacity, introduce sophisticated surveillance technology and hire more staff for crowd control.

2 **Limited advertising**
Advertising of UC at the club ground should be limited. You want the ground to keep its identity and intimate atmosphere. Too much UC advertising could upset the fans.

3 **Limited promotion by players**
Players' appearances and promotional activities should be limited to 10 days a year. Too much time doing promotion work affects performance on the field. If the team fails to reach the final of the European Cup though, you could increase players' availability by five days.

4 **Crowd control at home matches**
You are working actively with the local police to deal with the problem of hooliganism at home matches.

5 **An additional payment**
UC should pay an additional €16m towards the cost of buying one or two star players. Marco Conti says this is essential to Kensington's success in the European Cup.

6 **Diversification into other areas**
You have contacted baseball clubs in the United States. Two US clubs have agreed to play a competitive match at Kensington's stadium during the summer. This will greatly enhance Kensington's image.

7 **A deal with a football boot manufacturer**
You want to make a deal with Sprint plc, a football boot manufacturer. Sprint has developed an innovative football boot which gives players greater speed. It has offered Kensington €5 million to sponsor the product.

8 **Perks**
Try to get as many perks as possible from UC – for example, €20,000 for each goal that a player scores over his individual target of 20 goals. Also, free cars for players, memberships to clubs, etc.

You can offer UC:

- the advantage of being linked to the most exciting young team in English football;
- the opportunity to work with one of the best managers in the Premier League;
- the benefit of working with a brilliant Commercial Director, Ingrid Tauber;
- the possibility of becoming better known throughout Asia;
- the use of a hospitality box, with space to seat 10 people.

6 Risk, Case study, page 59

Director 2

The security risk
The country has been unstable for many years. There have been civil disturbances in the area recently. There was a demonstration calling for the release of a rebel leader currently in jail.
In some countries in the region, mining companies have been attacked by gangs of robbers, and some workers have lost their lives.

5 Job satisfaction, Starting up, Exercise D, page 44

Are you in danger of burning out?

You're turning up for meetings at the right time, but in the wrong week. You're pouring milk into the wastepaper basket rather than your coffee. You've lost your temper with half of the office, and the other half are cowering under their desks. You could be suffering from burnout, a debilitating condition caused by working too hard for too long and failing to prioritise. Try this quiz to see if you are in danger of self-combusting.

1 **Your boss asks if you can work late for the third night in a row. Do you:**
   a) say yes without giving it a second thought?
   b) laugh politely and close the door on your way out?
   c) say yes, but feel like crying?

2 **Some of your colleagues want to play a practical joke on your boss for April Fool's Day. Do you:**
   a) organise a brainstorming session to select the best idea?
   b) tell them that there are more important things to be done?
   c) go to your boss and tell them what they are planning to do?

3 **You arrive home one Friday night with a pile of work only to discover that your partner has arranged a surprise weekend away. Do you:**
   a) leave the work behind and take Monday off to catch up?
   b) tell him/her that you're sorry, but you can't afford the time?
   c) agree to go, but insist on taking the work with you?

4 **There is a rumour going around that a proposed company merger may mean some job losses. Do you:**
   a) take a cursory glance at the job adverts in the paper and look for your CV?
   b) bite your nails until your fingers hurt?
   c) find yourself hyperventilating?

5 **It's bedtime and you are exhausted after a stressful day at the office. Do you:**
   a) lie awake for two hours, then make a start on next week's assignment?
   b) lie awake for five minutes, then sleep right through until morning?
   c) lie awake for one hour, then read for a while until you fall asleep?

6 **Some colleagues ask if you could help them with a problem, but you're in the middle of a project with a tight deadline. Do you:**
   a) schedule some time in your diary to work with them when you're free?
   b) agree to help, but become irritated when they don't grasp the solution straight away?
   c) tell them to speak to someone who cares?

7 **There are a lot more things on your 'to do' list than you realistically have time for. Do you:**
   a) divide the items into 'urgent' and 'important' and start with the urgent things?
   b) pick out the easy tasks and start with them?
   c) work overtime until they're all done?

8 **An old friend you haven't seen for ages asks you to go out for a meal. Do you:**
   a) have a fantastic evening of reminiscence?
   b) refuse the invitation as you are always too tired to go out on weekdays?
   c) accept the invitation, and spend the evening telling them all about your job?

Check your score on page 143.

from *The Guardian*

8 Team building, Skills, Exercise D, page 79

Student B

You are a member of the team. You meet your team leader to discuss your performance at work. You are unhappy for these reasons:

- You feel you are working harder than everyone else. You are always the last to leave work.
- Your hard work is not recognised and appreciated by the team.
- You recently married and are missing your partner and young child.
- You do most of the boring paperwork for the accounts while your colleagues are given more face-to-face contact with clients. You are not happy with how the workload is being distributed.
- You think the team leader is too young and inexperienced, and is not managing the team well. This is the main reason why you are unhappy.

6 Risk, Case study, page 59

Director 3

The health risk

Mining the area could result in workers and inhabitants suffering from skin diseases because of industrial emissions.

The water in nearby wells is being contaminated, so they can no longer be used for drinking water.

Site waste and debris are contaminating the soil in the area.

These hazards could involve expensive legal costs for WCM, as well as heavy expenditure to remedy the problems.

5 Job satisfaction, Reading, Exercise B, page 46

Article B

KPMG

Audit, tax and advisory services	
Annual sales	£1,607m
Staff numbers	11,788
Male/female ratio	53:47
Average age	34
Staff turnover	16%
Earning £35,000+	49%
Typical job	Accountant

The phrase 'work hard, play hard' could have been invented for Sue Day, a high-flyer at financial services giant KPMG. The Corporate Finance Manager spends her working days getting the best out of her talented team, but KPMG makes sure she also has the time available to pursue her sporting career.

'KPMG recognises that if it looks after people, it will get more out of them,' says Day, who has been with the firm for 12 years. 'It is difficult to juggle the training and the competition of an international sport with a job. I've been here so long because KPMG is so supportive.'

It's that kind of caring culture that has seen KPMG top our list for the third time in four years. And its almost 12,000-strong workforce seems to agree with Day's assessment, according to our 66-point employee questionnaire. The company has top-ten results for 48 questions, and ten of those are the best scores nationally.

Corporate Citizenship Manager Uzma Hamid wanted to expand her career options and perhaps work abroad. She was given carte blanche by her manager and found a four-month secondment with the United Nations Global Impact initiative, which she says was 'like everyone's dream if you work in corporate social responsibility'.

'KPMG makes me feel empowered. I am taken seriously and I can make choices about my own career,' Hamid says. 'I am now using my experience proactively and to the benefit of the organisation.'

Employees say managers help them to fulfil their potential (a 70% positive score) and agree that the organisation is run on strong principles (78% – the top score nationally).

With an overall positive score of 75%, opportunities for personal growth keep staff happy. The expansion of KPMG Europe has increased opportunities for staff to work abroad. Its successful scheme to retain talented women encompasses Reach, a project aimed at encouraging women to become middle managers. It also has a programme for its own emerging leaders to help them move up to the next level.

Staff find their work stimulating (73%), agree training is of great personal benefit (74%) and believe the experience they gain is valuable to their future (83%), all top scores nationally.

When it comes to giving something back, KPMG has an impressive record. Last year, more than 4,500 staff contributed 43,000 hours to serve the community, helping it gain a score of 64%, again better than every other firm. All staff can use half a day of company time per month to volunteer.

As far as pay and benefits are concerned, KPMG staff are the most satisfied on our list (67%). The company has a flexible benefits scheme, including childcare vouchers, medical insurance for the whole family and the opportunity to buy up to ten days' additional holiday. There are occupational health and employee assistance programmes, and an 11.9% contribution by the firm to the pension scheme. Employees feel they are paid fairly for the work they do relative to their colleagues, too (62%).

Working across cultures 3, Task, page 91

Manager D

You think:

- the team leader should change every six months in rotation around the team, as this is the fairest way and will involve the most people.
- the six team leaders should make the decisions.
- there should be one initial face-to-face meeting to assign roles and videoconferences every time the team leader changes.
- team members should contact the team leader by e-mail to resolve any problems.
- any bonus should be for the whole team and be paid at the end of the project.
- all team leaders (six people) should attend a cultural training course.

8 Team building, Case study, page 81

Director 4

You want to:

- hear the opinions of the other directors before making up your mind. You are not sure whether to keep David Seymour or not.
- appoint Sonia as manager if the other directors think David should go. Sonia is tough, talented and dynamic, just what the team needs as a leader. She's also a very good communicator.
- replace Max with one of the other sales reps. He is not a dynamic person and has a poor record at getting new business.
- insist that Hank attends a course to improve his interpersonal skills.
- to think of other suggestions for improving the performance of the sales team.

6 Risk, Case study, page 59

Director 1

The exploitation risk

The 80-acre Kango site is located in the south-west of the country. Sites near Kango have previously produced good quantities of copper and basalt.
One site, just 50 kilometres from Kango, has produced large quantities of coltan, a precious metal used in many consumer electronic products, such as cell phones and DVD players.
Another site, 85 kilometres from Kango, has proved to have diamond deposits.
Geologists reports say that the site has potential, but there is no guarantee the deposits will be profitable.

8 Team building, Starting up, Exercise B, page 74

Score 1 point for each of the following answers:

Doers vs. Thinkers:	**a, d, f**
Mind vs. Heart:	**a, b, d**
Details vs. Ideas:	**b, d, e**
Planners vs. Improvisers:	**a, c, e**

Score 2 points for each of the following answers:

Doers vs. Thinkers:	**b, c, e**
Mind vs. Heart:	**c, e, f**
Details vs. Ideas:	**a, c, f**
Planners vs. Improvisers:	**b, d, f**

18–24 points
You are definitely a creative type. You value original ideas over detailed planning. You are likely to show consideration for others. You can get bored easily and sometimes need to be under pressure to get results.

12–17 points
Clear thinking and careful planning are of great importance to you. You are not afraid of challenging others in order to get results. You are likely to be ambitious and well organised.

8 Team building, Skills, Exercise D, page 79

Student A

You are the team leader. You meet a member of your team who is uncooperative and unhappy. Find out what the problems are and try to offer solutions so that the employee performs better as a member of your team.

8 Team building, Case study, page 81

Director 1

You are the leader of the meeting. You want to:

- get rid of David Seymour by asking him to resign. You think he has some good ideas for improving sales, but he is not a suitable person to manage the sales team. He's not a 'people person'. He's been given more than enough time to turn things round.
- replace him with a new person from outside the company. A new manager should be appointed – someone with good people skills and better managerial ability.
- discuss David's proposals and find out what the other directors think about them.
- think of some other ways of motivating the sales staff and improve team spirit.

Working across cultures 3, Task, page 91

Manager B

You think:

- there should be one team leader for the whole three-year project who should not change. This will keep the team stable.
- the team leader is in charge and should make the decisions.
- the team should meet face to face at the start of each year to plan for the next year.
- there should be monthly teleconference calls to keep people up to date and deal with any problems.
- there should be individual bonuses to motivate team members. These should be paid each year.
- all team members should attend a one-week cultural training course at head office in the Netherlands.

9 Raising finance, Skills, Exercise E, page 87

Student A

You are the business owner. You want to:

- get an equity investment of €500,000 to extend the range of your products and enter a new overseas market – France or Germany.
- keep a shareholding of at least 50% so that you continue to own and control your business.
- get management advice from the angel when necessary.
- keep control over recruiting senior managers.

In return, you expect to:

- offer the angel a 25% stake in the business.
- give the angel a seat on your board of directors, with voting rights.
- offer the angel a 10% share in the profits of any future business development.

Negotiate a good deal for your business.

9 Raising finance, Case study, page 89

Group A

Filmmakers

1 **Financial terms**
- First, find out if Concordia are happy with the detailed budget you sent them.
- After repaying 100% of Concordia's investment (€1 million) within five years, you will then share the net profits of the film on a 60/40 basis (60% for you, 40% for Concordia).
  Your budget is based on keeping costs as low as possible.

2 **Film title/location**
- Your title *All for one* is perfect. Everyone you have asked loves it. Paris is the ideal location for the scenario.

3 **Payment of instalments**
- You want the investment to be paid in full at the pre-production stage.

4 **Director/scriptwriter/music**
- Charles will direct the film; Gunnar has already written an excellent script and will write the music for the film. He received a prize in the film-studies course for a musical score he produced for a ten-minute film.

5 **Cinematographer/1st and 2nd camera assistant**
- Colleagues from the film-studies course will undertake these duties – fees to be paid from future profits.

6 **Actors**
- Two of the main characters will be unknown actors. The third main character will be played by a friend of Charles's who is a famous actor in Europe and will perform in the film for a low fee.

7 **Marketing and promotion**
- Concordia should pay for all the costs of marketing and promoting the film.

8 **Product placement**
- No product placement, if possible

9 **The way the film ends**
- The ending is important. It must be 'bitter sweet'. None of the three women get what they want, but their friendship is stronger than ever. In the final shot, they sit around a table in a café and put their arms around each other. The camera zooms in, they all have thoughtful expressions on their faces.

8 Team building, Case study, page 81

Director 3

You want to:

- move David Seymour to another department in the company.
- replace him with another member of the sales team. Chang might be a good choice.
- have a department meeting every two weeks, led by the new manager. Everyone should be encouraged to express their opinion.
- keep Hank in the sales team. You are Hank's closest friend – you went to school together. He is a difficult person, but a top-class salesman.
- reduce the sales team to five members and make the others work harder and be more productive (you decide who should go).
- reorganise the sales team (you decide how).
- think of other suggestions for improving the performance of the team.

10 Customer service, Vocabulary, Exercise D, page 97

Group B: Dealing with customer complaints

1 Keep an open mind at all times.
2 Do not end up arguing with the customer.
3 Do not be defensive.
4 Concentrate on the situation, not the personalities.
5 Don't force your solution on the customer.
6 Try to find out what result the customer wants.
7 Tell the customer what you can and cannot do.
8 Offer compensation of greater value than the goods or service complained about.

11 Crisis management, Skills, Exercise C, page 109

Student A

You are the presenter of the TV programme. Several consumers have contacted you to complain about the lamp, code-named BX 150, sold by a local electrical appliances manufacturer.

They say:

- the lamp overheats very quickly, which has caused some users to burn their hands.
- the vinyl coating on the electrical cord gets too hot, so the cord bursts and melts. As a result, in some cases, materials near the lamp have been set on fire.
- the bulbs in the lamp sometimes explode, which could harm people's eyes.

Try to persuade the company to recall all the lamps or to resolve the problem in a satisfactory way.

11 Crisis management, Case study, page 111

Group A

You are Directors of ExtremAction. Your objectives are to:

- defend your game
- work out an action plan to deal with the crisis
- handle the journalists' questions.

Your team will be lead by the Chief Executive of the company. You will support her/him at the press conference and answer journalists' questions.

1 Hold a meeting to discuss what actions you will take to deal with the situation.
Here are some possible actions. Add any others you can think of.
   - Postpone the launch until people have forgotten about Carl's report.
   - Withdraw the game and make it less violent.
   - Defend the game and go ahead with the launch as planned.

2 Try to predict what questions the journalists will ask and prepare answers to them.

3 Decide on an action plan to deal with the crisis. Be prepared to tell the journalists what you have decided.

9 Raising finance, Skills, Exercise E, page 87

Student B

You are the business angel. You want to:

- invest €1 million of equity capital in the herbal tea products business.
- help to expand the business in Europe and the United States.
- provide excellent contacts with sales outlets in France and Germany.
- put the owner in touch with other potential investors in the business.
- encourage the manufacturer to grow the business internationally.

In return, you expect to:

- have a 55% stake in the business.
- be offered a seat on the board of directors, with voting rights.
- have a 30% share in the profits of any future business development.
- advise on future recruitment of senior managers as the business expands.

Negotiate a good deal for yourself.

Working across cultures 1, Task 1, page 30

Suggested ranking

1 Setting up a take-out business rather than offering customers pizzas in an American-style restaurant with an attractive décor.

2 Not adapting the business model to the Chinese market.

3 Not making sufficient use of David Li's business knowledge.

4 Selling a product that was unsuitable, as it didn't appeal to Chinese tastes.

5 Gaining a reputation for unreliability because of late deliveries.

6 Making the pizzas too expensive compared to those of the competition. They were not considered value for money.

Working across cultures 1, Task 2, page 31

1 In India, it is likely that there will be some general discussion before people get down to business. Such discussion helps both sides to get to know each other better.

2 Decision-making may take longer in some Asian countries than in Western ones. It's important to be patient and not become frustrated by the slower pace of discussions.

3 Foreigners doing business in India should look for long-term benefits rather than short-term advantages.

4 Indian people need to trust those they are doing business with. They need to feel that the other side is sincere.

5 It takes time to build up relationships with business contacts in India.

Working across cultures 3, Task, page 91

Manager A

- You will lead the meeting and you should make sure the agenda is followed.
- You have an open mind about the items on the agenda, so you should listen carefully and try and
  see the different points of view.
- You are keen that the three-year project should run smoothly and avoid problems once the team is working together.
- You know that the company does not want to spend a lot of money on cultural training courses and is not keen on bonus schemes.

Encourage the other managers to give their opinions and reasons for their ideas.

Working across cultures 4, Task, page 121

Pair B

1 Look individually at the points to consider in an international negotiation listed on the right and add two more.
2 Choose the five most important points from your list.
3 Talk to your partner and agree the five most important points.
4 Join up with Pair A and try to agree the five most important points from your two lists.

1 Avoid an agenda. Let the negotiation develop naturally.
2 Ask a lot of questions to find out the position of the other side.
3 Try to disguise what you really want.
4 Be prepared to walk away without a deal.
5 Never compromise on your key points.
6 Be careful not to let the negotiation break down.
7 Make no concessions until the end.
8 Make sure you 'win' the negotiation and get the best possible deal.

6 Risk, Case study, page 59

Director 4

The economic risk
The cobalt and bauxite markets are booming at present, but the industrial metals market internationally is volatile. The stock-market prices of some smaller mining companies have been falling.
The slowdown in the Chinese economy is continuing to have an effect on commodity prices.
There will be a general election in the country in six months' time.

1 Communication, Skills, Exercise F, page 11

Student B

Role play 1
You are expecting a call from an overseas subsidiary confirming the details of a visit to your head office next month. You have been given some information by a colleague, but are not sure if it is correct.

Names of visitors: Bargaster? and Paz?
Contact number: 06875 413870?
Flight details: BA 3765 arriving at 17:10 on the 12th May?
Hotel: Hilton Plaza (12th–14th May)
Note: You have a rather quiet telephone voice.

Role play 2
You are the Marketing Manager of an electronics company. You phone an overseas agent to discuss plans for advertising the company's new range of up-market coffee machines. You and the agent have various ideas for promoting the sales of these items. Try to agree on a suitable advertising strategy.
Note: You are on your mobile phone and the battery is low, so check all the details carefully.

You want to:

- place special advertisements for the new products in lifestyle magazines
- have some in-store promotions and demonstrations at department stores (once a week for three months)
- advertise the products on buses, trams and in key outside locations (billboards)
- make sure the products are exhibited at a trade fair
- contact a local marketing consultant for advice on viral marketing:
  Markus Kaufmann, tel: 01782 550378
  E-mail: m.kaufmann@JHPAssociates.com

You will contribute €60,000 towards the cost of the advertising. You expect the agent to contribute €40,000 towards the cost of advertising.

While doing the role play, practise some of the expressions you can use for dealing with breakdowns in communication.

5 Job satisfaction, Skills, Exercise F, page 49

Student A

Headhunter

Use this information to persuade the TV Producer to discuss the offer further.

The job:	TV Producer at Barnard Media – a top company in the industry
Salary:	Around €180,000 pa + bonus – negotiable
Main benefits:	Insurance paid by company; top Mercedes car
Working hours:	Usually 40 hours a week
Vacation:	Six weeks a year
Office location:	Five minutes from mainline station

Add any other information you wish.

4 Success, Case study, page 43

Universal Communications negotiating team

Your negotiating objectives are listed below. Keep them in mind when you plan your strategy and tactics. You want:

1 **A four-year contract worth €50m**
In addition to €50m in sponsorship, you could offer Kensington (KU) an additional €20m if the club wins the European Cup. Decide how much you wish to pay each year and when payments will be made. If KU play badly and have to drop down to the next division, the sponsorship deal should be renegotiated.

2 **Maximum advertising at the football ground**
- Four huge billboards advertising the company at the sides and ends of the ground
- The company's logo on flags at all entrances
- The main stand to be renamed 'The Universal Communications Stand'
- The company's name on the surface of the pitch (playing area)

3 **Maximum promotion by players of KU**
- Players wear the company's logo on their shirts.
- The team's shirts and shorts should have blue and black stripes – UC's corporate colours.
- The two top goal scorers should do a minimum of 25 days' promotional work a year for UC (other players 15 days).

4 **Crowd control**
KU is totally responsible for controlling spectators at its home games. Any investment in crowd control should be paid for by the club, not UC. If there is any serious disorder in the crowd, the club should pay a penalty of €1 million to the company for each incident.

5 **Approval of Kensington's new ventures**
If KU wants to diversify into other businesses, UC should be consulted. The new ventures must be in keeping with the company's image.

6 **Cancellation of Kensington's deal with Sprint plc**
You have learned that Kensington plans to make a sponsorship deal with Sprint plc, a football boot manufacturer. You insist that their players must use the football boots made by a small firm you have just bought.

7 **Use of a hospitality box**
Two hospitality boxes at the ground should be provided for the exclusive use of UC staff and guests. There should be space for at least 30 people.

You can offer KU:
- a sponsorship package worth €50m;
- good exposure in China and India because of the group's strength in those countries;
- perks, for example:
  - a car with the company logo on it for all first-team players
  - free travel to holiday destinations
  - cheap loans for apartment/house purchase
  - media training courses for players to improve their presenting and interviewing skills
  - financial help for older players to attend coaching courses or obtain academic qualifications;
- a financial contribution of €5 million towards the cost of a new player.

8 Team building, Case study, page 81

Director 2

You want to:

- keep David Seymour as manager. You are a close friend of David's. You think he's an excellent manager of a difficult team. He just needs more time to put things right.
- send David on a management training course which focuses on teambuilding.
- get rid of Hank. He is rude and immature, and upsets the other members of the team.
- have fewer reports, meetings and web communications, so that the sales reps can focus on increasing sales and looking after customers' needs.
- think of some other ways of motivating the sales staff and improving team spirit.

3 Building relationships, Skills, Exercise D, page 27

Student B

Role play 1

You are a Canadian supplier of shellfish. A US restaurant owner phones you. You have never met the caller, so get more information about the person and his company.

1 Find out how the owner heard about your business.

2 Do not offer to supply the owner, as you have too many orders at present and are under-staffed. However, it may be possible later.

Role play 2

You are a speaker at a conference. You sit down next to one of the participants. You think you may have met the person before, but you're not sure.

1 Show interest when they introduce themselves.

2 If they want you to give a talk at their company, find out what date they have in mind and mention that your fee for an afternoon session is $2,000 + transport costs.

6 Risk, Case study, page 59

Director 5

The financial risk

The exchange rate of the local currency is fluctuating.

WCM will need to invest in expensive new machinery to exploit the site. The company will need to borrow money, in addition to using the proceeds of the share offer to finance the development of the site.

The transport services within the country are not reliable, which could increase the costs of mining the site.

4 Success, Skills, Exercise E, page 41

Student B

You are the Chief Buyer for the Swiss retailer. You want the manufacturer to agree to the following:

Delivery time:	Two weeks after receiving order
Place of delivery:	Individual retail outlets (16 around the country)
Price:	Top-of-the-range briefcase: €500
	Medium-priced briefcase: €270
Colours:	Black, brown, maroon, pink
Payment:	Two months after delivery
Discount:	10% for orders over 200
Returns:	All unsold briefcases returnable up to one year after order

5 Job satisfaction, Starting up, Exercise D, page 44

Are you in danger of burning out?

Key

1	a) 2	b) 3	c) 1
2	a) 3	b) 2	c) 1
3	a) 3	b) 1	c) 2
4	a) 3	b) 2	c) 1
5	a) 1	b) 3	c) 2
6	a) 3	b) 2	c) 1
7	a) 3	b) 2	c) 1
8	a) 3	b) 2	c) 1

19–24 points
The Olympic flame is more likely to burn out than you. You glow gently when necessary, but rarely get above Gas Mark 3. This is because your stress levels are comfortably low and you know what to do at the first sign that things are getting on top of you.

11–18 points
You are smouldering slightly, and any spark could set you off.You may not think that you are a candidate for burnout, but you are heading in that direction. Try to develop your life outside work, and if it's the job itself that's causing the problem, think about looking for a new one.

8–10 points
It is simply a matter of time before there is a little pile of white ash on the chair where you used to sit. Take some positive action to prevent total burnout before it's too late. Prioritise, delegate, improve your time management and, above all, ask for help immediately.

5 Job satisfaction, Skills, Exercise F, page 49

Student B

TV Producer
You are very happy in your present job and have a great group of colleagues.
The offer must be exceptional to persuade you to change your job.
Your present situation:

Position:	TV Producer, Universal Entertainment
Salary:	€140,000 pa + bonus, depending on company performance
Main benefits:	Working in a beautiful building overlooking the river Big discounts on theatre and cinema tickets
Working hours:	Very long: start at 6 a.m., finish late.
Vacation:	Four weeks a year
Office location:	Office not very accessible; takes one and a half hours to get to work

Working across cultures 3, Task, page 91

Manager C

You think:

- the team leader should change each year (i.e. three different team leaders). This will help to motivate the team.
- the whole team should be equally involved in decision-making.
- the team should meet face to face every six month to review progress and deal with problems.
- e-mail contact should be encouraged between team members. Time differences need to be considered, so replies may take longer.
- there should be different bonus schemes operating for team leaders and team members. These should be paid every six months.
- only team members with less than three years' experience in the company (four people) need to attend a cultural training course.

9 Raising finance, Case study, page 89

Group B

Concordia (independent distribution company)

1 **Financial terms**
- You want to be repaid 120% of your investment (€1.2 million) within five years of the launch of the film + a share of the net profits on 70/30 basis (70% for you, 30% for the filmmakers). Your reasons are:
  - the two filmmakers have no experience of making feature films
  - it is essential to use well-known actors in all main roles
  - there are other costs that the filmmakers have not considered (see below).

2 **Film title/location**
- You prefer the title *Friends forever*. It emphasises the main theme of the film.
- Berlin is a better location than Paris. The city is less well known and therefore the sites where the action takes place will be more interesting and mysterious.

3 **Payment of instalments**
- 20% when pre-production begins
- 50% at the start of the production stage
- 20% at the beginning of post-production
- 10% will be reserved for marketing and promotion

4 **Director/scriptwriter/music**
- You are happy for Charles to be Director and you approve Gunnar's script.
- You want to have a highly commercial soundtrack by a famous band. This will add to the production costs but also to the profits.

5 **Cinematographer/ 1st and 2nd camera assistant**
- You want to hire an experienced professional to be cinematographer, not someone from the film-studies course. You are willing to use students from the course as camera assistants. Hiring a professional will involve extra production costs.

6 **Actors**
- The main characters should be top film actors from the countries concerned. You will persuade them to take low salaries but offer them a share of the film's profits.
- Hiring top professional actors will add to production costs but greatly increase profits. Part of the increased cost will come out of the film's profits.

7 **Marketing and promotion**
- 10% of the budget should be retained to cover marketing costs.

8 **Product placement**
- This is a great opportunity for you to make money from the film. You believe you could persuade at least eight companies to place their top brands in the film.

9 **The way the film ends**
- You want an upbeat, happy ending. One of the women, Fabiola, should meet and marry the Frenchman of her dreams. The final shot should be of her kissing the bridegroom at the marriage ceremony.

11 Crisis management, Skills, Exercise C, page 109

Student B

You are the Sales Manager of the furniture company. The lamp is your best-selling product. It is a beautifully designed item which costs $60 in the stores.
You know that:
- the lamp could overheat if it was left on for many hours.
- there is a warning label on the lamp not to leave it on for more than six hours.
- as far as you know, there have been only two incidents when users have burnt their hands. This was because they were careless.
- the vinyl coating of the cord is top quality and very thick. You are surprised to learn about this problem and will look into the matter.
- the bulbs in the lamps have been supplied by a top-quality electrical goods manufacturer.

You believe that a competitor paid a reporter to write the harmful report.
You have been selling the lamp for two years to retailers and have had almost no complaints.
Try to make a good impression in the TV programme. Do not agree to recall the product.

10 Customer service, Vocabulary, Exercise D, page 97

Group A: Dealing with customer complaints

1 Show the customer you are listening by checking that you understand.
2 Allow the customer to show their emotions if they are upset or angry.
3 Say you are sorry that the customer is upset.
4 Admit that the problem was your fault as soon as possible.
5 Make sure you get full details of the problem.
6 Summarise and make sure that the customer understands what you have said.
7 Ask the customer to put the complaint in writing.
8 Be firm if you are sure of your facts.

11 Crisis management, Case study, page 111

Group B

You are journalists. Your objectives are to:

- ask probing questions to find out how the company is dealing with the crisis.
- gather information so that you can write a powerful and accurate article in your newspaper. You want to start a lively debate in the correspondence columns about *In Range*.
- get the company to answer questions about excessive violence in computer games, as you know many of your readers are very worried about the effects on their children of violence in computer games.

1 Work in small groups. Choose a newspaper, whether American or foreign, that you represent. Prepare some questions you would like to ask the Directors of ExtremAction.
2 Work as one group. Choose the best questions and decide who will ask each one.
3 When you ask questions at the press conference, make sure you 'follow up' questions. Don't let the Directors give you vague answers.
4 Take notes on the Directors' answers so that you can write an article about this press conference.

7 Management styles, Reading, Exercise B, page 68

Student B

Jim Buckmaster

What is the office atmosphere like?

'We don't really have the arcade games, fussball, ping-pong tables or that sort of thing, but I guess it's a cosy kind of non-corporate atmosphere, it just feels like you're sitting in a house, and there's no dress code. I spent a lot of years working in organisations that were regimented and we were told what to do in many different ways, and I developed a very anti-authoritarian mindset by the time I was put in a position of authority. The last thing I wanted to do was reproduce all of those things that I had disliked so much. Such that our employees aren't really told what to do, or when to do it, or when to come into work, or what they can wear, and we don't set deadlines at all – unless they are set for us by some external force like a regulatory agency. I don't think that artificial deadlines are a good idea. They just create stress where it is not needed.'

So there is no management?

'We do have a hierarchy, we do have managerial positions, but I personally don't like trying to impose my will on someone else or trying to hold it out that I'm in a position of authority. I hold that in reserve as an absolute last resort, and certainly years go by when I don't have to exert that kind of authority.'

How do you motivate people?

'One of the wonderful things about working at Craigslist is that the company philosophy and approach is such that people generally feel very good about working there. Because we have a non-traditional philosophy – it is very public-good centric – people feel good about coming to work … We are also very careful in hiring people who are a) talented and b) self-motivated. Then once we have people who fit that description, I've always found that it is just a matter of letting them do their work.'

And you really don't hold meetings?

'Of all the meetings that I've gone to in the past, virtually all of them, I've felt, were kind of useless. I don't like closed-door meetings because they always mean something bad is going to happen.'

Read your article quickly and decide which of these statements are true for the CEO you read about.

They …

1 think most meetings are a waste of time.
2 are good at making decisions quickly and firmly.
3 want people to know who is the boss.
4 think artificial deadlines are stressful.
5 believe in hiring the best staff they can.
6 think their staff feel happy working there.

Grammar reference

1 Idioms

In the language of business, idioms and metaphors are often used with reference to the domains of sport, war and gambling.

Sport

I don't know the exact price, but $500 is a good ***ballpark figure*** (= estimate).

She's smart and really ***on the ball*** (= quick to understand).

Follow his advice, and it'll be ***plain sailing*** (= easy to do or achieve).

You don't know where you stand – they keep ***moving the goalposts*** (= changing their aims or decisions).

There must be no unfair competition in the EU, and we shall continue to stress the need ***for a level playing field*** (= a situation that gives no one an advantage).

War

Bill's ***on the warpath*** (= very angry) *again – there are mistakes in the publicity material we sent out.*

You may have to ***do battle with*** (= fight it out with) *the insurers because they won't want to pay up.*

Manufacturers often feel they are ***fighting a losing battle*** (= making no progress) *against counterfeiting.*

If you can convince the commercial attaché here, that's ***half the battle*** (= the rest is easy).

I've been ***fighting a running battle*** (= having a series of arguments) *with the financial department, but they won't give us the money.*

She may want to convince you otherwise, but you should ***stick to your guns*** (= maintain your point of view).

She's ***up in arms*** (= very angry and ready to fight) *about the lack of safety procedures.*

Gambling

We are trying to ***hedge our bets*** (= reduce our chances of failure) *and not put all our eggs in one basket.*

The odds are stacked against us (= there are many difficulties), *but we're determined to succeed.*

It ***makes no odds*** (= makes no difference) *whether we get permission or not, we'll go ahead anyway.*

They're paying ***over the odds*** (= more than it's worth) *for the site, but it's a prime location.*

We had our doubts about Susan, but she has really ***come up trumps*** (= produced good, unexpected results).

If you ***play your cards right*** (= do the right thing), *you'll get the promotion.*

2 Noun compounds and noun phrases

1 When two nouns occur together, the first noun is used as an adjective and describes the second noun. The first noun answers the question 'what kind of?'.

a manufacturing subsidiary
a draft agenda
a phone conversation
a network operator

2 Noun + noun compounds can often be transformed into structures where the second noun becomes the subject.

an oil refinery (= a refinery that produces oil)
company executives (= executives that work for the company)
a travel agency (= an agency that sells travel)

3 Noun + noun compounds may also be reformulated using a preposition.

market research (= research **into** markets)
rail transport (= transport **by** rail)
leisure activities (= activities **for** leisure)
a web page (= a page **on** the Web)
their Paris store (= their store **in** Paris)
income distribution (= distribution **of** income)

4 The first noun is usually singular.

a five-star hotel (not *five-stars*)
consumer-purchasing behaviour (not *consumers*)
risk assessment (not *risks*)
brand names (not *brands*)
However, some words retain the plural form.
sales policy
needs analysis

5 Sometimes three or more nouns occur together.

line management system
production research centre
travel insurance claim form
Motorola's software development establishments
Hyphens can be used to avoid ambiguity in such compounds.
software-development establishments

6 Noun compounds can be modified by adjectives and adverbs.

inspiring *team leadership*
international *business development directors*
extremely boring *conference presentation*
increasingly volatile *mobile phone market*

3 Multiword verbs

Multiword verbs are formed when a verb is followed by one or more particles. Particles can be prepositions or adverbs.

The meaning of a multiword verb is sometimes very different from the meanings of the two words taken separately.

*How are you **getting on**?* (*get on* is not the same as *get + on*).

- There are two different types of multiword verbs.
  - Intransitive: without an object
    *The plane has just **taken off**.*
    *She **turned up** unexpectedly.*
    *What time did you **set off**?*
  - Transitive: with an object
    *We will **set up** a new subsidiary.*
    *They have **called off** the strike.*
    *She has **handed in** her resignation.*
- Multiword verbs can have two particles.
  *I'm **looking forward to** seeing you.*
  *She's trying to **catch up with** her work.*
  *We need to **make up for** lost time.*
- Multiword verbs are either separable or inseparable.
  - An **adverb** particle can come before or after the object if the object is a **noun** ...
    *We've **put by** some money.*
    *We've **put** some money **by**.*
    ... but you cannot put a **pronoun** after the particle.
    *She's **switched off** the computer.*
    *She's **switched** the computer **off**.*
    *She's **switched** it **off**.*
    (NOT ~~She's switched off it.~~)
  - If the particle is a **preposition**, the verb and particle are inseparable.
    Can you cope with your work?
    (NOT ~~Can you cope your work with?~~)
- We do not normally separate multiword verbs with two particles. However, there are some transitive three-word combinations that allow separation.
  *Multinationals can **play** individual markets **off against** each other.*
  *She **puts** her success **down to** hard work.*
  *I'll **take** you **up on** that suggestion.*

4 Present and past tenses

1. The **present simple** is used to make true, factual statements.
   *Established customers **tend** to buy more.*
   *Nokia **sells** mobile telephones.*
2. Verbs relating to beliefs, being, knowledge, liking, perception and appearance are normally only used in the simple form.
   *I **understand** what you **mean**.*
   *It **depends** on what the chairman **wants**.*
   *I **appreciate** your concern.*
3. The **present continuous** is used to refer to events in progress and temporary or changing situations.
   *I'll be back late, **I'm sitting** in a traffic jam.*
   *They**'re installing** a new switchboard.*
   *The world **is getting** smaller.*
4. The **past simple** is used to refer to events completed in the past. We frequently use a time expression to say when the event took place.
   *In the late 1940s, Ford **decided** it needed a medium-price model to compete with General Motors.*
   *2001 **was** a good year for our company.*
5. The **past perfect** sequences two or more past events.
   *Before he joined this company, **he had** worked for two competitors abroad.*
6. The **present perfect** is used to say that a finished past action is relevant now. There cannot be any specific reference to past time.
   *They **have changed** the address of their website.* (It's new.)
   *The share price **has plummeted**.* (It is lower than before.)
7. The **present perfect** covers a period of time starting in the past and continuing up to the present. An appropriate time expression takes us up to now.
   *So far, the company **has defied** predictions that its rivals will catch up.*
   *Stella McCartney **has been** one of the leading fashion designers since the mid-1990s.*
   *He**'s been** acting strangely lately.*
   *Over the last few years, e-commerce **has become** fashionable.*

5 Passives

We use the passive when the person who performs the action is unknown, unimportant or obvious.

*The file **was stolen**.*
*The roof **was damaged** during the storm.*
*She**'s been given** the sack.*

1 The passive can be used in all tenses and with modal auxiliaries.

*A new fitness centre **is being built**.*
*The job **was going to be done** on Friday.*
*He **had been asked** to do it twice before.*
*She **may be required** to work on Sunday.*
*The best employees **should be given** a performance bonus.*
*He **would have been told** eventually.*

2 If we know who performed the action (the agent), we use *by*.

*The file was stolen **by** a secret agent.*

3 In a passive sentence, the grammatical subject receives the focus.

a) *Giovanni Agnelli **founded** Fiat in 1899.*
b) *Fiat **was founded** by Giovanni Agnelli in 1899.*

In a), our attention is on the agent – Giovanni Agnelli. In b), it is Fiat rather than Agnelli that is the topic of the sentence.

4 The subject of the sentence can be a pronoun.

*We **were informed** that the firm was going to be taken over.*

5 Passive constructions are common in formal contexts, for example in reports or minutes, and they help to create an impersonal style. Using *it* as a subject enables us to avoid mentioning the person responsible for saying or doing something.

***It was felt** that the system needed to be changed.*
***It was decided** that expenditure would be limited to $250,000.*
***It was suggested** that staff be given stock options.*
***It was agreed** that the proposal should be rejected.*

6 Adverbs of degree

1 If we want to amplify the quality an adjective describes, we use an intensifying adverb. These are some of the most common.

*The presentation was **really/very** good.*
*She's **dead** certain to get the job.*
*The new design looks **pretty** good.*
*I was **extremely** surprised by her reaction.*
*She's a **thoroughly** efficient organiser.*

2 The relative strength of adverbs is shown on this scale:

Strong: *absolutely, altogether, awfully, completely, greatly, highly, quite, terribly, totally, very*

Moderate: *fairly, mildly, moderately, partly, quite, reasonably, somewhat*

Weak: *a bit, a little, marginally, poorly, slightly.*
*The whole thing is **quite** amazing.*
*The goods are **reasonably** cheap.*
*I was **slightly** surprised by what she said.*

Note that *quite* also means *fairly*.
*The restaurant is **quite** cheap, but the food isn't wonderful.*

3 Intensifying adverbs modify adjectives that are **gradable** – that is, they can signify degrees of a given quality. Adjectives that are not gradable or identify the particular class that something belongs to are not normally used with intensifying adverbs. We cannot say:

~~*a very unique idea*~~
~~*a fairly free gift*~~
~~*a very impossible solution*~~
~~*some slightly financial news*~~

4 However, you can use an adverb such as *absolutely* or *utterly* with an ungradable or classifying adjective to show that you feel strongly.

*It doesn't cost anything – it's **absolutely** free.*
*The task is **utterly** impossible.*

7 Text reference

Read this text and note how certain words refer forward and back to other words in the text.

> Although more **women** are becoming sales managers, *they*'ll have to tailor *their* management styles to the gender of *their* employees if *they* want to have continued success. According to **a study** carried out by John Doyle and Jill Harris of the University of Hull, both female and male sales personnel welcome the newcomers. But *it* also points out that there can be a difference between **the management style** males prefer and *the one* that elicits their best performance.
>
> In particular, the researchers wanted to discover differences in satisfaction and variations in sales performance under female supervision. **Two management styles** were identified. A transactional style is the more traditional of *the two*. Male managers are hands-off until something goes wrong. The philosophy is 'When *you*'re doing OK, *you* won't even know I'm around. But, when *you* mess up, *I*'ll be right next door.'
>
> Women take a more hands-on approach. A transformational mode encourages a more hands-on, individual-orientated manner. **Women** more than **men** tend to motivate by encouragement and personal attention. *The former* relate to their staff emotionally and tend to foster new ways of thinking, whereas *the latter* rely on rewards and punishments.

Grammatical reference

In paragraph 1:

- *they/their/they* refer back to *women*
- *it* refers back to *a study*
- *the one* refers back to *the management style*.

In paragraph 2:

- *the two* refers back to *two management styles*
- *you/you/you* refer back to any employee working under a male manager
- *I* refers to the male manager.

In paragraph 3:

- *the former* refers back to *women*
- *the latter* refers back to *men*.

Lexical reference

Very often in texts, words belonging to the same family, and synonyms and antonyms occur closely together.

gender ... men ... women, male ... female
John Doyle and Jill Harris ... the researchers
the newcomers ... women sales managers
employees ... personnel ... staff
differences ... variations
hands-off ... hands-on
something goes wrong ... you mess up ... do OK
style ... mode ... approach ... manner
individual ... personal
encourages ... motivate ... foster
encouragement ... rewards ... punishments

8 Modal perfect

1 We use past modals to speculate about events in the past.

*I thought I saw Yolanda in the car park, but it **may/might/could have** been someone else.*

*The project **might/could have** been a terrible failure, but turned out to be a great success.* (We know it was a success, therefore *may* is not possible here.)

*I wasn't there myself, but from what I hear, it **must have** been a very stormy meeting.*

*She says she met me in Brazil, but it **can't have** been me because I've never been to Brazil!*

2 Past modals can also be used to express irritation.

*She **could/might have** given me the information, but she didn't bother.*

3 Missed opportunities are also expressed using *could* or *might*.

*She **could/might have** had a brilliant career, but she gave it all up for love.*

4 *Would have* and *wouldn't have* are used to make hypotheses about the past.

*The team **would have** been stronger if she had been with us.*

*We **wouldn't have** achieved such good results if we hadn't worked together as a team.*

5 *Should have*, *shouldn't have* and *ought to have* are used to criticise.

*The report **should have** been submitted a lot earlier.*

*He **shouldn't have** resigned without having another job to go to.*

*You **ought to have** made a reservation – there are no seats left now.*

6 Note the difference between *needn't have* and *didn't need to*.

*I **didn't need** to come into the office because there was no work for me to do, so I stayed at home.*

*I **needn't have** gone into the office because there was no work for me to do when I got there.*

9 Dependent prepositions

1 Here is a list of common verbs and the prepositions that follow them.

complain about	*insure against*	*react against*
hint at	*account for*	*hope for*
long for	*opt for*	*pay for*
strive for	*emerge from*	*stem from*
suffer from	*invest in*	*result in*
bet on	*insist on*	*rely on*
amount to	*lead to*	*object to*
refer to	*relate to*	*resort to*
associate with	*contend with*	*sympathise with*

2 Some verbs may be followed by more than one preposition, with a corresponding change in meaning.

How did you ***learn of*** *his sudden departure?*
I hope you will ***learn from*** *your mistakes.*
The team ***consists of*** *(= is made up of) two Americans and two Japanese.*
For her, job satisfaction ***consists in*** *(= is based on) having almost no work to do.*

3 Here is a list of common adjectives and the prepositions that follow them.

lacking in	*aware of*	*capable of*
representative of	*contingent on*	*intent on*
reliant on	*conducive to*	*essential to*
parallel to	*prone to*	*susceptible to*
vulnerable to	*compatible with*	*filled with*

4 This is a list of common nouns and the prepositions that follow them.

admiration for	*aptitude for*	*bid for*
demand for	*need for*	*remedy for*
respect for	*responsibility for*	*room for*
search for	*substitute for*	*threat to*
access to	*alternative to*	*contribution to*
damage to	*exception to*	*introduction to*
reference to	*resistance to*	*solution to*
ban on	*comment on*	*constraint on*
curb on	*effect on*	*tax on*
contrast with	*dealings with*	*dissatisfaction with*
involvement with	*relationship with*	*sympathy with*

10 Gerunds

1 The gerund is the *-ing* form of the verb used as a noun, either as the subject or object of the verb.

Selling *is all about persuasion.*
Getting through to *the right person isn't always easy.*
My idea of relaxation is ***going to*** *a fitness centre.*

2 Gerunds follow prepositions.

We are committed <u>to</u> ***giving*** *the highest quality.*
We depend <u>on</u> ***having*** *fast communications.*

3 They are often used to begin an item in a list.
Good leaders are skilled at:

- ***fixing*** *goals*
- ***motivating*** *people*
- ***producing*** *creative ideas.*

4 Gerunds can be made negative, used in the passive and used with past verb forms.

It's wonderful ***not having*** *to get up early for work.*
Being kidnapped *is not a pleasant experience.*
He mentioned ***having met*** *our main competitor.*

5 Many verbs are followed by a gerund (e.g. *admit, avoid, consider, deny, dislike, involve, mention, recommend, risk, suggest*).

He denied ***fiddling*** *his expenses.*
I dislike ***having*** *to eat at my desk.*
She suggests ***raising*** *the price.*

6 Some verbs are followed by either a gerund or an infinitive. The choice of one or the other usually leads to a change in meaning.

Increased production may ***mean taking*** *on extra staff at the weekend.* (= involve)
I didn't ***mean to cause*** *any offence.* (= intend to)
He ***remembered to buy*** *his wife a present.* (= He didn't forget.)
He ***remembers buying*** *his wife a present.* (= He has a clear recollection of this.)

7 The gerund is formed by adding *-ing* to the base form of the verb.

She's ***talking*** *to a client.*
However, some gerunds require minor spelling changes.

- For verbs ending in *-e*, take away the *e* before adding *-ing*.
  He's ***making*** *some coffee.*
- For verbs ending in consonant + vowel + consonant, double the final consonant and add *-ing*.
  Is anyone ***sitting*** *here?*
  But do not double the final consonant if it is in an unstressed syllable.
  developing, marketing

11 Conditionals

1 We use conditional sentences to make hypothetical statements and questions.

*We'**ll** deliver within 24 hours **if** you **order** online.*
***If** we order now, **will** you **give** us a discount?*
The use of *if* + *will* + verb suggests that these arrangements are feasible.

2 If the proposal is more tentative and possibly less feasible, *would* + past verb forms are used.

*I'**d need** some venture capital **if** I **was/were** to start my own business.*
***If** I **got** a guarantee for the loan, I **would lend** them the money.*
***If** I **had invested** my savings in the company, I **would have made** a fortune.*

3 If the verb is *had*, *were* or *should*, we can leave out *if* and put the verb at the beginning. The sentence is now more formal.

***Had** it not been for his help, we would not have survived.*
***Were** it not for Patrick, we'd be in a terrible mess.*
***Should** you require any further information, do not hesitate to contact me.*

4 These words are also used in conditional sentences.

*We'll meet tomorrow **providing/provided (that)** no one has an objection.*
*Even the best management teams won't be successful **unless** they are given the resources.*
*You can say what you like **as long as** you don't make any criticisms.*
***Supposing (that)** we decide to use the Topsite service, how much would it cost?*

5 Mixed conditionals follow a variety of patterns.

*If you need help, just **ask**.* (an offer)
*If Peter **wants** to see me, **tell** him to wait.* (an instruction)
***If** you **hadn't invested** in e-commerce, our sales **would be** much lower.* (This is true now, so *wouldn't have been* is inappropriate.)
*I **would** be grateful if you **would** give me an early reply.* (a polite request)

6 These are other examples of conditional sentences.

Ignore the media, and we'll never be able to protect our reputation.
Tell us what you need to get the job done and you'll have it.
Should you need any further information, please contact the crisis team.
Given time, our company can recover from the current crisis.

12 Prediction and probability

1 A number of modal verbs are used to make predictions. The modal indicates the speaker's degree of certainty.

*They **will** be there by now.* (100% certain)
*They **won't** have any trouble finding our office, they've been here many times.* (100% certain)
*They **must** have arrived by now.* (80% certain)
*They **can't** have arrived yet.* (80% certain)
*They **should** have arrived by now.* (60% certain)
*They **may/could have** arrived by now.* (40% certain)
*They **might** have arrived by now.* (20% certain)

2 Conditional statements contain hypotheses about the way the future may turn out.

*If we **use** solar power, we'**ll probably** save money.*
*If you **tried** harder, you **would be able to** do it.*

3 The **future perfect** and the **future continuous** predict what will be in progress or will have been accomplished in the future.

*By 2050, businessmen **will be taking** orders from the Moon.*
*By 3000, scientists **will have discovered** how to transmit objects by electronic means.*

4 There are a number of lexical expressions of likelihood. These include *about to, bound to, going to.*

*He's tapping his glass – I think he's **about to / going to** make a speech.*
*She's **bound to** be late, she always is.*

5 The following lexical phrases can be used to discuss the future: *certain, probable, possible, unlikely* or *impossible.*

*There's **certain** to be more changes in the world's weather systems over the next few decades.*
*It's quite **probable** that an economic upturn will start next year.*
***Maybe** there'll be a change of management in the coming months.*
*It is **unlikely** that the retirement age will be increased to 75.*
*It is just **impossible** to imagine the World Wide Web having serious problems in future.*

6 There are a number of useful time phrases that can be used to talk about the future.

***In my lifetime,** I will see China becoming a dominant world power.*
***Before long,** the company will decide to merge with a bigger company.*
***In the near future,** everybody will be using wind power.*
***In the next ... years,** there will be a huge change in the way we travel.*
***Over the next decade,** governments will start reducing air traffic.*
***By this time next year,** I will be promoted.*
***By the end of this century,** the way we conduct business in the world will be very different from now.*
***Sometime in the next decade/century,** man will inhabit other planets.*

Audio scripts

UNIT 1 COMMUNICATION

CD1 TRACK 1

Good communicators really *listen* to people and take in what is said. They maintain eye contact and have a relaxed body language, but they seldom interrupt and stop people talking. If they don't understand and want to clarify something, they wait for a suitable opportunity.
When speaking, effective communicators are good at giving information. They do not confuse their listener. They make their points clearly. They will avoid technical terms, abbreviations or jargon. If they *do* need to use unfamiliar terminology, they explain by giving an easy-to-understand example. Furthermore, although they may digress in order to elaborate a point and give additional information and details where appropriate, they will not ramble and lose sight of their main message. *Really* effective communicators who have the ability to engage with colleagues, employees, customers and suppliers are a valuable asset for any business.

CD1TRACK 2 (I = INTERVIEWER, AD = ALASTAIR DRYBURGH)

I How do you advise companies to cope with modern communication?

AD I think the thing to remember is the principles of communication haven't changed and I don't think there's anything inherent in technology that makes good communication easier. It can make it better, but there are also many ways it can make it worse. So, I think there's four things that you need to remember. The first thing is that you've got to remember people have limited attention – if you like, limited bandwidth – which puts the onus on you as the communicator to think hard about what it is exactly you're trying to communicate and make sure that you get it down as succinctly as possible.
Um, second point is, recognise that, you know, communication is about meaning. It's not about dumping vast amounts of data on people and expecting them to deal with something. Now, I went to a presentation once and someone started off. He said, well, I've got 41 slides here, but I think I'll get through them all in 30 minutes. And they were really dense slides – lots and lots of graphs and pictures. Now, I was actually at the back of the room, and these glasses are not quite what they should be. I need new lenses. I couldn't read any of the slides because they were so fine, so that's what you've got to remember: don't dump lots of data on people. You have to distil the meaning into, into a small number of points.
Um, the third point about communication is, it's just as much about listening as it is about telling things, and the biggest communication problems I come across in organisations are actually failures of listening rather than failures of, of outward communication, particularly the inability or unwillingness of senior management to listen to what other people are actually telling them.
And the fourth ques-, point is that, um, you know, if a communication is going to be effective – if you are actually going to get someone to do something or stop doing something or do something differently – there's got to be some sort of emotional connection in it.
And so, if you think about all those four points, there's no obvious reason why technology would make any of those easier. There are certainly ways you can use it to make it easier; there are certainly ways you can use it to make it an awful lot worse. So, I think that's what you've got to watch. The principles remain the same. The tools could help or could hinder.

CD1 TRACK 3 (I = INTERVIEWER, AD = ALASTAIR DRYBURGH)

I Do you think that in general companies are now communicating better with their customers?

AD In general, I would say no, and I think there are, there are examples of excellent communication and there are examples of awful communication. If you think about two examples, perhaps, of companies who've used technology to change the way they communicate with customers, one is absolutely fantastic, the other is completely abysmal, awful.
The fantastic one I would say is Amazon. The thing about Amazon – you always know where you are. You order something, you get a confirmation. Um, as soon as it's been sent, you get another confirmation. So you always feel exactly … you know exactly where you are. You know exactly what's happening, when your thing's going to turn up – which anyone could do, but most people don't. The other thing about Amazon is they are, in a sense, listening to you because they're looking at the things you've bought in the past and suggesting – well, based on that, there are other things you might like. I think that's very effective communication. It certainly resulted in me buying quite a lot more books than I otherwise would. Or things like, you know, people who bought, other people who bought this also buy that. That's, that's really good because again they are using the opportunity of having you on this wonderful technological platform where they don't just know what you buy, they know everything you've ever looked at – to tell you useful things. I think it's great because if I want books on a particular subject, it will suggest books I've never heard of. And I'll buy them, so it's, it's good for them as well. So that works really well.

CD1 TRACK 4 (AD = ALASTAIR DRYBURGH)

AD Because what they've done is they've built this amazing computerised voicemail maze, which seems to be designed to prevent you ever from getting to talk to a real person who could actually answer your question or solve your problem. So you go through – push one for this, dial one for this, dial two for this, dial three for that. Neither option seems to answer my question, so what do I do? Sometimes I arrived at points where literally my options were to hear the message again, which was no use, or hang up. There are some points where, if you just don't do anything and hang on the line, you will actually get to talk to a human being … but it takes you a while, you know, many minutes on the phone, repeated attempts to find out where those are. And so, I don't really know what they're trying to do. They've obviously put, I suppose, put an emphasis on efficiency, but, in the process, they've actually made themselves almost impossible to deal with.

CD1 TRACK 5 (KS = KOICHI SATO, BK = BERNARD KLEBERMANN)

KS Yamashita Electronics, Koichi Sato speaking.

BK Hello, Koichi, this is Bernard Klebermann. How are you?

KS Very well, thank you. How can I help?

BK We need some more sales literature. We're planning a big advertising campaign for your new laser printer, the HG903 model. And there's a lot of demand for your other products too, by the way.

KS Good.

BK Could you send some more brochures – 5,000 would be good – plus some updated price lists, the same amount? Also we need point-of-sales literature, especially posters – at least 200 – and, um, yes, some of those pens and pencils with the company logo on, also 50 or so of the bags that we give out at exhibitions.

KS OK, I don't know if I can remember all that … can you …

BK Good. Another thing, you might like to know, we've managed to get a big new customer, Seelmayer.

KS Seel-… I don't think I know the company …

BK We're very excited about it. They're a big restaurant chain. They've placed an order for 518 of the new lasers. Please tell your boss, Hideo. He'll be very pleased, I'm sure.

KS An order for 580 laser printers? Great! I'll let my boss know. He'll probably want to write to this company … er … Seelmund …

BK Yes, please tell him to write to them. That'd be good PR. They're expanding very fast in Europe and they'll probably order some computers from us as well. They're planning a big roll-out here in the next two years. Tell him that.

KS Um, yes, a big, um, roll-out, you say, um, interesting. I'll tell him immediately. I'll need some details about the company, an address and the right person to contact and …

BK Sorry, Koichi, I can't hear you, it's an awful line. Anyway, nice talking to you. Speak to you soon.

CD1TRACK 6 (KS = KOICHI SATO, BK = BERNARD KLEBERMANN)

KS Yamashita Electronics, Koichi Sato speaking.

BK Hello, Koichi, this is Bernard Klebermann. How are you?

KS Very well, thank you. How can I help?

BK We need some sales literature. We're planning a big advertising campaign for your new laser printer, the HG903 model. And there's a lot of demand for your other products, too, by the way.

KS That's good. Could you hold on a second while I get a pen? … OK. What do you need?

BK Could you send some more brochures – 5,000 would be good – plus some updated prices lists, the same amount? Also we need some point-of-sales literature.

KS Sorry, Bernard, I didn't catch that. Could you slow down a little, please? I need to take some notes.

BK Oh, sorry. Right – I said, we need more brochures.

KS Right, I've got that so far. Could you give me some more details?

BK Certainly. Um, 3,000 brochures for Switzerland, 1,000 for France and 500 each for Spain and Italy. Also, I'd like some of those posters, pens and pencils with the company logo on – a couple of hundred – and 50 or so of the bags we give out for exhibitions.

KS Let me check that: 200 posters, pens and pencils and 50 bags. Got it.

BK Good. Another thing you might like to know, we've managed to get a big new customer, Seelmayer.

KS Seel-… sorry, could you spell that for me, please, Bernard? I don't think I know the company.

BK Certainly, S-E-E-L-M-A-Y-E-R.

KS Thank you.

BK We're very excited about it. They're a big restaurant chain. They've placed an order for 518 of the new lasers. Please tell your boss, Hideo …

KS Sorry, did you say 580 lasers?

BK No, 518 – five one eight.

KS Right, I'll let my boss know. He'll probably want to write to this company to thank them.

BK Yes, please tell him to write to them, it'd be good PR. They're expanding very fast in Europe and they'll probably order some computers as well. They're planning a big roll-out here in the next few years. Tell him that.

KS Sorry, I don't follow you. What does 'roll-out' mean?

BK A roll-out is when a company plans to expand throughout a country. It's a nationwide expansion, if you like.

KS Ah, I see. I'll tell my boss immediately. But I need details about the company … Sorry, it's a bad line. Could you speak up, please? I can't hear you very well.

BK Yes, the line's awful. What did you say?

KS Could you e-mail me the details – the address, the right person to contact, etc.?

BK Sorry, I still can't hear you. I'll call you back, maybe the line will be better.

CD1 TRACK 7 (WH = WILLIAM HOOPER, BF = BETTY FRIEDMAN)

WH I'm not happy with this report, Betty. I don't think the consultants understand how we work. I mean, do the directors and I have time to read weekly reports from department managers? It's information overload, surely.

BF Mm. Well, you do need to keep informed, Bill.

WH Yeah, but there are other ways of doing it. That isn't the answer. Another thing, they want us to hire a key account manager. Now, I can't see that's a good idea. It'll just add to our costs, and we certainly don't want to do that at the moment. Our most important customers like the personal approach. They're people I've known for years and they wouldn't do business with us if they were dealing with some new person.

BF Mm. What about their other recommendation – you know, about the Customer Services Department?

WH Customer Services should inform the other departments as soon as someone complains about a product? I mean, where will it all end? We'll become a bureaucratic company, like a government department. You know my feelings about paperwork, Betty. There's already too much in the company, and for that matter, too many e-mails floating around, instead of staff having face-to-face contacts.

BF Mm. OK, Bill, I get the picture. You're not too keen on the recommendations. Well, we can talk about it at the next board meeting, see if everyone else agrees with you.

CD1 TRACK 8 (BF = BETTY FRIEDMAN, JM = JOANNA MERKOWITZ)

BF So, uh, you've seen the ideas that the consultants have come up with, Joanna. What do you think?

JM Mmm, I don't know. I'm not too keen on the idea of sending in daily sales reports.

BF Oh. What's the problem?

JM Well, I think it could be a distraction. It's difficult enough to get orders at the moment, so I want to focus on getting new business, not on sending in reports all the time. Surely, a monthly report is sufficient – or is it simply that Head Office wants to keep an eye on us and know what we're up to each day?

BF No, no, I don't think that's the case. They just want to improve communications between you people on the road and the admin staff back at base.

JM Maybe. You know, I think our CEO has got things right. Paperwork doesn't generate sales, we do. He believes selling is about personal contact and building relationships, and he doesn't want reports to interfere with that. I totally agree with him. That's why I enjoy my job so much here.

UNIT 2 INTERNATIONAL MARKETING

CD1 TRACK 9 (I = INTERVIEWER, SH = SVEND HOLLENSEN)

I How can products be designed to be suitable for international markets?

SH Well, basically, there are two different strategies. There is one strategy where you have one product and you sell it all over in the same format, and there is another strategy where you try to adapt your product to the different cultures, to different countries that you are in. And I would like to show one example of a company who has really marketed one product concept for the whole world. And that is the OneCafé company. And this product is actually selling all over in the same format and, er, it is a small company, it is based in Denmark and in Sweden. So, it is a company which is kind of 'born global'. This means that it is getting into the global markets very fast and it is doing this by setting up production in Uganda in Africa and then from there, it tries to sell in other countries of the world. So, by setting up, for instance, a website from where they also sell these coffee products, they can sell to all kinds of hotel chains and to airline companies and to different retail chains. So, this would be an example of a global product concept.
And of course, then there is the other situation where you have to adapt to the different cultures that you are in. So, you have to adapt to the cultural traditions, er, in China if you are going to China, or to India, and that means that you have to adapt your product and your concept, your communication, to the culture you are in and to the different environmental, er – environment that you face. That means that you have to adapt all levels of the marketing mix to the different regions and the different countries that you are in. And, er, that can be done in different ways, but, basically, again, two different strategies – one strategy where you have one product for all global markets and another strategy where you go into different markets with different product concepts.
I like to mention another global company that will do one product concept and, for instance, the soap brand, Lux, is one example of a global brand that will sell all over. But, actually, most brands in the world are local brands. Um, most people don't realise that, but that is actually the case. So most brands that you buy in retail stores in global markets are manufactured for local markets.

CD1 TRACK 10 (I = INTERVIEWER, DK = DARRELL KOFKIN)

I How can people be trained to be international marketeers?

DK Of course, people can learn on the job. One minute they may be asked by the Head of Marketing, 'Go away and develop a global marketing strategy. We want to enter X country.' And, therefore, they may learn by doing. We wouldn't necessarily say that is the best way and certainly, since 2007, what we have done is to work very closely with Ashcroft International Business School at Anglia Ruskin University, and with our global faculty and with our global advisers in shaping a new curriculum that enables marketers worldwide to have the latest practices, the latest knowledge and techniques, to enable them to become international marketers.
And the way we have also looked at doing it is to ensure that we enable really global relevance, but real world learning. So there are no exams for this programme. It's purely based upon work-based assignments. So our students are asked to write a report, develop a business plan, develop a presentation, write a webcast, present an internal briefing paper – just as they would do in the workplace. Because we know in talking to employers worldwide that they want marketing professionals that have the capabilities and skills required of today's demanding global business environment.

CD1 TRACK 11

1 really impressive advertising campaign
2 new customer relations department
3 highly competitive mobile phone market
4 incredibly successful product launch
5 loyal customer base
6 extremely thorough sales report
7 absolutely brilliant global campaign
8 increasingly competitive marketing environment

CD1 TRACK 12 (MT = MARTIN THOMAS, CH = CAROLINE HOLLOWAY, GR = GUILLEM ROJAS, CR = CAROL RUECKERT)

MT Hi, good morning everyone, so the purpose of the meeting this morning is to have a look at the international sales conference we're having next, um, year in January, and our objective here is to come up with location, activities that we can do in the, um, in the conference and look also at the accommodation and also some leisure-time activities so … What I'd like is for us to, um, brainstorm some ideas. OK, guys?

CH Yeah, it sounds great.

MT OK. So maybe Caroline, do you want to … have you got any ideas for where we can have this?

CH Yeah, um, I was thinking, maybe we should go to Amsterdam and we've had a few, um, conferences there in the past and they've been really successful, the facilities were great, so I think that would be a really good idea.

MT OK, anyone else?

GR Actually, yeah, I also tend to like the summer conferences, like in Amsterdam, it was great, I … I'm just a bit worried about, you know, like the time of the year because it's January, so it might just as well be just like a location more like in southern Europe, maybe like south of Portugal which would be, you know, it could be interesting like for everybody, you know.

MT That's great. Any other ideas, any options?
CR Well, I, my … my suggestion would be Florence. I think it's a great city, um, lots of things to do there, there's great food obviously, um, and they have very nice accommodation as well.
MT Mm-hm, OK, that's great. Now, can we think of some, um, activities that, er, we can do in this sales conference?
CH Mm, um, product launches, um, we always have something coming out, um, ah, at the beginning of the year, so, um, that'd be a great, um, session to have.
CR Mm, and probably following that would be some product training?
CH Good idea, yeah, mm-hm.

CD1 TRACK 13 (MT = MARTIN THOMAS, CR = CAROL RUECKERT, CH = CAROLINE HOLLOWAY, GR = GUILLEM ROJAS)

MT That sounds … that's an excellent suggestion, yeah, that's great. OK, what about the accommodation, anybody any ideas on that?
CR Well, I suppose we could do some different things, um, I mean, we could just go for a four-star hotel or, um, look at maybe some boutique hotels.
CH Mm, that's a good idea, but, um, yeah, I think it'll end up coming down to price, but, um, accommo- um, there's great accommodation in all the locations we've mentioned, so …
GR Definitely, let's see if we can get a good deal, you know, like research a bit on each, on each case, you know?
CH Yeah.
GR And it depends on the deal, I guess that will decide.
CH Yeah.
GR The budget is always important.
MT Yeah, any other ideas about what we … what we can do with the participants in their free time, what they – you know, all the delegates – can do?
CR Well, I think it'll depend on how long we're actually going to have the conference …
MT Mm-hm.
CR … um, but it would be nice to maybe take a half a day or something and go and see some of the sights.
MT That's a good idea, yeah.
CH Mm, excursions, yeah, you're right, um, what's always been successful, I think, is, um, gala dinner, the … um, it's quite nice in the … in the evening to get to know, um, other delegates from all over the world, so dinner is a great way to interact with other colleagues.
MT That's true.
CR It's a good idea.
GR And finally, you know, ah, maybe like, just like to indicate some time you know, like doing, like I don't know how many cases we're going to like to have the conference, but like for networking, you know, because during the gala dinner you are not usually like discussing about too many issues about work. So just that you know there are no like, ah, an hour, a day, you know, where the people can meet to discuss about anything.
MT OK, good, that's really great, yeah.
CH Mm-hm, that sounds good.
MT Thanks, guys, that's … there's some really brilliant ideas, so OK, we need to look at the location, then – we've got some ideas of Amsterdam, southern Portugal or Florence; we need to look at the … the timing more, but we know that we should take a half day out for some kind of leisure-time activity to do with, um, the delegates for this. And the accommodation, we'll look at depending on price, and also who can accommodate these, um, these people, and also we need to look at the, um, the workshops that you've suggested and the different sessions. OK, that's great, thank you very much for some brilliant ideas.
CH No problem, thanks.

CD1 TRACK 14 (CF = CARLA FERNÁNDEZ, PM = PIERRE MARTIN)

CF We've had some interesting results from the focus groups in the markets, Pierre. It seems we may have to change the group we're targeting when we have the international launch. From the research, it looks as if we'll need to target a lower age group. And perhaps reposition the brand, targeting the masculine, adventurous, energetic male, rather than the sophisticated, aspiring urban man.
PM Oh, why's that?
CF It's really about the competition. A lot of top producers are coming out with premium brands aiming at the urban man. It seems that this segment of the market is well catered for – in fact, it's becoming rather over-crowded. Givenchy, Jean-Paul Gaultier, Hugo Boss, even Kylie Minogue – they're all launching male fragrances at the top end of the market.
PM I see. Well, it'll mean changing the brand image of *Physique*. That'll be a big step, and we'll need to think it through.
CF Absolutely. Another thing that's come out of the focus groups is, *Physique* is seen as a French brand, and it seems that won't work in many of our target markets. We may need to change its name to appeal to an international audience, especially a younger one.
PM Mmm, does that mean *Physique* should no longer be a premium product? Are they saying we should market it as a high-volume, mass-market fragrance?
CF Perhaps it may come to this. Certainly in the emerging markets – for example, China – we could make a lot of money if we promoted it as a mass-market fragrance, at an affordable price.
PM OK. Tell me about packaging. What did the research come up with? It's essential that we get the packaging right.
CF Not good news, I'm afraid. The packaging we're using here just isn't appealing for most of the international markets. We're going to have to think again, and create a new look that'll have universal appeal. And our creative team is going to have to produce a really exciting advertising campaign that we can use in all the markets, with a few changes here and there.
PM OK. Anything else the research found?
CF You'll have a full report on your desk tomorrow. But one other thing, we'll definitely need a new slogan if we change the audience we're targeting. So that's something else the Marketing Department must start thinking about.

UNIT 3 BUILDING RELATIONSHIPS

CD1 TRACK 15 (I = INTERVIEWER, GB = GILLIAN BAKER)

I Gillian, what are the key factors in building good business relationships?
GB I'd say one of the best ways of building a lasting relationship is to give the customer or supplier superior value and satisfaction. It's all about not just meeting the customer's expectations, but trying to exceed them if possible. If you satisfy and also delight the customer, this will produce greater customer loyalty, and that in turn will lead to a better company performance.
Let me give you an example. It was reported in a marketing book written by the famous American marketing expert, Philip Kotler. He gives the example of Lexus Cars. It's well known that the manufacturer of this luxurious car makes immense efforts to satisfy their customers and exceed their expectations. Apparently, a customer bought a new Lexus car, and while driving it home, he decided to try out the radio. As he tuned in to some radio stations, he noticed that they were set to either his favourite station – music, news or whatever – or to his daughter's favourite station – in this case, it was rock music. Every button was set to his or his daughter's tastes. How did it happen? Quite simply, the mechanic who checked the car he'd traded in to buy the Lexus noted the radio settings. He then transferred these to the new car. Of course, the customer was highly impressed.
I I see, so you're suggesting customers will remain loyal to a company if it makes that extra effort to satisfy and if possible delight them?
GB Exactly.

CD1 TRACK 16 (I = INTERVIEWER, AW = ALISON WARD)

I Can you tell us about the Cocoa Partnership and how it came to be developed?
AW We launched the Cocoa Partnership in 2008, and it's a £45-million investment into cocoa sustainability. But the inspiration for it came from a piece of research which was done in the UK and in Ghana. And we looked at what was happening to cocoa farms in Ghana, and cocoa in Ghana accounts for about 70 per cent of our cocoa-bean supply, so it's an important country for us. We found that farmer yields were declining, and they were actually only getting 40 per cent.
So, a 40-per-cent yield from the land, compared to what they could get – so a real gap between the potential of the land and what they were getting now.
We also found that farmers were ageing. So the average age of a farmer is 50 – young people don't want to become farmers in Ghana. And we also found … Through the research, we looked at the social aspect in the village, and it was clear that we needed to take some action in terms of helping people have a sustainable livelihood from cocoa. So, that's really where the investment came from, um, and, already, we're working with partners in Ghana, including the United Nations Development Programme, and then with social experts like Care, VSO and World Vision, to actually look at how we create, create action at a farming level in Ghana.
But there's also a real commercial element to this because, quite simply, if we don't have the beans, we don't have the bars that, for our great chocolate brands around the world. So, it's really important that this isn't just a social programme, but it's actually a commercial programme as well.

CD1 TRACK 17 (I = INTERVIEWER, AW = ALISON WARD)

I What are the benefits for each side in this relationship, and are there consumer benefits, too?
AW Well, we're really proud that we've achieved Fairtrade certification for our Cadbury Dairy Milk brand, and that's in the UK and Ireland, and

Canada, Australia and New Zealand. So it means that people around the world can now make an ethical choice and know that the money, some of the money from their chocolate-bar purchase is going right back to farmers in Ghana.
I was privileged enough, um, to meet some of the farmers from the Fairtrade co-operative and really saw the empowerment that trade had brought these women, um, and how that it was trade that was giving them a helping hand out of poverty. Fairtrade's an interesting marque in that it's not only very powerful in consumer markets – it's very well understood – but it also has great power back in cocoa-farming communities. And we're really proud to be their partner and looking forward to really helping these farmers in Ghana as well.

CD1 TRACK 18 (I = INTERVIEWER, AW = ALISON WARD)

I Are there other examples of Cadbury building long-term business relationships?

AW We see partnership as part of the way we do business and we also have a great partnership with our milk farmers in the UK. We use fresh milk in our chocolate, and there's a co-operative of farmers who supply only milk that makes our UK chocolate. We've been working with them on their carbon footprint, so that's the metric that measures how much carbon is produced from, to make milk.
And we found in our Cadbury Dairy Milk bars that 60 per cent of the carbon footprint comes from milk. So, by working with this co-operative, we've begun to help them and help us make some changes in our supply chain. So that includes different types of animal feed, it includes investment, so that the lorry that brings the animal feed only delivers once rather than three times, and actually helping them really make some changes on their farms, so it's more efficient.
So our partnership spans not only for farmers in Ghana, but back into the UK and our dairy, dairy farmer partners in the UK as well.

CD1 TRACK 19

A So, how's the relationship with Toyota going?

B Ah. It's fine now, but at the start of the year, it was disastrous.

A Oh, what went wrong?

B Well, I went over my contact's head and went directly to his boss at Toyota Motors Europe. I was really trying to clinch a deal.

A Was he annoyed?

B They were both annoyed. My contact thought I had let him down, and his boss simply decided not to turn up at the meeting. We'd set up a meeting in Brussels by e-mail, but he called it off at the last minute. I'd already checked in at the hotel.

A How did you turn it round?

B Well, I had to build up my relationship with my original contact again. At first, he kept putting me off. But eventually we met up and I focused on our relationship, not the next sale. Now we get on really well and sometimes play golf together.

A Glad it worked out. Anyway, are you free for a drink later?

B Well, I'm going to carry on working until about six. We could meet after that.

CD1 TRACK 20 (HC = HOWARD CLARK, JM = JUDY MASTERS)

HC Hello. Haven't we met somewhere before?

JM Yes, it was last year, wasn't it – at the conference in St Petersburg?

HC Right! I remember now, we were sitting next to each other at the presentation. Howard Clark, Trustwood Marketing.

JM Hi, Judy Masters, Delta Systems. How are things going? I seem to remember you were having a good year when we last met.

HC Yes, but this year our online business isn't doing at all well. We've run into a few problems with our website. We need to completely reorganise it. There've been a load of complaints from customers, it's just not working well.

JM Hmm. I see. If you don't mind me asking, have you got anyone to do the job for you?

HC No, not yet. We don't have the expertise to do it ourselves. We need someone really experienced, but we don't really know where to look.

JM Maybe I could help you out there. I know someone who's a top-class web designer – he's one of my former colleagues, Martin Engelmann. He's now working freelance. I'm sure he'd be interested. Why don't you contact him?

HC Great. You haven't got his phone number, by any chance?

JM Yeah, I can give it to you now. Um, I still see him socially from time to time, so I've got his number here. Hold on ... it's ... um, 07825 300646. Got it?

HC Yep ... 07825 300646. Can I mention your name when I call him?

JM Of course. You could try calling him during the week, but he does travel quite a lot and he's often in meetings or giving presentations.

HC OK, I'll try to reach him. Thanks very much for the contact.

CD1 TRACK 21 (HC = HOWARD CLARK, ME = MARTIN ENGELMANN)

HC Hello, my name's Howard Clark, Trustwood Marketing.

ME Hello.

HC I was given your name by Judy Masters. I met her recently at an exhibition.

ME Oh, yes?

HC She told me you're a website designer and suggested I should call you. I hope you don't mind.

ME Not at all. How can I help?

HC Well, it's our company website. We really need someone to completely reorganise it. We've had dozens of complaints from customers recently, saying it's not working properly, it's very hard to navigate, they can never find what they want on it and the product information is insufficient. So it's clear we need to do something about it. I was wondering ...um, well ... would, would you be interested in helping us to redesign it?

ME Yes, I'd be very interested. I'm really busy for the next two weeks, but after that I'd be available and we could discuss it.

HC Good. Can I suggest meeting at our office, say, at the end of the month? You could meet our Systems Manager and one or two of our staff. We could take it from there.

CD1 TRACK 22 (AH = ABD AL-HALIM HAMDI, VS = VANESSA SCHULTZ)

AH OK, the main reason why most guests aren't returning is pretty clear. They don't feel they've had a 'memorable experience' in your hotels during their stay. They aren't made to feel special and valued – that was often mentioned. They want you to pay more attention to their needs and they expect to be treated as individuals. They are looking for a more personalised service, I'd say.

VS Can you give me some examples?

AH Yes, one guest said that there was no facility in his room for making coffee. He often works in his room before attending meetings and, and he likes to drink a lot of coffee. Another said she was a vegetarian, but couldn't order the food she liked. What else? Yeah. A number of guests with families mentioned the lack of facilities for children, no special menus for them, that sort of thing. No play area and so on.

VS Mmm, OK, interesting. Um, please go on.

AH Well, it seems your staff need to respond much more quickly and positively to requests. A businesswoman made this point very well. She said she needed to use the business centre at all hours of the day and night. But very often when she went there, it was closed. She mentioned this to the staff, but nothing was done about it.

VS I see. Any other points you'd like to mention?

AH Well, you need to have more information about guests – more *accurate* information – if you want to build up good relationships with them and get them coming back again and again. You don't know enough about them to give them a personalised service.

VS So we've gotta have more information about each guest – at our fingertips, as it were.

AH Exactly. Staff must know who are returning guests and who are new ones. If the guest is returning, for example, they shouldn't have to fill out forms again to use the health-club facilities. Staff should be able to greet returning guests warmly, so they feel special. Another thing – many guests mentioned the staff didn't seem particularly motivated. They gave the impression that they didn't really enjoy their job.

VS OK, thanks a lot, Abd Al-Halim – that's plenty of food for thought. I'm grateful for the work you've done to collect this information. I'm sure we can build much better relationships with our customers in future. We just need to rethink our customer-relations management.

WORKING ACROSS CULTURES 1: DOING BUSINESS INTERNATIONALLY

CD1 TRACK 23 (B = BOB, M = MELISSA, C = CHRISTINA)

B I spent 18 months trying to set up a franchising network in China for our Munchem pizzas. I hired a local guy, David Li, to deal with the details of the business, like choosing sites, getting the necessary documents, checking agreements – that sort of thing. But I made it clear to him we had a successful business model for the pizza restaurants and we'd use it in China. We were doing really well in the other regional markets like South Korea, Japan and Malaysia, so we knew we had a winning concept.

M Bob, was there much competition in the Chinese pizza trade?

B Yes, but we felt our tried-and-trusted marketing approach would work well there. And certainly we expected to get a foothold in the market pretty quickly. OK, we got on with it, and within six months, we'd opened 10 outlets in some of China's biggest cities. My only problem was that David Li kept trying to give me advice about our business when I didn't want it. He really got on my nerves. After a while, he seemed to become very demotivated and I felt he wasn't giving me a 100 per cent effort.
Our relationship got worse, and eventually I fired him.

C I see. So ... did you sell a lot of pizzas to the Chinese, Bob?

B No, I'm afraid we didn't. The whole project was an expensive failure.

C Oh really? Too much competition, then?

B Well, there were a lot of aggressive pizza businesses springing up, but that wasn't the problem. We just didn't get it right from the start. For one thing, the product wasn't right. Our thick, 15-inch pizzas, which were so popular in the other markets, were much too big for Chinese tastes. Another problem was, customers weren't able to eat them out of boxes as they were walking along. And the Chinese like to do that. Also our toppings didn't seem to appeal to them. The pizzas just didn't taste and smell delicious to them. It surprised me, because people loved them in our other Asian markets.

M OK, so the product wasn't right. What about pricing?

B Well, we slipped up there, too. We went for the top end of the market because we thought our pizzas were better quality than the competition, but the Chinese didn't see it that way. For them, our pizzas were too expensive and they weren't value for money. They thought we were ripping them off!

M Mm. I suppose you had a home-delivery service, did you, as well as the take-out business?

B Yes, we did; we thought it was one of our USPs. We guaranteed to deliver to any customer within 20 minutes. Unfortunately, we hadn't reckoned with the traffic problems in the big cities. It was murder to get across the cities at peak times. Sometimes it was over an hour before customers got their pizzas. That really damaged our reputation. The word soon got around we weren't reliable. But our biggest mistake, without a doubt, was to sell our pizzas through a take-out business. If the customers wanted to eat on our premises, there was only standing room. Now, Chinese people are very sociable. They like to take their friends and relatives to a restaurant and stay there for a long time. We should have offered them American-style restaurants with an attractive décor. They'd have enjoyed that.

C So … are there still any Munchem restaurants in China?

B Nah, my feeling was there was no way back. Our brand had no credibility after a while. I told Head Office we should sell off the restaurants and cut our losses.

CD1 TRACK 24 (B = Bob, M = Melissa, C = Christina)

C Well, my trip to India wasn't easy either, but I'd call it a partial success. I went there to negotiate an agreement with Mumbai Enterprises, to distribute our products nationwide. It's a well-known company with food stores all over the country.

B Yeah, isn't it owned by the Duleep Singhs, one of the richest families in India?

C Yeah, that's right. It was a pretty important assignment for me. If I could get them to be our distributor, it'd really be a feather in my cap, it'd really raise my profile in Drew Corporation.

B I can understand that. A deal with Mumbai Enterprises would be worth a lot of money to the company.

C Exactly. Well, it started quite well. I met the President and some top executives and was given a tour of their flagship store in the city. When the meeting began a couple of days later, there was a lot of chit-chat at the beginning, mostly about the Indian cricket team. That frustrated me a little, but I didn't show it. Anyway, we followed the agenda for the meeting, and the President did most of the talking.
At one point, the question of storage came up. I told him his stores would need special refrigerated cabinets for some of our foodstuffs, and that I could give him details of an Australian supplier we use for this purpose. 'Was that OK?' I asked him. 'We shall see, we shall see,' he repeated, 'everything is possible in India.' And he smiled at me. I took it that he agreed with this suggestion. At a later meeting, the subject of storage came up again. 'That's no problem,' the President said, 'all our stores have the latest refrigeration equipment. We'll use the cabinets we have for your products.' 'But I thought we'd agreed you'd buy them from our Australian supplier,' I said. 'No, no,' he replied, 'our technology is the best in the world, we don't need to use foreign suppliers.' He seemed displeased, so I didn't push him on this point.

M Mmm, there seems to have been a bit of a misunderstanding there.

C Yeah, that was my impression. By the end of the week, I was getting very frustrated by the slow progress. Also I was suffering from a stomach upset and I was a little short-tempered. Maybe I showed it.

M Do you think you came across as impatient?

C Yeah, it could be – perhaps they thought I was rather rude. It was just … we'd spent hours and hours during the week talking about the long-term objectives of the deal and what sort of relationship we would have in the future. It was exhausting. To be honest, I was thinking more short term, how to get to the point when we could shake hands on the deal.

M So what was the effect of that?

C Well, the atmosphere in the meetings started to change. It was as if they didn't trust me any more. I had the feeling they didn't think I was sincere. And when I made a mistake with a couple of figures I gave them, I had the distinct impression that they thought I was incompetent.

B So, did the deal fall through, Christina?

C Fortunately, it didn't. There was a turning point at the beginning of the next week. The President invited me to his home for dinner. We had a splendid meal. I brought some lovely flowers for his wife and toys for his young children – that went down really well. And we had a fascinating conversation about Indian art, which I'm really interested in.

B So that's what turned things around?

C Yes, I'd say so. It all changed after that. The meetings became more friendly. The President's colleagues seemed to take their lead from him and began to show me a lot more warmth and respect.

M So did you complete the deal? Will Mumbai Enterprises be our distributor in India?

C I'm not sure, to be honest, but we did make progress. I've got to go back to Mumbai with a team and work on the finer details of the deal. But I'm more optimistic now. I think they really like and trust me.

CD1 TRACK 25 (GK = GALINA KOZNOV)

GK It's not surprising that Georgy Volkov didn't want to give Melissa a five-year sales forecast for the products they were supplying because there are so many permissions and certificates you need in Russia before you can set up a joint-venture deal. Also, Volkov probably didn't want to give figures he might have to change at a later stage in their relationship. He didn't want to be stuck with those figures.
Melissa should have known that the joint-venture process was likely to take longer to set up in Russia than in some other countries.
Relaxing and socialising is important to Russians. So the trip to the *dacha* at the weekend was a good opportunity for both sides to develop their relationship.
Melissa shouldn't have been upset about Volkov's comments on the organic products. He was trying to be helpful and friendly with his advice about the products. Russians tend to be direct when they speak English, just as they are in their own language, and foreigners shouldn't be shocked if Russians appear rather abrupt at times.
For Russians, personal relations when doing business are important. That's why Volkov wanted to settle the legal matters by using his schoolfriend – a person he knew well and trusted. He would feel more comfortable consulting a friend in a small legal firm than going to a large organisation where he knew nobody.
Finally, Melissa made a big mistake by not delaying her flight back to Dallas. The meeting with the Minister would have been an important step in setting up the joint venture. The Minister would have expected to meet someone of importance in the American company. When he learned that Volkov would be accompanied by the General Manager in Moscow, he probably thought that the lower-level officials in the ministry were more appropriate to attend the meeting. The right person to be there was either Melissa or her own boss.

UNIT 4 SUCCESS

CD1 TRACK 26 (I = Interviewer, TH = Tom Hockaday)

I What are the essential qualities of a successful business?

TH I think that the absolute essence of a business is, or a successful business, is one which manages to manufacture and sell something, whether that's a product or a service, but manages to sell it for more than it cost to produce it. So, you are generating profit from delivering a product or service and you're getting more money in than is going out and that is absolutely at the heart of a successful business.
Now, in our context at Isis, we are creating businesses which are based on developing very early-stage technology. So, actually, it's going to take quite a few years for the company to go from those initial phases to actually having a product or service to sell. So, at the early stage of a technology business, really what we're doing is we're investing in the technology to take it through various stages of development, so that we can demonstrate it has increasing value, so that we might be able to attract more rounds of venture capital investment or finance from other sources.
But, one day, of course, we are aiming for a product or service which we can sell for more than it cost us to produce.

CD1 TRACK 27 (I = Interviewer, TH = Tom Hockaday)

I Which business success stories inspire you?

TH I think the ones that are based upon a great team of people, where you can see the passion and the vision and the clarity of thought that has led to the creation of a successful business. So, from within Oxford, um, the work of Isis Innovation, in the last 10 years, we've helped set up 65 new companies – what we call university spin-out companies – based upon Oxford University technologies, Oxford University researchers, where we've got investment and management. And it's probably unfair to pick out one from that list or, um ... Nevertheless, there is a company called Natural Motion, which was set up in 2002, so already has had many years of development, and from its start – and I had the good fortune to be involved working with the people who set that company up at the beginning – um, it's had those qualities of passion, vision and clarity. And it's gone on to be a very successful software animation company. So, its software tools are used in the film industry, in the computer game industry, to help make software characters look more realistic in those formats. And it's been fantastic to see the individuals involved working together from their early vision for what this company might be and seeing that being delivered, um, with, you know, passion and enthusiasm throughout those years. Of course, there have been some challenges along the way, but it's been the clarity with which the team have taken forward their vision, over the years, which has been so impressive.

CD1 TRACK 28 (I = INTERVIEWER, TH = TOM HOCKADAY)

I Which types of business do you expect to succeed in the next five years?

TH That's a very difficult question to answer, of course, because we're predicting the future. But it does seem to me that one of the areas in which there's so much attention and so much focus, at the moment, is in environmental technologies, low-carbon technologies, alternative-energy technologies.
So, in that overall area, um, within Oxford, we are already seeing an increased focus of research attention on those areas and we've successfully created some companies based upon developing technologies all aimed towards reducing carbon emissions, reducing energy consumption, to address the global challenge that we face at the moment. So, for example, we have set up a smart-metering technology company, so that domestic households will have far more information about their energy consumption and, with that, with that information, they can begin to modify their behaviour.
And we're also working on projects for tidal energy and wind energy and lightweight electric motors for the next generation of cars, all aimed at addressing this extraordinary problem we face of the, er, carbon emissions.

CD1 TRACK 29 (E = EXPORTER, B = BUYER)

E If you place an order for only 50 rugs, we can offer you a discount of five per cent off list prices. So you'll be paying just under 2,400 euros for our standard rug. It measures 184 by 320 centimetres.

B What if we ordered rugs of different sizes?

E I'm afraid the discount would be less and you'd pay according to the rug's size.

B Supposing we increased our order for your standard rugs, what discount would you give us?

E Well, what sort of quantity do you have in mind?

B OK, if we ordered 100 rugs, made in Esme, would you double the discount?

E No, not double it, but we'd be willing to increase it to seven per cent. That's pretty generous, I'd say.

B That sounds fairly reasonable. I'd like to ask a question now about delivery. Could you get the rugs to us by the end of this month?

E Mmm, that's asking a lot, I honestly don't know. I'd have to check our stock levels.

B Are you saying you don't have that quantity in stock?

E No, I'm just not sure how many we have in the warehouse at the moment.

B I'd like to make a proposal. I'd be prepared to place an order for 150 standard rugs if you could give us a discount of 10 per cent, and provided you delivered the goods by the end of the month. How about that?

E Hmm, 150 rugs, made in Esme? OK, if I'm certain we can supply you that quantity by the end of the month, you've got a deal. We'll give you 10 per cent off the list price for that amount.

B Great. When can you confirm the order?

E I'll check with our warehouse supervisor this afternoon to find out if we can meet your delivery date. I'm pretty sure we can do that.

CD1 TRACK 30 (P = PRESENTER, B = BILL)

P Let me ask you about Kensington United now, Bill. Do you think they can get into the final of the Champions League?

B Frankly, I can't see it happening. Not with the present team. They lack a real star player who can score goals that win matches.

P I see. But there are rumours they're trying to buy the African player, Henry Obogu. He would be a real star, wouldn't he, if they could get him?

B Well, he's young, but he was African Player of the Year, so, yes, he could be a huge asset to the team if he signed with them.

P What about the problem the club's having with its fans? I believe it's looking for a new sponsor, maybe Universal Communications. They won't be very impressed with what happened last week at the stadium.

B Right. The fighting in the crowd was a disgrace, it went on for too long. Some of the fans are hooligans, there's no other word for it. And those sort of fans are harming the reputation of the club, no doubt about it.

P It'll be a problem in any deal they make with Universal Communications, that's for sure.

B Yeah, but let's face it, Kensington has a great future if they can buy more players. The club's making a lot of money, you know.

P Can you expand on that a bit?

B Ingrid Tauber, their Commercial Director, is a really smart woman. She's done a lot to exploit the Kensington United brand. The club owns a travel agency that their fans use a lot. Their hospitality facilities are popular with businesspeople. Companies pay a lot of money to entertain clients in the boxes. They have a joint venture with an insurance company, and they run training courses on leadership in their conference centre. Just recently, I've heard they want to have a sponsorship deal with Sprint, the football-boot manufacturer. They've got a finger in every pie.

P Very impressive. Ingrid Tauber seems to be a bit of a whizz kid.

B She is. She's been responsible really for the club's commercial success. They'll make even more money soon, because the TV rights will be renegotiated, and Kensington will get a share of the income. And then there's the sponsorship deal, if they can pull it off.

P Things look pretty rosy for them, then.

B I'd say so. They'll be in a strong position to negotiate with Universal Communications. Who knows, in a few years' time, they could be the new Manchester United.

CD1 TRACK 31

Now some hot news for football fans. Kensington United have announced that the brilliant African player, Henry Obogu, will be joining the club for a transfer fee of 20 million euros. Obogu is a superb player. The club's President describes him as the next Pelé. However, Obogu is known to be very quick-tempered on the football pitch. This will probably appeal to the club's fans, but his fiery temperament is likely to give the Head Coach nightmares! The question is: will Obogu provide the winning touch that will enable Kensington United to win the European Champions League Cup? Time will tell.

UNIT 5 JOB SATISFACTION

CD2 TRACK 1

I suppose I do have great people around me, which is good, and I do enjoy coming to work, but my main motivation is the financial incentive. Being in sales means that I can really increase my salary because of my efforts – the more I sell, the more I can earn. The only thing that worries me is that things are a bit unstable at the moment – I don't think anyone is really safe. I just try to keep my head down and do a good job.

CD2 TRACK 2

What really motivates me is the variety I have at work. There are a lot of challenges. No two jobs are the same. I'm learning all the time, you know – developing. The other thing is, the company offers plenty of chances to talented people. You can climb the ladder quickly if you're good. That's very motivating – you feel that if you do good work, it'll be rewarded.

CD2 TRACK 3

It's a huge company, so I'm just a small part of a very big machine. I don't really get to see the results of my work. The company could do more. Someone saying 'well done' now and again would be nice. The main thing for me is flexibility, and I guess freedom. I'd like to work from home some of the time and be able to organise what I do and when I do it, but the company is keen on people being in the office.

CD2 TRACK 4 (I = INTERVIEWER, MB = MADALYN BROOKS)

I A recent survey rated Procter & Gamble as one of the best workplaces in the UK. How do you encourage job satisfaction among your staff?

MB I think attracting, retaining and motivating employees is key to any successful business. And that's core of how you drive job satisfaction. At Procter & Gamble, I think we achieve this really in two main ways. The first way is that we seek to be a business that's committed to its people. Most of our leaders of the organisation have grown up through the organisation. So they know it very well. They've come through individual, personalised career paths and development plans, committed to invest in them as they've developed their careers with us. We reward and recognise people individually as a company, for their individual contributions. Not as a group or as a total, but individually – driving their connection to what they work on to the reward and recognition that they get. Diversity and celebrating difference of people is another core principle by which we operate. Recognising that great innovation comes from diversity. We seek to make this part of what we call our DNA in our company.
So, I think it's commitment to people, but, beside that, we also focus on challenging our people. People need to be challenged to drive job satisfaction. We are in a very tough market place. We operate in the fast-moving consumer goods arena and this drives constant challenge and dynamic change. Our consumers are very demanding. They constantly want new products, new ideas that are going to improve their lives, which is company purpose. So, our people are constantly challenged to come up with new innovation, new ideas and build ever-stronger and better customer relationships and supplier relationships. So, I think through two-pronged approach of committed to people and driving challenging opportunities for them has driven our job satisfaction.

CD2TRACK 5 (I = INTERVIEWER, MB = MADALYN BROOKS)

I Do you think that job priorities among employees have changed much over the last 10 years?

MB Yes, I do. I think job priorities have changed in the last 10 years, since I've been working in this field. I think there are several areas that I can think of that come to mind. The first one, I think, is flexibility. A stronger demand these days for flexibility in the way … when people work, where they work and how they work. This was initially driven, I think, by the changing role of women in the workplace. As more women entered our workplaces, the demand for flexible hours, flexible timing, started.
But, as time's moved on, it's the new, emerging generations in the workplace who are demanding even greater flexibility of where they work through new, emerging technologies, of, of remote communications and also the demand for sabbaticals and opportunity to take time out, which is changing the workplace of today.
I think another key area that has changed is the drive for personal learning and growth – a second area where, I think, people really want to take personal control of their growth. I think, before, individuals looked at the company to do that for them. People don't expect to stay with the same company, or even doing the same type of work, all their lives, any more. So, there's a much stronger drive towards my growth, my development and what am I learning in everything I do.
And I think the third area I'd pick up on for the change is people's requirement that the organisations they work for are socially responsible. That's clearly moved a huge amount in the last 10 years. People now want to work for companies that are committed not just to greener environmental issues – such as reducing carbon footprint and recycling and, and these areas – but also things like how we're committed to supporting our local communities.
Can they get involved in charitable work and other voluntary areas? And these are hugely different to how I remember it being just 10 years ago.

CD2TRACK 6 (I = INTERVIEWER, MB = MADALYN BROOKS)

I Looking forward, what changes do you see in the way people feel about work?

MB I think it's more of what I was talking about with the changes. I think we're on a journey. I think we'll see an increase in this desire for training. Self-actualisation, building self and skills will be a constant demand. People are encouraged to be lifelong learners, to grow and develop, and we really see this demand increasing in the workplace. People want opportunity to grow through training, through opportunities of challenging assignments, and I think that will get ever, ever bigger.
I think P&G is well set up to deal with that. Leadership and ownership are core of our principles, so that will come through as we, as we move ahead into the future.
I do think this drive for feeling a company is socially responsible will also get higher. We are seeing, today, a drive for people's desire to have time out, to get involved in voluntary work, to think how they can put back into the society that they've taken out of up until now. And I think people will want to feel proud of their workplaces in that respect. They'll want to feel that they can share with their families and their friends an environment they are working in to be responsible. They'll want to be able to take time to do voluntary work, such as working in schools, working in local communities and, and giving back. So, more of the changes we have already seen getting deeper into our workplaces, will be the challenge for us employers in the future.

CD2TRACK 7 (EW = ENID WONG, PE = PATRICIA EVANS)

EW Enid Wong.

PE Good morning, Ms Wong. My name's Patricia Evans. I work for an executive recruitment agency.

EW Oh yes?

PE I was given your name by Edward Zhang, I believe you know him quite well.

EW That's correct.

PE He suggested I call you. He thought you might be interested in a position that's become vacant at KB Financial Services. It's for a chief negotiator. Would you like to meet to find out a bit more about the job?

EW Well, I'm flattered you've called me. It's nice to know I'm still in demand. But honestly, I don't think there's any point in us meeting. I'm very happy in this job, and I don't want to go anywhere else – well, not at this stage of my career, anyway.

PE OK, I quite understand. Can you recommend anyone I could contact and sound them out about the job?

EW Well, let me see … no, not off the top of my head, I'd have to think about it. Why don't you give me your number and I could probably think of someone if I had a bit more time.

PE Great. I'd appreciate that. My number's 0207 644 8981…

CD2TRACK 8 (PE = PATRICIA EVANS, FG = FEDERICO GONZÁLEZ)

PE Good morning, Mr González. My name's Patricia Evans. I work for an executive recruitment firm. A friend of yours, Enid Wong, gave me your name.

FG I see. What's it about?

PE A position has become vacant at KB Financial Services. Head Negotiator. I was wondering if you'd be interested.

FG Mmm, KB Finance? They are a very good company. But I don't know. I'm fairly happy here, actually.

PE People often say that to me, Mr González, but they change their mind when they hear more about the offer.

FG Well, it would have to be a really good one to interest me.

PE It is. KB are offering a top salary and great benefits package …

FG Are they?

PE Would you like to know the salary range?

FG Sure.

PE Well, it's over six figures, I can tell you that: probably in the region of a hundred and fifty for the right person.

FG Is that pounds or euros?

PE Euros. There's another thing you should bear in mind. It's a very attractive part of the package they offer. They give staff a substantial bonus at the end of the year – usually well above the industry average.

FG Mmm, interesting.

PE Look, why don't we get together and I'll give you some more details? Then, if you're still interested, we can take it from there.

FG OK, where can we talk?

PE How about meeting at the Chamberlain Hotel? There's a nice bar there, it's quiet during the afternoon. And it's not too near where you work!

FG OK, let's do that. I know the Chamberlain Hotel well.

PE Fine. What day suits you?

FG Well, how about next Wednesday? Say, at three o'clock. Is that OK for you?

PE Let me see … I'll just check my diary … Yes, that time's OK.

FG Right, see you in the Chamberlain at three.

PE I look forward to it. Bye.

CD2TRACK 9 (PM = PATRICK MCGUIRE, VS = VERONICA SIMPSON)

PM I've thought a lot about this problem, whether we should have a company policy about close relationships. I think we've got four options, Veronica.

VS OK. What's the first?

PM We could just ban all special relationships at work. Insist that staff go elsewhere if a romance develops. I believe some companies have that policy.

VS Mm-hm. What about the second option?

PM We could do what a lot of companies here are doing, we could ask staff in special relationships to sign a love contract.

VS A love contract? How does that work?

PM Simple. It's a document that staff sign. They declare that they have a special relationship, and the document specifies what behaviour is acceptable. It could also indicate what action we might take, such as transferring one or both staff, altering their reporting lines or even what disciplinary action we could take.

VS Mm-hm. I see. And the third option?

PM Our policy could simply be that staff must inform their team leader if they have a special relationship and they must agree to behave appropriately at work.

VS And what's the last option?

PM Do nothing. Have no policy at all. Just accept that it's human nature and we can't do anything about it.

UNIT 6 RISK

CD2TRACK 10 (I = INTERVIEWER, SF = STEVE FOWLER)

I What are the main types of risk that companies face?

SF Well, there are two ways of looking at risk. One way of looking at risk is to divide risks to an organisation between internal risks and external risks. Now, some examples of internal risks include injuries to employees within a factory or, alternatively, a fire in a warehouse, for example. Examples of external risks can include an earthquake or a tsunami affecting a site or, alternatively, a change in exchange-rate mechanism.
Now, I mentioned there were two ways of looking at risk. The other way of looking at risk is to divide up risk into four categories – hazard, operational risks, financial risks and strategic risks. I'll give some examples of each of those four.
Hazards can include natural events – um, typhoons, hurricanes, fires, floods and so on and so forth. Operational risks can include risks such as information technology, supply chain and employment risks. Financial risks include the non-availability of reasonably priced credit or a lack of liquidity within an organisation.
And finally, and most importantly, strategic risk. Strategic risk looks at the area of competition, also looks at the area of changing customer demand, the availability of new technologies, changing social and political pressures on an organisation.

CD2TRACK 11 (I = INTERVIEWER, SF = STEVE FOWLER)

I How can companies begin to manage risk?

SF Well, the good news is that risk management is actually applied common sense. The other good news is there are plenty of guides out there to help organisations focus on the way they manage risk. Now, one such guide is a new standard available from the International Standards Organisation, ISO – ISO 31,000.

In addition, my own organisation, the Institute of Risk Management, have published a very simple, free guide on how organisations can manage risk. Now, this is freely downloadable from IRM's website in 16 different languages and it sets out the basics of how to manage risk.

There are five key steps to the management of risk. The first step, which is most important, is to recognise the strategic objectives for your organisation and the key processes that your organisation uses.

Following on from step one, step two then goes on to identify what the, what the risks affecting the organisation might be. Now, the best way to identify risks is look at them from two directions – both top down, from a management point of view, but also bottom up, from the shop floor. Only that way will one identify the full spectrum of risks affecting an organisation. Only at that stage does one then go on to assess and prioritise risks.

Point three: after identifying risk, the next stage is to assess and prioritise those risks. Now, a useful tool to recording prioritised risks is called a risk register. It's a way of an organisation recording those risks that are most critical to the organisation and, more importantly, what the organisation is doing about those risks; when they're planning to do it, if they haven't started yet; and who owns the risk.

Point four: mitigating risk. There are four ways of dealing with risk once risk has been identified. Firstly, treating the risk – putting in place some counter-measures in order to deal with that risk. Two examples could be the installation of a fire protection system, in order to prevent a fire, or improved driver training in order to stop accidents on the road. Secondly, terminating a risk. Terminating a risk by stopping the process that leads to the risk. Thirdly, tolerating risk – living with the action that gives rise to the risk. And, finally, transferring the risk by means of insurance or other contractual arrangements.

Finally, point five: after identifying strategic objectives, identifying risks, assessing and prioritising risks and then mitigating those risks, it's important that those actions are flowed back through to one's strategic objectives again. In life, it's not always possible to deal with every risk and, therefore, a systematic analysis of your approach to dealing with risk will reinform your strategic objectives. It will affect the way that the company thinks about itself.

CD2TRACK 12 (I = INTERVIEWER, SF = STEVE FOWLER)

I Can you give us some examples of companies that failed to manage risk?

SF A great example involves the banking industry worldwide, because of actions taken throughout the banking industry over the last 10 years, in particular, the systematic and reckless risk-taking undertaken by many banks. There are massive implications, not just for those organisations and their shareholders, but also for the world generally – public finances and economic growth and so on.

Moving to a, um, a lower level of risk, there's a great example of an organisation – actually an American-based clothing retailer – that managed to lose 45 million credit-card details two years ago, giving rise to an $80 million loss and untold impact on its own reputation.

Finally, there are plenty of examples of organisations that have failed to anticipate changes in customer demand. A great example is the video-cassette industry. There are lots of organisations worldwide producing … were producing video cassettes and retailing those cassettes to the public through shops. Now, the world has changed in the last few years and, increasingly, people are now reverting to the use of digital media, which they can download through the Internet. I suppose those organisations have faced the ultimate risk of being replaced by another technology.

CD2TRACK 13 (MT = MARTIN THOMAS, CR = CAROL RUECKERT, CH = CAROLINE HOLLOWAY, GR = GUILLEM ROJAS)

MT OK, guys. so thank you for all your comments in the last meeting. Now, just to sum up, we've looked at some different locations, so we talked about Amsterdam, Portugal and Florence for the sales conference. We also looked at the different activities, some sessions that we could do within that, and the type of accommodation and also some of the, um, leisure-time activities for the participants. OK, Carol, what did you come up for the location?

CR Well, um, I was looking at Florence and I think it's a really great place, um, again because of all the things that we can do in our free time, and the accommodation that I found was quite good, and I also found a venue that is willing to give us quite a good deal, um …

MT OK.

CH That's actually great news because, um, Amsterdam was, um, not so great because of the venue, the venue was much too small, the 350 delegates that we have just wouldn't fit in the one hotel, so, um, that's great news that you found a place in Florence.

MT So can we all agree, then, that we go with Florence?

CH Yes.

CR I think we have to, don't we?

GR Is it very cold in Florence in, in the winter?

CR Well, it can be cold, but I … I think that most of the time we'll be spending indoors. So, you know, I think with the budget, we really have to go with Florence and …

MT OK, that's great, then, OK, so we're agreed we're gonna go with Florence. Now, what about the activities? Um, what did you come up with, Carol, for the actual workshops?

CR I thought it might be a good idea to use, um, role play within, um, the workshops, so maybe pick a scenario for, um, people to use and then, um, in groups discuss how they could, um, overcome, um, the scenario, so …

MT OK.

CH I think some kind of interaction is a good idea in these conferences because sitting and listening to different presentations for three straight days gets really quite dull and …

MT OK, so we go with the workshops, then?

CH Well, I don't know about role plays, though. I like the idea of interaction, but I … I was thinking maybe something like, you know, a simple quiz, um, and we've had quite a few quizzes in the past and it went over really well because it doesn't take a lot of time, and it's something to look at, to focus you while you're listening to the presentations.

CR Yeah, actually, I've been to a conference before where they've had a game-style quiz, so basically each person in the room gets a little, um, button to press and it has A, B, C, D, and the person asks the question and then the delegates all answer A, B, C or D …

CH Exactly.

MT So can we, we, we'll put that into, definitely put that into the programme, that's, yeah, that's a brilliant idea, OK then. And I know that, Caroline, you talked about the gala dinner – what did you find out about that, to be able to have the gala dinner?

CH Oh actually, um, with the hotel that you were thinking of, I called them up and they said they are fine for a huge banquet-style buffet.

MT Oh fantastic.

CH So we could, um, have it there, um, and that would be really convenient because everyone's in the hotel anyway.

MT Well, that's great, so we're gonna go to Florence, and we're gonna have this in January, then, yeah?

CR Yes, exactly.

MT OK, we know that there are some issues with the product, with one product being ready in January, but I think we can overcome that as we said by pre- um, you know, different styles of presentation, so that's great. And the accommodation we've got, you know, ah, a hotel that can accommodate everybody – 350 you said? Yeah?

CR Yeah.

MT That's, that's brilliant, OK, and we're gonna have a great banquet. Well, that's fantastic, thank you very much, OK, this is brilliant.

GR Thank you.

CR Great.

GR Cheers.

CD2TRACK 14 (DH = DANIEL HABERSHAM, DC = DENISE COUTURE)

DH I think we ought to mention the ATZ project in our prospectus. It's a very exciting venture, and if we're successful, it'll put us in another league in the mining industry. It'll also raise our profile and help us to get finance for other projects. Investors will want to know about this project, surely.

DC Let's think about this rationally. We haven't signed an agreement yet with ATZ, and maybe we won't. We're still assessing the risks. The area's not politically stable for one thing. It wasn't so long ago they had a civil war, and thousands of people were killed.

DH OK, but you have to take risks to make money. We've grown fast because we're not afraid of taking risks – let's say calculated risks. Remember Kazakhstan? Everyone was saying it was too risky to invest in the area, so we stayed away. What happened? A few companies went in, and they made a fortune there.

DC Yes, I accept we missed a great opportunity when we stayed out of Kazakhstan. But this share offer, it's a different matter altogether. We don't want investors to hold back from buying our shares just because they think we're a high-risk company, one that's going to go bust soon.

DH I'd say you're exaggerating a little. OK, let's give this a little more thought. As you say, we haven't decided yet to sign with ATZ, but it's a decision we're going to have to make pretty soon.

DC Well, our New Business Department are doing some research now. They'll report their findings at our next management meeting, and that'll help us to make up our minds.

WORKING ACROSS CULTURES 2: WORKING IN NEW MARKETS

CD2TRACK 15

Thanks for coming to my talk today. I know that most of you are here because you have an interest in doing business in Kazakhstan in the future. My purpose today is to give you a basic understanding of the country and of its business culture.

Let me start with a few basic facts. Kazakhstan is in Central Asia and it has a population of just under 15 million. It's a big country, with the ninth largest land area in the world – equivalent in size to western Europe. It's rich in natural resources and has received over 40 billion dollars in foreign investment since 1993.

A key feature of the country is the diversity of its population – there are more than 100 ethnic groups. The two biggest are the Kazakhs and the Russians, but other ethnic groups include Chechens, Ukrainians, Tatars, Germans and Koreans, to name but a few. However, Kazakhstan is basically a mix of Russian culture and Kazakh oriental traditions.

I'll give you one striking statistic: 51.8 per cent of the population are Kazakhs and 31.4 are Russian. By the way, Russian is the official language and the language of business.

Now, there is one Kazakh tradition which is important when you first meet businesspeople. If you want to make a good impression, you shouldn't immediately talk about business. You should start by asking how they are, and how the family is. Two or three questions like that go down well, and then you can start getting down to business.

A word now about verbal and non-verbal communication. Usually in Kazakhstan, people keep at arm's length during a conversation, and it's important to keep good eye contact when talking to people – they expect that. Touching is not acceptable in formal situations, especially between members of the opposite sex. When you meet a man, you should shake his hand. Nowadays, it's becoming more common for business and professional women to shake hands, but it's better to wait for a woman to take the initiative in this case.

Kazakhstanis tend to speak fairly quietly and less directly than in some other cultures, such as North America. And when someone from Kazakhstan explains something, they may give a lot of background information when answering your question. Be patient, because they want to give you a thorough answer.

UNIT 7 MANAGEMENT STYLES

CD2TRACK 16

1 considerate, consideration
2 competent, competency
3 creative, creativity
4 diplomatic, diplomacy
5 efficient, efficiency
6 flexible, flexibility
7 inspiring, inspiration
8 logical, logic
9 loyal, loyalty
10 organised, organisation
11 decisive, decisiveness
12 responsible, responsibility
13 sociable, sociability
14 supportive, support

CD2TRACK 17 (I = INTERVIEWER, LM = LAURIE MULLINS)

I What are the key qualities for a successful manager today, compared to the past?

LM I see two major factors which influence the managerial function today. The first one is the ability to manage in an increasingly competitive, volatile, changing, business environment. An example of this is the growth of the so-called BRICK nations, B-R-I-C-K, which is Brazil, Russia, India, China and Korea. Arising from this development is, there's greater concern for recognition of the individual person within the work organisation. Um, people will bring their own cultures, their own, uh, situations to diversity. We now have a far more diverse workforce, uh, their culture, um, the importance of non-verbal communications, and international human resource management.

Secondly, the manager today has to manage with an increasing rate of technical change – this is allied to the competitive and challenging business environment. A particular example of this is the so-called information communications technology, which is often shown as ICT. So if we take just one example of this, if you think of developments in computer-based technology and consider managing a remote team. Um, so people today may no longer be at the same desk, the same location, or they may not work together in face-to-face contact. So this means that, through ICT, a manager may have to interact with staff who may not be at the same desk, may not work together, may not be in the same building, may not even be in the same location and may not even be in the same country.

CD2TRACK 18 (I = INTERVIEWER, LM = LAURIE MULLINS)

I Which management style do you think gets the best out of people?

LM The underlying consideration here is that people are not owned by the organisation, um, people bring their own perceptions, biases, attitude, personality, cultures to work. So arising from that, I see six key fundamental managerial philosophies. One is consideration, respect and trust. Most people respond according to the way they're treated. So if you treat people with politeness and dignity, the chances are, the majority of staff will respond in a similar manner.

Recognition and credit – people can be praised to success. Let people know you acknowledge good work. An example of this, if you have a junior member of staff who, on your behalf, prepares an excellent detailed report for senior manager, when you as the departmental manager submit that report, why not add the name of your junior colleague as joint author?

Three: involvement and availability. Take an interest in your staff, maintain an open flow of communication, the so-called 'management by walking about'. The key feature of this is not to give the impression to staff that you don't trust them, that you're supervising their work, but you're taking an interest in their work.

Four: a sense of justice. Treat people fairly, but according to merit. If difficult decisions have to be made, staff are more likely to accept those decisions if they feel they've been treated fairly, and with a sense of justice. This requires good human resource management.

Five: positive action on an individual basis. If colleagues are working in a, a team, and one or two colleagues need to be criticised, criticise those people in private, on an individual basis.

And lastly, point six: emphasis on end results. The ends do not always fully justify the means, but wherever possible, place emphasis on not time-keeping, or what people appear to be doing, but the level of performance actually achieved.

CD2TRACK 19 (I = INTERVIEWER, LM = LAURIE MULLINS)

I As more managers work internationally, how should they adapt their styles to suit this situation?

LM An underlying precept is that managers must be fully aware of their own predisposition towards people, and their preferred natural style of management. For example, some managers believe in the need for direction and control through an organised system of central control, formal organisation structure, um, systems of routine, and the belief that it's natural for people to try to get away with what they can; therefore management has a job to stop them doing that and to control and supervise them – the 'carrot and stick' assumptions.

Other managers believe in the integration of individual and organisational goals and that people can be committed to the goals of the organisation, in which case they will exercise self-direction and self-control.

CD2TRACK 20 (JH = JASON HARDING)

JH First of all, thanks very much for coming to my presentation. I'm Jason Harding, Sales Manager of Quench Products. I'm going to tell you about our new iced tea that'll be launched early next March. I hope by the end of my presentation, you'll understand what a unique product we're offering and want to place a large order for it.

OK, what is Quench Iced Tea? What are its unique features? Quench Iced Tea is available in several flavours – lemon, green, strawberry and grape – and it comes in sweetened, unsweetened and diet versions of the drink. It's a delicious, healthy, thirst-quenching drink. And the fact that we offer it in different versions will give it a definite edge over the competition. I want to stress that. In other words, it's got a wide appeal. As you all know, I'm sure, customers buy iced drinks for different reasons. For instance, many people are watching their weight, so they'll buy the diet version. Others do sports and will want to buy the sweetened version that'll give them extra energy.

Another key feature of Quench Iced Tea is that it contains a very high percentage of vitamins, especially vitamins C and E. This will undoubtedly appeal to health-conscious customers. And that's a major selling point of our product.

CD2TRACK 21 (JH = JASON HARDING)

JH Turning now to the tea itself. As you know, our company uses only high-quality tea, selected by hand, and we add pure spring water. What about the packaging? It's so important to get that right, isn't it? Please take a look at the slide. As you can see, the drink is packaged in single-serve and multi-serve bottles. What about sizes? Fourteen ounces for single serve, 55 fluid ounces for multi-serve. What does this mean? It means that once again, we're offering customers choice.

You can see from the slide that the bottles are beautifully designed, very eye-catching and appealing. They'll really stand out on the shelf.

So to summarise, we're offering customers a unique, delicious, thirst-quenching product. A product that'll appeal to different tastes and which has outstanding design. It'll be available for supermarkets and retailers early in March, and will be supported by a comprehensive marketing programme. We're confident it'll be warmly welcomed by health-conscious consumers.

I'll be happy to answer any questions you may have. I've provided you with an information pack. In it, you'll find a link to a website where you can download photos and more information about Quench Iced Tea. Thanks very much, everyone. Any questions?

CD2 TRACK 22

I don't think Paul had any idea how to run the team. He worked very long hours, but that was the problem. The next morning, he was always in a terrible mood because he hadn't had enough sleep. He was really unpleasant to us most of the time. He was the kind of boss who makes a decision and that's it. He didn't encourage us to agree or disagree, he just wasn't interested in our opinions.

He was good at telling us what to do, but not how to do it, how he wanted us to do it. For example, I interviewed a couple of our big retail customers. I thought it went well, but Paul said I hadn't asked the right questions. When I tried to get him to explain, he just said, 'You should know by now the kind of questions you need to ask customers.' I was really annoyed, we'd never discussed that in detail before.

I'm really glad he's going. I got no feedback from him. He never spent time with us socially, so we had no opportunities to get to know him.

CD2 TRACK 23

Did Paul have some good points? Yes, he was a strong manager, very decisive, and I liked that. He gave brief instructions and expected you to do the job properly. Some people didn't like that, of course. He wouldn't accept any excuses if things went wrong. But that was fair enough, I suppose.

He had one weakness that upset everyone in the team. He didn't set clear goals. For instance, none of us realised we had to collect information about the incentives offered to regular customers. We didn't know that was part of the brief. And we had no idea that we had to complete our survey in France in two weeks. He simply didn't make it clear to us.

He treated everyone fairly, but never really got to know us as individuals. He was too distant as a manager, I'd say. Too focused on results, not a people person.

CD2 TRACK 24

I got on OK with Paul, but he didn't give me any work that was really interesting or challenging. I spent most of the time making appointments for the other members of the team. I got bored and sort of lost interest. I don't think he trusted me – or anyone in the team, for that matter. He tried to do too much himself, so he was always under a lot of pressure and seemed very stressed.

I know that quite a few of the team felt Paul didn't adapt his style to suit individual members. He seemed to have no cross-cultural skills at all. He treated everyone in the same way, and you can't do that when the team has such a mix of nationalities and personalities.

UNIT 8 TEAM BUILDING

CD2 TRACK 25 (I = INTERVIEWER, DC = DAN COLLINS)

I How can businesses build successful teams?

DC The key thing with a team is that it's really just a group of people working towards a common goal. The leader's role in a team is to make sure that goal is well understood and is clear and then to encourage people along the way as they work towards that objective. Where necessary, steer them back on track if they veer off, but a team really is a group of people who are feeling enthusiastic towards achieving the same objective and they're feeling encouraged by their leader throughout.

CD2 TRACK 26 (I = INTERVIEWER, DC = DAN COLLINS)

I Can you give us some examples of companies that you have helped?

DC Yeah, we work in a variety of sectors, including pharmaceuticals, telecoms, banking, retail. And the issues that they have are very common. Communication is always an area of challenge, more so now because as people have got hi-tech communication devices, they have conversations, but they are conversations with a subject heading. So they are responding to an e-mail with a subject heading or they're having a discussion in a meeting to a set subject. What is harder is for people to find time to do is to have those more spontaneous conversations which explore new opportunities. And so, part of our role is to take people away from their normal work environment and to give them the opportunity to have meaningful, significant conversations about what they want to achieve as a team and the strengths that each individual brings to that team.

CD2 TRACK 27 (DC = DAN COLLINS)

DC So, in addition to communication, we spend a lot of time helping people to discover their area of strength and their contribution to the team. So, there are a number of ways of splitting up the roles and the behaviours that people perform in a team. But, in simple terms, we have people who are the leaders, and that's self-explanatory – they take a leading role, either because they are appointed to that position or simply because they're natural leaders and they have a leading style in the way they do things. There are creative people who solve problems either by being creative as we would expect insomuch as they have random ideas and they, um, they're are able to really think outside of the box. But there are also those who solve problems, um, creatively, but using analysis and, er, research. So, they are the creators. We have the leaders and the creators. We also have the 'gluers' and they are the people who pull the team together. So, they are people who are motivated by a relationship and they're keen to ensure that people are feeling good in the team and they're looking after some of the pastoral needs of the team. They're the sort of person who might arrange for a lunch out or arrange the Christmas party, will ensure on somebody's birthday they are given a card – an essential part of a team, which is often overlooked.

And finally, there are the doers and they're the people who like to look at process and project management, ensure that things are done on time and to a level of accuracy and quality. It is that mix of those four types that makes a team really effective. So, one of the things we do is analyse the team that exists and say, 'Well, where are the gaps?' or 'Are you biased one way or the other?' And, for certain roles, that's OK – it is quite good to have a very analytical team if their role is, say, financial, where analysis is important.

CD2 TRACK 28 (I = INTERVIEWER, DC = DAN COLLINS)

I Do attitudes to team-working vary in different countries?

DC Um, to some degree and, I think, attitudes to the way in which teams are developed and led varies. So, in the West, certainly in the United States and, increasingly, in Europe – but United States is probably leading the way – we're very open to an empowered form of leadership where somebody is given an instruction and then really allowed to get on with that and do it the way they want to do it without too much interference. And people are allowed to do the work that they do in their way, more so than in, um, developing countries, such as India and China, where there's more of a command-and-control approach. And there are very specific instructions and people work to those instructions. I don't know that either one is better than the other, but there is a difference in leadership styles and, consequently, the way in which a team is, is led and behaves. And the expectations of that, the team members in terms of their, um, their relationship with the team can vary from place to place.

CD2 TRACK 29 (K = KAREN, L = LARISSA)

K OK, Larissa, I think I understand now. What you're saying is, you're unhappy with Sophie, you don't think she's pulling her weight in the department, and it's putting pressure on you and the rest of the team. Right?

L Yeah, we're meant to work as a team, aren't we? And she's the most experienced member. But she's not doing her job. She's never around to give us advice or help us deal with difficult clients. Preparing the annual report is a big job, but we're getting no input from her at all. Another thing …

K OK, I've got the picture. I understand your feelings, Larissa …

L I hope you do. I'm really fed up with her – it's not just me, it's the whole team.

K OK, let's keep calm. What do you want me to do? Fire her?

L Oh no, not that … of course … but you could give her a good talking to. You know, tell her to make more effort, and then if she doesn't do anything, well, you'll have to take serious action, won't you?

K Mmm … I think there's one thing you could all do – maybe you should talk to her, tell her how you feel. That'd help, I think. But I'd like to put off doing anything else for a while.

L Oh, why's that? How would that help?

K Let me explain. Sophie's getting married early next month. She's got a lot on her mind at the moment, and it's not work, it's the wedding. That's her priority at the moment …

L Yeah, OK, but even so …

K Why don't we wait for a while? Let her get the wedding out of the way. I think you'll find she'll be the Sophie we used to know then … she's always been a good member of the team. She hasn't changed overnight, has she?

L Mmm, I don't know, maybe …

K Look, let's talk about this in a few weeks' time. We can review the situation then. Meanwhile, you and the others can talk to her, in a friendly way, I hope, and, OK, I'll have a quiet word in her ear.

L All right, we'll see if that works. Thanks for listening, Karen.

CD2 TRACK 30 (D = DAVID, M = MAX, H = HANK, L = LAURA, N = NATALYA, S = SONIA, C = CHANG)

D I'd like to talk about training today. I've got a proposal to make – see what you think about it. I feel that you'd all benefit from more training. Even if you're very experienced, you can always add to your knowledge and update your skills. So, my proposal is you should all go on at least two training courses a year to update your knowledge. You could either choose which courses you go on from a list I've drawn up, or make suggestions to me. How do you feel about this? Yes, Max?

M Well, an obvious question really: would it be compulsory to go on two courses?

D Yes, it would. I think everyone would benefit from more training.

M Then I'm sorry, I don't think it's a good idea. Personally, I don't enjoy courses, I don't think I need them. I'm the top salesman here, and I've been that for the last three years. I certainly don't need any more training. I need to spend all my time looking after my customers' needs. That's my priority.

D I see. OK, what about you, Hank?

H Well, frankly, Max is talking rubbish as usual. We all know he's top salesman because he's been given the best area to work in, and he's been there for years. I mean, anyone could sell kitchenware in West London. Put a monkey in there and he'd be salesman of the year.

D Hank, you're being very offensive, you know.

M Sorry, Hank, I can't let you get away with that. I've built up sales in this area steadily over the last 10 years, and it hasn't been easy at all to get into some of the top stores, but I've stuck at it and now it's paying off. My customers are loyal to our company. They like me, and I really look after them. That's the reason I'm the top salesman, it's not about being in the best area.

H OK, OK, sorry if I offended you, Max – I just like to speak my mind, that's all.

D Right, we'll take that as an apology. All I want to know from you is, do you think my idea's a good one?

H Yeah, right, I suppose so … uh, well, a good idea for some of our team, anyway. Natalya could certainly benefit from a *lot* more training.

D I'd like you to keep your personal comments to yourself, if you don't mind.

H All right … I thought you wanted my opinion.

D Thanks, I've noted what you said. Laura, what do you think of the proposal?

L Er, well, Hank's right, it is a good idea, more training courses, but not for all of us. If we want to increase sales, we can't have everyone running off at a moment's notice. We need to focus on meeting our sales targets.

D OK … Well, what do our younger members think? Sonia? Natalya? Yes, Natalya.

N Er, well … I don't think it's a good idea for experienced people like … Max. If he went on a course, he'd probably end up teaching everyone. I'd like some more training, if possible, to improve my sales and negotiating skills, but I think once a year is enough.

D Sonia?

S I've already been on two sales courses, that was in my previous job. For me, it'd be a complete waste of time. I'm more interested in the way you pay commissions here. I think …

D Sorry, Sonia, I must stop you there. Commissions are not on the agenda today. Chang, you'd like to say something?

C I think, David, it is a good idea to offer more training to the team. You're on the right track here. But why do you want to make it compulsory? Why don't you have a talk with each member of the team, find out if they are interested in more training, and then draw up a training plan for each person – that's the way I'd do it.

D Yeah, I see what you mean, Chang. That's a useful suggestion. OK, um, who haven't we heard from yet?

UNIT 9 RAISING FINANCE

CD3 TRACK 1 (I = INTERVIEWER, SD = SIMON DAVIES)

I In which ways can a business raise finance, and what are the advantages of each way?

SD There are probably, I guess, three ways in which I would see business raising finance. Um, first, er, equity, either current shareholders or new shareholders. Er, a business can raise finance by effectively selling shares to its – more shares to its current owners, or shares to new owners.
Um, secondly, I would see a business being able to raise, er, money by borrowing, through debt. Um, and thirdly there's a hybrid, um, effectively a combination of the two, um, something that starts out as borrowing that could convert, um, into shares or equity, er, at some stage in the future. Within that, there are two markets that a – a business could raise finance in, a private market or the public market.
A private market is what it is, it is a private market, private individuals, private relationships, has the advantages of confidentiality, um, and remaining, um, below the radar screen. Um, the public markets, um, selling shares to the public markets has the advantages of having a much deeper pocket. There is a greater source of funding available from the public markets, um, and that's the same for, er, for debt as well, so if you're borrowing money, um, the bond markets, the capital markets, tend to have a far greater, um, amount of funds available, so the larger your business is, the more public you're likely to want to be in the way in which you raise finance. And then finally, um, hybrid finance, er, as an example, convertible bonds.

CD3 TRACK 2 (I = INTERVIEWER, SD = SIMON DAVIES)

I And what are the disadvantages of the different ways of raising finance?

SD For shares, um, equity carries a fairly significant capital cost, um, people who, er, invest in shares expect a return that reflects the risk that they're taking. Um, shareholders obviously carry the full business risk and don't have a right to be repaid their money. Um, they can receive dividends over time, but only after the company has covered its costs and other liabilities, such as interest on the debt. Um, for debt, and the disadvantages are that obviously, um, the interest burden on debt is required to be paid over time. That reduces the amount of cash that a company has that would otherwise be available, er, for it to use for investment purposes.
Um, there's also advantages and disadvantages in the public versus private markets. Um, the public markets, um, while they give you a broader, um, amount of capital available, um, they don't create that type of private relationship that you would get in the private markets – you could have a dispersed shareholder base. Um, in the public debt markets, you could end up with, er, effectively bondholders of whom you don't know their identity, um, whereas in the private markets you very closely know who your lender is or who your shareholder is. Um, for the private markets, the disadvantages are potentially a lack of capital available if you're a significant business. Um, in addition to that, um, private markets will tend, on the equity side, to want a significant return, and some significant change to shareholder control features, um, to the extent that you will lose a certain amount of control over who your executive management is and how that management effectively runs the business.

CD3 TRACK 3 (I = INTERVIEWER, SD = SIMON DAVIES)

I Do you think finance is always a short-term business, or can borrowers and lenders develop more long-term relationships?

SD Finance has become somewhat short-term business, to a very great extent, and there are, I think, three or four reasons, um, for that. One, um, is the breadth of opportunity available, um, gives people such a range of investment choice from a funding perspective, that, um, they are almost spoilt in their ability to invest and then sell and reinvest. Um, so the whole attitude has become quite – quite short-termist from an investing perspective.
Um, the second is the speed of in… – the speed and quality of information. Um, information is key in making investing decisions, and the better the quality of information, the easier it is to make a decision. But the speed with which investment decisions can be made now, is, um, incredible compared to only say 10 years ago or 20 years ago. But it does give people the opportunity, effectively, to become a short-term investor.
Um, I think thirdly, er, what has also happened is that the banks have become less relationship-driven from a financing perspective and more relationship-driven from a sales and distribution perspective. So the relationship between a – a lender and its borrower has changed fundamentally at this time, um, and effectively, the person who used to be the lender is now distributing, um, finance to a syndicate of other people who are – who are becoming lenders but who are more naturally, um, inclined to be able to buy and sell the investments that they make. Um, so the loans become a more tradable feature, um, and less static, um, creating a short-term relationship between the lender and the borrower.
Um, and fourthly, I think from an equity perspective, um, it has become so easy, er, to buy and sell shares, that, um, the – the – the churn of shares is so great, um, that people have very short-termist nature. They trade off sentiment as much as they do, um, fundamental value.
Um, I think there is still a place for long-term investing and long-term relationships from both an equity perspective and from a lending perspective. Um, it is rare at the moment. I think the one big example is probably Warren Buffet's fund. Um, his whole structure is different to that of the majority of the financial markets, in that he does not earn, um, his money from, um, effectively taking a portion of the profits. He earns his money by being invested alongside his investors and he runs businesses and asks the people who run his businesses to run them as if they're running them for their – the generations of their family to come, not on a short-term basis.

CD3 TRACK 4

a) Can you offer any collateral?
b) There seems to be something wrong with your figures.
c) Let's go over what we've agreed.
d) What sort of loan are you looking for?
e) Let me clarify my last point. What I meant was, we would want to retain control of the business.

CD3 TRACK 5 (B = BANK MANAGER, C = CLIENT)

B I've looked at your business plan and I like some of your ideas for expanding your business. Could I ask you, what other people are providing finance for you?

C Well, two family members have offered 100,000 euros for a small stake in the business. I haven't decided anything yet, and my partner is also investing some more money. We're still discussing the exact amount.

B Have you approached any other bank, if I may ask?

C Yes, two banks, but they turned me down.
B Oh, sorry to hear that – these are difficult times to raise money. I'd like to make a suggestion. Why don't you revise your business plan? And especially, put in a bit more about your competitors, for example. That'd help.
C Certainly, I can do that.
B Good. Could I ask what sort of repayment terms you have in mind?
C I'm pretty sure we could repay a loan – the whole amount, that is – within three years.
B Right. That might be a bit optimistic, I'd say. Anyway, suppose we were to offer you a loan of, say, 250,000 euros, once you've revised your business plan? How would you feel about that?
C Let me clarify what the money's for. The 250,000 would be for working capital, and to hire more staff, a finance director, marketing people, money for the extension of the factory …
B Well, we can talk about that a little later. Your first task is to strengthen the management as we discussed earlier.
C OK. Well, in that case, 250,000 would certainly help me to achieve some of my objectives in expanding the business.
B Good. We seem to be getting somewhere now. Let me sum up what we've agreed so far, then we can talk about your marketing strategy.

CD3 TRACK 6

Hi, Charles, hi, everyone. Some great news. I sent your business plan to an independent film distributor over here called Caplyn Entertainment. They're interested in buying the rights to distribute your film here in the States. They like the concept a lot and think the film would do really well over here. They own cinemas throughout the country and are highly regarded in the industry. I'm sure you'll all be very excited about this. They really believe in the film and support your creative vision. One final thing, you might also be able to negotiate with them about DVD and cable rights in the US.

WORKING ACROSS CULTURES 3: MANAGING INTERNATIONAL TEAMS

CD3 TRACK 7 (P = PRESENTER, J = JULIE, D = DALE)

P Good evening and welcome to another edition of *Business Time* with me, Steve Langley. On tonight's programme, we'll be talking about managing and working in international teams from a cultural perspective. I'm joined by tonight's guests Julie D'Angelo, business psychologist and author of the bestselling book *Business in Mind*, and an old friend of the programme and cultural expert, Dale Hawkins. Hello, Julie, and welcome back, Dale.
J Hello, Steve, and thank you for having me.
D Hello again, Steve.
P Well, I guess we should start by saying that international teamworking is becoming increasingly common, not only with teams of mixed nationalities in the same location, but also in virtual teams. This could involve a group of individuals based all over the world who rarely communicate face to face. Businesses really need to think about the potential problems as well as benefits attached to this way of working. Could I ask you both: what are the important points to consider when putting together or working with international teams. Julie?
J Well, Steve, one thing to bear in mind right at the start is actually the way a team is seen in different cultures. In some parts of the world, a team is composed of so-called specialists, each with clearly defined roles and responsibilities, whereas in other cultures, individual roles are much less clearly defined, and responsibility is shared.
P Interesting.
D Yes, that's right. And of course whether team members expect tasks to be very clearly set out by the manager or team leader, or if team members are expected to use their own initiative. This means there may be very different ideas about roles and attitudes to things like empowerment.
P I see, but how could this cause problems?
D Well, for example, the competitive nature of some teams may mean giving individuals praise for particular things they've done. This is a recognised way of motivating people. However, in a more collective culture, praising an individual may be less acceptable, as it's felt that the whole team takes either the praise or the blame for things. There may also be another difference, as some cultures tend to give financial rewards for achievement, whereas others value loyalty more highly.
J Mm, yes, Dale … In more collective cultures, asking for assistance or seeking advice from another team member, whether you truly need it or not, is a way to build team spirit, solidarity and unity. Also, from a psychological point of view, this idea of group responsibility is important. In some cultures, a team member with a problem will consult another colleague for advice or assistance, whereas in other cultures they will go straight to their boss.

CD3 TRACK 8 (D = DALE, J = JULIE)

D Yes, and while we're on the subject of so called 'individual' and 'collective 'cultures, what I think's really interesting is the way individuals relate to each other as far as knowledge is concerned. For some cultures, 'knowledge is power' – so knowledge is only shared on a need-to-know basis. This sort of culture again favours the idea of the individual expert. Other cultures are more collective in spirit and will work and share knowledge for the common good. Knowledge is built up through group discussion and trust, and it's not felt to be the 'property' of an individual. For these cultures, knowledge cannot be stolen, as it's owned by everyone. A good example of this is that there is no real concept of 'copyright' in the sense that it belongs to an individual or a specific company.
J Yes, I think you're right. This is a really important consideration for international teams and, for me, the most interesting area. There's also a group of cultures which operate at the level of mutual debt, which is the idea of an exchange. What this means is, one person will give information if someone does something for them in return – you know, I'll scratch your back if you scratch mine! Knowledge here confirms someone's status and is not readily shared. It's elitist in the sense that to benefit from knowledge, people will need to be part of the same network.

CD3 TRACK 9 (P = PRESENTER, J = JULIE, D = DALE)

P Right, and what are some of the practical considerations involved?
J Well, management of international teams leads to particular problems. Team members will have expectations about something simple like the number and purpose of meetings. In some cultures, team meetings are simply for planning. People then expect to be allowed to get on with the work. For others, meetings are more about keeping track of what's going on – to share ideas about progress, to talk about problems and mistakes and how to rectify them. Obviously, with virtual teams, another factor is the difference in time zones, which can make the scheduling of meetings problematic.
D Yes, and don't forget if teams do meet face to face, there are other considerations like body language, dress and manners. A good example is the simple handshake. This can be very different from culture to culture, with different connotations and meanings. Should you look the person in the eye? How firm should the handshake be? In some cultures, a firm handshake while maintaining eye contact is seen as a sign of trustworthiness and sincerity, whereas in other cultures it can be seen as challenging and over-assertive.
P Thanks very much, Dale, you've really given us something to think about. So, Julie, moving on – can I ask you about the sort of training which …

UNIT 10 CUSTOMER SERVICE

CD3 TRACK 10 (I = INTERVIEWER, PNH = PHILIP NEWMAN-HALL)

I Can you tell us a little about the Le Manoir?
PNH Yes, Le Manoir aux Quat'Saisons is Raymond Blanc's dream of excellence within a hotel and restaurant in the UK. We are a 32-bedroom luxury hotel with a stunning restaurant. The heart of the house is the food and the cuisine, and everything else that we do in the house is … The ethos of the kitchen spreads into everywhere else in the house. It is a retreat from the norm and is supposed to be a house where you can come and feel comfortable. We like to think that the house tells you what you can do in it rather than what you can't do in it. It's a two-Michelin-starred restaurant and we have now been running for 25 years.

CD3 TRACK 11 (I = INTERVIEWER, PNH = PHILIP NEWMAN-HALL)

I At Le Manoir, how do you define top-quality customer service?
PNH It's very difficult to answer that, but I would say that we try to exceed customers' expectations, we try very hard to see that customers are wanting something before they even know they want it. So, therefore, we have to have empathy with the client and we have to try and judge each client individually, so that we sense what they're looking for and try and provide that service all the time.
We also must provide consistent standards of service. If we don't provide a consistent standard, then one guest's expectations will be met and another guest's won't be met. We try very hard to have a phrase within the house that 'the standards you set are the standards you get'. And once you have set those standards, we try to offer those to guests at all times.

CD3 TRACK 12 (I = INTERVIEWER, PNH = PHILIP NEWMAN-HALL)

I How do you train staff to deal with demanding customers?
PNH Get them to empathise with the customer, the guest. Try to put them in their place, try to see it from their point of view. We particularly allow every single member of the staff to have a guest experience. So, they stay in the house overnight, they eat in the restaurant and they understand what the experience is like for a paying guest. So, therefore, if it was their own money they were paying for it, they would understand what they should expect for that, and I think that gives them an edge in

understanding what a client is looking for when they come into the house.

It's very … high-end here, so, therefore, people's expectations are very high, and we have to try and exceed those expectations. And I think by only getting the staff to understand what those expectations are, we can then meet them and, and exceed them.

CD3TRACK 13 (I = INTERVIEWER, PNH = PHILIP NEWMAN-HALL)

I Do you think that customer service requirements are changing, or have they always been about the same things?

PNH I think they're becoming much more demanding. I think people are expecting a lot more for their money nowadays and I think the way the world is now, people are more open and more questioning of what they're receiving for their money. So, I think we have seen a definite increase in the number of people who would complain, when perhaps they wouldn't have complained before – which is no bad thing because it gives us great feedback. But I think people in general are much more demanding nowadays than they used to be. And therefore, we've had to up our game to actually provide better service. So, yes, I really think it has changed over the last few years.

CD3TRACK 14

A Good morning, Madam, how can I help?

B Well, you see, I bought two bottles of wine from you on Monday. It was a special promotion, your 'wine of the month' offer.

A Oh yes, I remember, we gave you a very good price on that one, 30 per cent off if you bought two bottles, wasn't it?

B Yes, that's right. It was one of the main reasons I bought the bottles, the price was right. But when my husband and I tried one of the bottles, we found the wine was much too sweet.

A Really? What exactly do you mean by 'much too sweet'?

B Well, like fruit juice. And when I offered a glass to my neighbour, she took one sip, then said, 'Sorry, this wine's too sweet for me. Do you have anything else?'

A Mmm, I can't understand that, I'm afraid. Well, what did you do next?

B We tried the other bottle, but it was even sweeter! We were hoping … you see, we were hoping you'd give us a refund or let us choose two other bottles, er, free of charge.

A A refund! I'm sorry, but that's not our policy at all. We can't give refunds to customers, just because they're disappointed with their purchase. You understand that, surely?

B I see, well … to be honest, I was hoping you'd be a little more understanding … I mean …

A I'm sorry, Madam, but when you buy wines, you need to check what the label says. Medium wine's not the same as dry wine.

B I know that. But all the same, it was far too sweet …

A So you're saying it was too sweet and I'm saying medium wine is always sweet. I can't do anything more for you, Madam. I can only say, 'Better luck next time' and … don't forget to read the labels.

CD3TRACK 15

A Good morning, Sir. I'm carrying out a consumer satisfaction survey for the airline you've just travelled on. Could you possibly answer a few simple questions for me?

B Certainly. Go ahead, please. I'll do my best to answer them.

A OK … well, were you, on the whole, satisfied with the service you received?

B Satisfied? Certainly! In fact, I was more than satisfied.

A That's great. What did you like especially about our service?

B Well, you see, we weren't expecting much, the flight was very cheap, so we knew there wouldn't be any meals. It's a no-frills airline, isn't that what they call it?

A Right. No surprises, then?

B Well, yes, there were, actually. The stewards and stewardesses were absolutely fantastic, really friendly and helpful. Nothing was too much trouble for them. And they were really good with our young children, brought them games to play with – it kept them quiet and occupied during the flight. We weren't expecting that. It was a pleasant change, I can tell you!

A I'm pleased to hear the staff looked after you well. What else impressed you?

B OK, er, everything, really. The plane took off on time and arrived on time. The service was great, and we were even given free rolls and a coffee or orange juice. We'll definitely be flying with your airline again. And we'll tell all our friends how satisfied we were. I can't say more than that.

CD3TRACK 16

A Something so irritating happened recently with a delivery that I'd ordered. I certainly won't be using the supplier again.

B What happened?

A Well, I work from home as a translator for a leading bank. My printer had broken, and I needed a new one urgently. The person who took my order was extremely friendly and promised it would be there the next day.

B OK.

A Mm-hm. It didn't arrive, and I had waited in all day to receive it! When I phoned the supplier, I got the same friendly, helpful treatment again – they were very sorry, it would definitely be there the following day. But they let me down again. This went on for the rest of the week.

B How awful!

A I was very put out indeed. It was all talk and no action.

CD3TRACK 17 (P = PASSENGER, CS = CUSTOMER SERVICES AGENT)

P I'm calling because I've just come back from Italy on one of your flights. And I want to complain about the service before I flew and when I was on board the aircraft.

CS Oh, sorry about that. What happened, then?

P Well, I had some hand luggage and it was just a little over the limit, only a little bit, and I was charged an extra 30 dollars – I couldn't believe it! You know, I don't think the scales are very accurate. Anyway, then I had to pay three dollars for two plastic bags to put my toiletries in. I don't know if your company or the airport got the money for them.

CS Well, I don't know, but I'm afraid if you're over the limit … well, go on.

P Right, then we went by bus to the plane, the bus was freezing cold, and when I got there, there wasn't a proper stairway to the plane. It was just some sort of flimsy mobile steps and it was really dangerous climbing up them. I was so afraid of falling and breaking my leg. No one helped me, of course. Everyone was in a mad rush to get a good seat on the plane.

CS Oh dear! It can be a bit of a scramble at times, I know.

P Anyway, during the flight, the stewards and stewardesses seemed to be more interested in talking to each other than serving us. I'd asked for one of those entertainment boxes, you know, a sort of DVD player – I think you call it a TV box. I paid 15 dollars to have it, but I didn't know how to work the machine, and the attendants were too busy, they said, to help me. So I didn't see anything on the box.

CS Well, that shouldn't have happened, should it?

P No. Another thing, I was given a sandwich, I had to pay three dollars for it, and the roll was really stale. I don't know about the meat in it, but when I went to the hotel, I was sick and had an awful stomach all night.

CS Oh, I'm so sorry … Of course, your bad stomach could have been caused by anything. There are a lot of nasty viruses around …

P I don't know. But I certainly won't be using your airline again, I can promise you that.

CD3TRACK 18

Hi, my name's Francisco López. I want to tell you what a great flight to Chicago I had with your airline. The service was fantastic for a budget airline. The cabin crew were really friendly. I was sitting at the back of the plane, and I had a long conversation during the flight with two of your stewardesses. They were lovely people. The captain was great, too. He warned us of any turbulence well in advance and kept in touch with us during the flight. He had a very friendly and reassuring manner. He helped the nervous passengers to relax. We arrived on time, and the landing was so smooth that all the passengers clapped. The tickets were a real bargain, I'd say – I'd fly again any time with your airline. You're doing a great job of providing low-cost flights for people like me who are on a limited budget. So, keep up the good work!

UNIT 11 CRISIS MANAGEMENT

CD3TRACK 19 (CS = CRAIG SMITH)

CS Right now, ah, the Toyota Motor Company is facing a, a huge crisis, a crisis as a result of a – a product defect. So it has this problem of what's called 'unintended acceleration', and it's a problem that, ah, the company frankly has been very slow to, ah, acknowledge and very slow to respond to. There are – it's reported – incidences – reported instances, ah, of this unintended acceleration going back se- six or seven years. Ah, there have been some two thousand reported incidents, so pretty substantial evidence of a problem, and it was only September 2009 that the company really truly acknowledged there was a problem and said, 'we're gonna have a recall'.

The, the problem is, ah, put down to a couple of causes, ah, one is that the floor mat in the car can get jammed against the accelerator, ah, the other is that for some models there is a sticky accelerator, a design materials problem with the accelerator pedal itself.

Ah, and part of the problem Toyota is experiencing is that its communication around the causes of the problem has been unclear, and consumers have been left confused, and perhaps le- left with the feeling that Toyota itself doesn't really know, ah, what, what the problem is. The, the classic advice here is tell it all and tell it quickly. And the, ah, the, the … the thing to do is to get out there and, and, and let people know that you acknowledge that there is a problem, and know that you're doing something about it.

And you can see in the, in the Toyota story, ah, evidence of the company seemingly knowing there was a problem but not really getting out there and acknowledging the problem and saying, ah, we're going to get it fixed and, and, and here's how.

CD3 TRACK 20 (I = INTERVIEWER, CS = CRAIG SMITH)

I How can companies prepare themselves to manage crises?

CS The model, ah, I think that, ah, is useful in laying out the approach is, is a three-, three-part model, ah, that says you need to attend to, ah, the possibility of a crisis beforehand, so there's the before piece, ah, there is then the during piece – what's happening during the crisis – and then the after piece, what you do after the crisis has passed.
And if we, if we look at the before piece, ah, three particularly critical activities here: firstly an audit which is essentially asking the question 'What could go wrong?'. Ah, secondly, having identified what could possibly go wrong, say 'Well, can we reduce the likelihood of that happening? Can we avoid the avoidable?', so taking steps to avoid the avoidable, or in some cases, it may be a possible problem that you could, you could, ah, insure against. So there it could be business interruption insurance that you might want to take, take out if the company will need to close at some point.
And then I think, um, ah, fairly obviously in terms of preparing, you need to have some contingency plan in place and a dedicated team that will be ready to, to step in, ah, should a crisis arise.

CD3 TRACK 21 (CS = CRAIG SMITH)

CS Secondly, then, coming on to what happens during the crisis, the first, ah, thing that needs to happen is to recognise that there is indeed a crisis, so crisis identification is a … is an important, ah, first part of what takes place during the crisis.
The second, um, of, of, of the three considerations during the crisis is containment. Clearly you want to try and contain the crisis as, as best as possible.
And, ah, this means thinking about the actual problem itself, ah, but also the, the indirect challenges that come about through a crisis and here's, this is where communication is very important.
And then thirdly within, ah, the during phase, it's, it's resolving the crisis, and obviously very important here is figuring out what the cause is, and causes can come from within the organisation. It may be some, ah, clear defect in the product design or product materials, um, or indeed they could come from outside the organisation, they could be a problem from a supplier, some material that came into the organisation that is problematic, ah … Or indeed it could be a prob- a problem downstream, ah, with the, with the retailer. The, the problem could be something do with consumers and their misuse of the product, ah, or indeed in some cases there have been instances of product tampering where products have been tampered with and there's a, ah, there's a safety problem.

CD3 TRACK 22 (CS = CRAIG SMITH)

CS Once the crisis has passed, the, the 'after', ah, phase if you will, you've got then the, the recovery. So how do you, ah, reintroduce the product if that's, if that's the problem, how do you recover from the storm that has hit all your, your stores damaged your, damaged your stores, dislocated, ah, or, um, caused, caused employees to, to lose their homes possibly and they're, ah, they're dislocated. Um, and then there's the auditing of the management of the crisis. So what can be learnt, ah, as a result of seeing what worked, what didn't work. And then thirdly, ah, and finally there's rebuilding, so if this, if this has been a major crisis that the organisation's had to deal with, how does it rebuild its reputation externally, how does it, ah, restore the confidence of its customers, of other stakeholders and indeed internally of its, of its employees?

CD3 TRACK 23 (MG = MICHAEL GOODRICH, TB = TIM BRADSHAW)

MG Good evening, my name's Michael Goodrich. I'm the presenter of *Consumer Watch*. Tonight, we're investigating toy products. How safe are the imported toys products you're buying for your children? Not very, it seems, if you're buying toys from TG Products, one of the biggest toy retailers in the country. We've had dozens of complaints from parents about some of the toys sold in TG stores. Tonight, the company's Chief Executive, Tim Bradshaw, has agreed to answer questions about his company and to defend its reputation. Good evening, Mr Bradshaw.

TB Good evening. May I thank you for inviting me on to your programme, I welcome the opportunity to answer your questions.

MG Thank you, Mr Bradshaw, it's a pleasure to meet you. Now, I believe your company sells a range of stuffed toys. Is that correct?

TB Yes, they're one of our best-selling products. Children love the grey rabbits, the dogs and penguins we market. I'd say the reindeer and elephant are our most popular items. Why do you ask?

MG Could you please tell me how many of these items you import each month?

TB Oh, I don't know off the top of my head. A very large number, that's for sure. It's one of our most popular lines.

MG Could you be a little more precise? What quantity are we talking about, roughly?

TB Well, I'd say … um … about 30,000 a month.

MG That's a lot, isn't it? Roughly how many complaints about the toys do you receive each week from your customers?

TB Oh, we get a few complaints, but no higher percentage than any other company.

MG A few complaints? Mr Bradshaw, isn't it true you've been receiving dozens of complaints from customers every week? Do you deny people have been phoning you and e-mailing you constantly to complain about the toys?

TB What do you mean exactly? What are you trying to say?

MG I'm saying the toys are defective, they should be recalled by your company immediately.

TB Could you clarify that comment, please?

MG Certainly, I'd be glad to. The stuffed toys have a defect. They have button eyes, and these get pulled off very easily by children. They put the buttons into their mouths and then start choking. The toys are highly dangerous, Mr Bradshaw, you know that. Why are you still selling them?

TB I'd say you're exaggerating the problem. There may have been one or two cases, but not dozens.

MG Isn't your real reason for not recalling the toys very obvious, Mr Bradshaw?

TB What do you mean?

MG Simple. You've got over 50,000 of the items in your warehouse and if you recall the toys, it'll cost you a lot of money!

TB Good heavens, where did you get that information from? Who gave it to you?

MG I'm sorry, I can't possibly comment on that. But what are you going to do about these defective toys?

TB Do about it? Well, I'll look into the matter, of course, and I'll get back to you. But I don't think …

MG When will that be? When exactly will you get back to us?

TB Oh, as soon as possible.

MG Would you answer my question, please? I think you owe it to your customers to give us an exact date.

TB I'm sorry, I don't know the answer to your question, but I'll get our Customer Services to check our records. We'll treat this matter very seriously, I promise you.

MB That's good to hear. Now let me ask you another question …

CD3 TRACK 24

1 Could you please tell me how many of these items you import each month?
2 Could you be a little more precise?
3 Roughly how many complaints about the toys do you receive each week …?
4 Isn't it true you've been receiving dozens of complaints from customers every week?
5 Do you deny people have been phoning you and e-mailing you constantly to complain about the toys?
6 Why are you still selling them?
7 Isn't your real reason for not recalling the toys very obvious, Mr Bradshaw?
8 But what are you going to do about these defective toys?
9 When exactly will you get back to us?
10 Would you answer my question, please?

CD3 TRACK 25 (LT = LINDA THOMSON, BM = BOB MORGAN)

LT OK, it's pretty clear we've got a crisis on our hands, Bob, but before we decide how to handle this one, could you run me through our plans for the launch?

BM Yeah, sure, um … well … the big event, of course, will be the extracts from the game that we'll show in the Universal movie theatre. There'll be an invited audience, famous people in the arts and entertainment business, movie stars, artists, musicians, media people, anyone with influence, even a few politicians – only those who support us, of course!

LT OK, sounds good. What about the big party afterwards?

BM You'll really enjoy it – I hope. It'll be at the All Seasons hotel. There'll be over a thousand attending, we've got Q7 performing at midnight, they're the hottest group in the country at the moment – they love our game by the way …

LT Great!

BM Let's see, what else can I tell you? Oh yeah, all the service staff will be dressed like mercenaries in combat gear and they'll all look really tough, perhaps a bit intimidating.

LT That's a nice idea. It'll get us good coverage in the press. They'll put those photos on their front pages.

BM Exactly. A bit of controversy won't harm sales at all!

LT What a cynic you are, Bob! But you're right, of course. How about our advertising and promotion? Are you happy with it? It's coming in for a lot of criticism.

BM I'm totally happy with it, just look at the sales projections.

LT We'll come to them in a moment. What about advertising?

BM OK, well, we started with a teaser campaign, as you know, followed it up with TV and movie-theatre commercials, sent advance copies to reviewers of gaming magazines – they were all full of praise for the game. In fact, one magazine awarded it their Gold Medal – that gave it a big boost – then we backed it all up with viral advertising, 500 18-year-olds got a copy of the game and they spread the word to their friends, relatives, classmates and so on.

LT OK, what about the latest sales projections? You got them from Marketing?

BM Yes, you'll love the figures. We expect sales of seven million in this country, bringing in a revenue of around about 350 million dollars, and in the UK, four million with a revenue of 200 million dollars. Those figures are just for the first month.

LT Mmm, it's looking really good. That'll more than cover the 200 million dollars we put into the project. And we'll really knock out the competition with those figures. But … I'm very worried about all the criticism we're getting. How should we handle it? We don't want to screw up at this late stage. Our opponents aren't playing around, they're really out for our blood.

UNIT 12 MERGERS AND ACQUISITIONS

CD3 TRACK 26

Well, moving on to the idea of restructuring. The terms *takeover* and *acquisition* are to some extent interchangeable, although in recent years the term *acquisition* has become more popular. Strictly speaking, a takeover refers to one firm gaining control of another by buying over 50 per cent of its shares. This takeover may be either friendly or hostile, which is when the company being targeted doesn't want or agree to the takeover. If a company acquires a part of another company's shares, which may be less than 50 per cent, this gives them an interest, holding or stake. Over 50 per cent would become a controlling interest. A merger, on the other hand, involves two companies or organisations coming together to form a larger one. Although a merger sounds more like two companies coming together on more equal terms, many mergers are in fact more like takeovers for one of the businesses involved, as usually there is a dominant partner. A joint venture involves two quite separate companies co-operating for a limited time, or for example in a particular geographical area on a particular project, but maintaining their own identities. This could be something such as building a plant – which is quite common in the oil and gas industry – or developing a new technology which would benefit both companies. Now, if I may, I'd like to look in more detail at some other …

CD3 TRACK 27 (I = INTERVIEWER, SM = SCOTT MOELLER)

I Why is it that a number of mergers and acquisitions don't work as well as expected?

SM It is true that somewhere between two-thirds and three-quarters of all acquisitions fail, uh, so the success rate in acquisitions is obviously quite low. And the reason for that is due to a number of different factors. First off, inadequate planning. Uh, that is to say that the strategic plan behind the acquisition tends not to be grounded in too much of what the future strategy would be, but more of an opportunistic basis as to whether a company is able to be acquired or not.
Secondly, the due diligence done on the target company tends to be done much too quickly, and in many cases doesn't focus on the key factors that are going to drive that particular deal to success in the future. More time should be spent trying to understand what it is that really makes that target company successful – if it is already successful – or why perhaps it has failed, uh, and whether that can be turned around if, in fact, the company is being acquired because, uh, it is a company that's now available, because of lack of success.
And then lastly, um, there's really a lack of planning for the post-merger integration period. Many, many times a deal is done, and then once the company is acquired, the focus of management tends to disappear. They go on to the next deal, they go on to some other strategic initiative and forget that the really hard work comes, and the work that takes years and years, comes after the deal is closed, when in fact the integration really takes place. The people have to start working together from two different companies now as one. The customer databases have to be put together. Back-office systems need to be integrated, suppliers need to be contacted, and basically, two companies need to be made one.

CD3 TRACK 28 (I = INTERVIEWER, SM = SCOTT MOELLER)

I Once the merger has taken place, what can be done to ensure the successful integration of the businesses?

SM In order to assure the successful integration of the businesses, one first must determine whether, uh, you want to integrate the companies completely, and at what speed. That is, there are many deals where you actually want to make sure the newly acquired company is kept separate for a period of time, perhaps to understand that company better, uh, perhaps because you want that company to operate as a separate subsidiary.
Uh, other times, you'll want to integrate the newly acquired company very, very rapidly in order to make sure that you don't lose customers, that you don't lose employees, uh, perhaps because there's something that has a very time-critical element, uh, driving the purpose of the acquisition in the first place.
Once you've determined whether you want to do it quickly or slowly, you also need to determine whether you want to impose your own culture and way of operations on that company, or in fact to keep that company's own culture separate, perhaps for a period of time, or again, for a longer period of time.
So determining the speed of the acquisition, and determining how, uh, fully you want to integrate it are the two critical things driving then what you are going to do afterwards. Uh, are you going to appoint somebody from the company itself to run that division, or do you want to bring in new management, perhaps from the acquirer's own management, or perhaps from the outside?

CD3 TRACK 29 (I = INTERVIEWER, SM = SCOTT MOELLER)

I Can you give us an example of an acquisition that has worked really well?

SM One example of an acquisition that has worked really well is actually the merger between Bank of New York and Mellon Bank, which took place back in 2007. Those two banks had actually, interestingly enough, eight years earlier, uh, had an unsuccessful attempt at coming together where Bank of New York had made a hostile attempt to, uh, overtake, uh, Mellon Bank.
Uh, however, in the second try, what they did is they understood some of the mistakes from previously, so experience is very important.
But most importantly what they did is they met very early before the deal became public, and they determined what it was that were showstoppers – things that could derail, that could stop the deal in the future from being successful, and they did determine what those items were very, very early on.
Each side put their cards on the table, they identified what those potential problems were very early, and said if we can't get those, past those problems now, if we can't agree on what those problems are, if we can't agree about how we're going to deal with them once we have merged, then we shouldn't go through with this merger. We want to make sure it's friendly. We want to make sure it's going to be successful.
What they then did is having worked through those showstoppers – those items that might not be successful – they then put together a team from both sides of very, very senior people, uh, ultimately announcing the deal, including the identification of who was going to be running the firm with about an equal number of people from both sides.
Everybody therefore knew who their boss was going to be, they knew which businesses were going to be retained, they had some idea as to how the business was going to drive forward, and most importantly, they knew that very deeply engaged in the deal strategy, as well as the integration process, was the CEO and Chairman of the company, who took a very, very public role in identifying what the company was going to be doing post-acquisition.

CD3 TRACK 30 (SD = SUSAN DRAKE)

SD Right, well, as I mentioned earlier, we see the acquisition of Highview as the foundation for our drive into the budget-hotel market here in the UK. We have very ambitious plans for the future of the Highview brand – I'll outline these later in my presentation.
OK, why did we buy Highview? I'd say there were three main reasons: the gap in the market, the market conditions and the opportunity for growth.
Firstly, the gap in the market. It's well known that business travellers to the UK are tending to stay in mid-price and budget hotels nowadays rather than in the more up-scale, prestigious hotels. Economic conditions are difficult, everyone's trying to cut costs. But, the truth is, there are not enough budget hotels to meet the demand. Let me give you a simple statistic. Only 13 per cent of hotels in the UK are in the budget section. That's about half the level of budget hotels in Europe and the US.
What about the market conditions? Well, this is the ideal time to develop a budget hotel brand in the UK. Hotel occupancy and room rates are continuing to rise. Revenues from available rooms in large cities are at a record high. But, as I mentioned, the demand for rooms is much greater than the supply.
We're incredibly excited about the growth potential of the Highview brands. With our experience in owning and running budget hotels, our

unique training programme and our financial strength, we see unlimited possibilities for increasing profits from the acquisition and we firmly believe …

… Right, I've told you why we've acquired Highview. And I've explained that this purchase gives us the opportunity to develop a portfolio of branded budget hotels in the UK.

What are our future plans for the group? We have a clear, realistic and ambitious strategy for the Highview brand. We plan to buy other hotels in the UK, improve their performance and market them using the Highview brand. Although all the hotels will be budget hotels with limited service, we'll make sure that customers really enjoy the experience of staying at a Highview hotel. Good value for money will always be our main objective.

So where do we see Highview in five years' time? By that time, we'll have built new Highview hotels on the company's four development sites. We'll have integrated a number of US hotels into the group, renaming them Highview. And finally, we'll have developed a portfolio of budget hotels which will make us leader in this sector of the market. Highview will be the future of budget hotels in the UK. Highview will lead the way. Highview will set a new standard for value for money. Right, are you now clear about why we bought Highview and the direction we plan to take? Is there any area I haven't covered? Anything missing? Yes, you have a question, I see. Go ahead, please.

CD3 TRACK 31

We focus today on four companies we believe could be targets for Rinnovar International's planned expansion. How have they been performing recently?

Let's start with Mumbai Herbal Products. Last year, it reported strong growth, with sales of 26 million dollars and net profits increasing by 16.9 per cent. In the three previous years, turnover increased by 48 per cent and profits by 32 per cent. MHP has been very successful: it has introduced new 'star' products in its domestic market and they're beginning to sell overseas.

Next, Good Earth, the Brazilian company using natural ingredients to make cosmetics, perfumes and health products. Its main market is Brazil, but it also operates in other Latin American countries. Last year, turnover was 55 million dollars, with net profits of only 3.2 million dollars. In the three previous years, profits grew by 8 per cent. Good Earth is planning to open new plants in selected foreign countries in the near future.

Hondo Beauty Products is another company Rinnovar International will probably be looking at. This Korean company manufactures not only cosmetics but also bath and shower products. It could give Rinnovar the opportunity to expand into Asia and to develop the bath and shower segment of the market. Hondo, with sales last year of almost 62 million dollars and net profits of 14 million dollars, is a tempting target for Rinnovar. The company grew fast in the previous three years, with profits increasing by 48 per cent.

Finally, will Rinnovar International go for a company near home? Some say they're taking a close look at Sheen Hair Products, based in Palm Beach, Florida. SHP is one of the top manufacturers of haircare products for professional salons in North America. Ninety-five per cent of its sales are in the home market, but SHP also distributes hair products in two European countries. Sales topped 94 million dollars last year, with net profits of 8 million dollars. Profits have increased by less than 10 per cent in the last three years, but the company has a strong position in the professional salon industry.

WORKING ACROSS CULTURES 4: INTERNATIONAL NEGOTIATIONS

CD3 TRACK 32

Thanks for that, Gary – and now, in this part of the day, I'd like to take a quick look at negotiating across cultures.

Many people assume that international negotiations are no different to domestic ones, but that's a big mistake to make. Tactics which work well when doing business with people from your own culture do not necessarily apply internationally – for example, the idea that everyone likes to get down to business and focus on the result and get a contract drawn up. One thing to realise right from the start is that it's not only national culture that determines behaviour in negotiations. Other factors include company culture, gender or even the level of international negotiating experience. The other point to make is that preconceptions and regional generalisations are often simply incorrect. For example, the Japanese and Koreans share some similarities, but are very different in other respects. The same is true of the Italians and Spanish. It's not really possible to talk about regions in any meaningful sense. So I don't really want to talk about specific cultures, but to outline a few general principles and differences which are worth bearing in mind when getting involved in international negotiations.

I'd like to look at three main areas before you break into smaller focus groups to examine some of the issues in more detail with the trainers.

First of all, a major difference between cultures is the perception of the business relationship. For some cultures, business is seen in terms of a contract – objective and impersonal. The encouragement of personal relationships is generally seen as inappropriate. Emotion and sentiment can interfere with sound business decision-making, which it's felt should be rational, cool and logical. In other parts of the world, business is all about personal relationships, where businesspeople will only do deals with people they get to know well, feel at ease with and trust.

Secondly, moving on to the contract itself … for some, this is expected to be a formal, written, legal document, which outlines the responsibilities, duties and deadlines of all concerned. In other cultures, it's the handshake or verbal agreement which is much more important, and in some cases it could be said that a formal contract is seen as a sign of a lack of trust or respect. A contract may also be the sign of the *beginning* of a business relationship rather than the final stage in the conclusion of a deal. In fact, in some cultures, the signing of the contract is a signal that negotiating for better terms can now begin! It is really an intention to do business and nothing more. Similarly, it may be claimed that because the person who signed the contract has left the company, then that contract needs to be renegotiated. This is because there is a feeling that contracts are made with individuals rather than with organisations or companies.

Finally, the way that negotiations are conducted can vary. I know my colleague spoke at length this morning about body language, eye contact and the role of silence, but it's also important to bear in mind the social aspect. Should you greet your new business partners using first names, surnames or by titles? The amount of time allowed for small talk is another issue to consider. Handshakes can be too soft and be seen as untrustworthy, or too strong and therefore overly assertive. Gift-giving is expected in some countries, but viewed negatively and suspiciously in others. One last point is whether it's more usual to negotiate in teams, rather than alone. Are decisions made by consensus or by one person? It may also be that the person doing the talking is not the decision-maker. So all these things …

Market Leader Extra: Business skills
Audio script Upper Intermediate

1.1 SMALL TALK

BSA1.1.1 (JO = JEFF OLD, PC = PROFESSOR CHAUDRI)

JO Hello, excuse me, I'm Jeff Old from Bador International. Are you Professor Chaudri?
PC Yes, I am. How do you do?
JO Pleased to meet you. I was given your name by a colleague, George Landers.
PC Oh, yes, we met at a conference last year. How is he?
JO Er ... oh, very well. He says 'hello'.
PC That's nice. Have you worked together long?
JO About two years. He suggested I give you a call.
PC How's his family? I believe he has three children now.
JO Yes, he does.
PC Do you have family, Mr Old?
JO Um ... I'm not married, Professor. Not yet, anyway.
PC Ah, so you're engaged then?
JO Well ... er ... um ...
PC That's OK, I didn't mean to embarrass you, Mr Old. I forget how the British like to get straight to the point. You said George gave you my name. How can I help you?
JO We're looking to set up branch offices in India and he told me you might be able to help me navigate my way around the system.
PC I can do my best, certainly. Here's my card. E-mail me when you are planning to visit.
JO Thank you so much. That's very kind of you. Here's mine.
PC Thank you. Have you got George's phone number by any chance? He wrote his number down for me when he ran out of cards, but I can't make head nor tail of his writing and I'd like to contact him before I go back to India.
JO Oh dear. Yes, here it is. I'll write it on the back of my card. I'll make sure my writing is clear! Thank you.

BSA1.1.2 (JO = JEFF OLD, CH = CHIZUKO HAYASHI, WC = WAYNE COULTER)

WC This is a great venue for a conference, isn't it? I'm Wayne Coulter, by the way, from the San Francisco division.
JO Wayne, hi, I'm Jeff Old. I think we met briefly at that conference in Dubai last year. Can I introduce you to Chizuko Hayashi. She works in the Tokyo design division. Ms Hayashi, this is Wayne Coulter from the San Francisco division.
WC Chizuko, great to meet you at last. I've heard good things about you from colleagues in the Tokyo office. How are you?
CH Very well, thank you, Mr Coulter.
WC Please, call me Wayne. Everyone does.
CH I prefer Mr Coulter if you don't mind.
WC Haven't we met somewhere before?
CH I don't think so, Mr Coulter. I would have remembered, I'm sure.
WC Sorry, I must be mistaken. You look familiar. I was sure I'd met you before ...
JO Ms Hayashi, I believe you're interested in visiting the Design exhibition in York.
CH Yes, I'd like to, but I don't think it opens before I return to Japan.
JO Well, there's a private viewing the day after tomorrow if you'd like to go.
CH Don't I need an invitation?
JO Yes, but I know someone on the committee who can arrange it for you. Why don't I give him a call now?
CH That would be wonderful. Thank you.
WC Any chance of you getting me an invite, too? I'd love to go.
JO Oh, I've arranged for you to meet the other members of our production team tomorrow as you expressed an interest in meeting them.
WC Oh, of course. I forgot. No problem.
CH Well, if you'll excuse me, please, Mr Old, Mr Coulter. I must go and speak to Ms Jones over there.
WC Good to have met you, Ms Hayashi.
CH You too, Mr Coulter.
JO I'll e-mail you the invitation and all the details for the York exhibition later tonight.
CH Thank you. Bye for now.
JO Bye. Are you free for a drink later, Wayne? We need to discuss the new project.
WC Yes. Meet you in the bar at seven?

BSA1.1.3 (JO = JEFF OLD, PC = PROFESSOR CHAUDRI, EF = EMILIA FULLER, LC = LOK CHEN, CH = CHIZUKO HAYASHI)

JO Ms Hayashi, I don't believe you've met Professor Chaudri, have you?
CH No, I haven't. Pleased to meet you, Professor Chaudri.
PC Nice to meet you, too, Ms Hayashi. I've heard a lot about you. Jeff speaks very highly of your work.
JO And this is Lok Chen from our Beijing office.
PC Pleased to meet you, Mr Chen. Have you been to one of these conferences before?
LC No, I haven't.
JO Professor, I think you and Ms Hayashi have something in common. You've both won awards for design.
PC Oh, really? Congratulations, Ms Hayashi.
CH If you don't mind my asking, what was your award?
PC It was for our new office building. What about yours?
CH A little different I think. It was for a computer advertising campaign.
EF Hello, everyone.
JO Oh, hello, Emilia. I'd like you all to meet our Design Director. Emilia Fuller. Emilia, Ms Hayashi, Mr Chen and Professor Chaudri.
EF Ah, but I know Chizuko and Prisha already. Lovely to see you both again.
CH You, too. You're looking very well.
PC Yes, you are. How's business?
EF Very good at the moment, thanks.
CH Mr Chen has won an award, too.
LC Well, er ... Our company has.
EF Excellent.
CH Mr Chen is too modest. He was the lead designer on that project. He's very talented.
EF Really? You'll have to tell us more. Now tell me, Chizuko, last time we met, you'd just won your award, hadn't you? I hear you've just won one, too, Prisha. That's great.
PC Thank you, Emilia.
EF Well deserved I say. It's a beautiful building.
PC Mr Chen, what was your award for?
LC Erm ... well ... We designed a park for a new town.
PC Oh, that must have been interesting to do.
LC Yes, it was.
EF And how's your family, Prisha?

PC Very well, thank you. The children are growing up fast. What about yours?

EF The same. All well, thanks. John has just got into a new school, so we're very happy.

PC Chizuko, are you married?

CH Er ... no.

EF How are your parents Chizuko?

CH Getting a little older by the day, but they're well, thanks.

1.2 E-MAILS

BSA1.2.4 (I = Interviewer, JH = John Harrison)

I In your opinion, John, is e-mail better than face-to-face meetings for problem solving in international teams?

JH Good question. Most managers complain about the e-mails they receive at work: there are too many, usually badly written and all too easily creating bad feeling among colleagues. Yet it may be the messenger more than the medium that's causing the problem.

I What do you mean exactly?

JH Well, recent research, curiously, has indicated that e-mail has many advantages over face-to-face interactions, particularly as a problem-solving tool in international teams, with three seen as 'big advantages'.

I ... and they are?

JH Firstly, e-mails can allow senders to put down on paper all their ideas and support these with relevant data in the form of attachments. This is important as it helps face-to-face discussions to be effective. In meetings without pre-presentations of ideas by e-mail, we found that people listen poorly, interrupt more often and generally just push their own solution.

I I see. How interesting.

JH Additionally, e-mail is a slower process, which allows more time for creative and analytical thinking in groups, more so than in meetings when time pressure to solve the problem and take a decision acts against open and creative thinking.

I That makes sense. So what's the third big advantage?

JH Importantly, for non-native English speakers, often marginalised in meetings with their US and UK colleagues, e-mail gives them an equal place and voice in the exchange of ideas and possible solutions. This is because people get more time to digest and understand text, rather than having to cope with the high-speed noise of typical exchanges. E-mails, however, only have the advantage if they're well-written.

I Thanks for your time.

2.1 NEGOTIATIONS

BSA2.1.5 (AL = Alan, AG = Agata)

AL So, Agata, you've been with us for six months now. You've done some excellent work as a Key Account Manager.

AG Thanks.

AL You seem to have adapted well to the team. How has it been from your point of view?

AG Well, I get on well with everyone, I've got a lot of initiative, I'm organised and I've got a very good relationship with the client. However, now that six months have gone by, erm ... I'm not sure how to put this ...

AL Go on. The point of this job appraisal interview is that we can be frank about how things are going for you.

AG OK. Well, to be honest, I was hoping you'd pay a little more.

AL I see. Erm ... what did you have in mind?

AG I was thinking 10 per cent.

AL Sorry, I didn't catch that.

AG I'd like a 10 per cent salary increase please. That's what Kumar got last month.

AL Yes, but Kumar has been working for us for three years.

AG I know, but I think you'll agree I've brought a lot to the company in a short time, and I've negotiated a contract with a big client. Kumar's great, but I know my sales are almost double his ...

AL Yes, but sales are not the same as profits. Kumar's client is actually more profitable for the company.

AG Another thing, Kumar's always joking about me in front of the others ...

AL Well, he does have a particular sense of humour. Let's keep on track about your situation, Agata, rather than discussing Kumar. The thing is, I'd love to pay all my team more, but you haven't been here long. You've done well, but you still have a lot to learn ...

AG I realise that. I'm prepared to do more training. If I did some sales training, I'm sure I'd bring in even more clients!

AL Are you saying you would like to be promoted?

AG That's right.

AL Let's look at this another way. You're already a Key Account Manager, the next step would be Assistant Sales Manager, but that is Kumar's position.

AG So what you're saying is, you can't offer me a salary increase at the moment. Would you be prepared to consider performance-related pay?

AL Well, you already get a five per cent commission on sales.

AG Yes, but my client brings in more sales than Kumar's clients. I don't think it's fair that he earns more than me.

AL I see.

BSA2.1.6 (AL = Alan, AG = Agata)

AL Agata, can I ask a question? Are you happy working here?

AG Er ... yes. I love my job and I want to stay motivated. However, if I don't see the opportunity for a pay rise in the future, that's not very motivating, is it?

AL Right. Let's see what we've got so far. You would be interested in doing another training course and you are suggesting performance-related pay. On the other hand, you seem upset that Kumar was promoted instead of you, although he's been with the company for longer and has more experience.

AG I guess, that's right.

AL The thing is, pay is not the only benefit here, is it? We provide training and help new staff, we organise staff appraisals, there's a positive working atmosphere. We also do fun events, like the fun run and the karaoke evening last month. You can also take unpaid leave if you want to go on a longer holiday and there's the pension scheme we offer ...

AG Yes, I realise that.

AL There would be other benefits if you became a manager. If you worked for us for three years, you'd get free parking and free gym membership.

AG That would be great, Alan, if I had a car, or if I were interested in going to the gym ... This is a great company to work for if you want to meet young people. Don't get me wrong, I think you're a fair boss, but I'd like to feel more valued and I'd like to be able to save for the future.

AL We value your good work, Agata, but 10 per cent seems very high ... I'd like to make a proposal. I think we should leave this discussion for a few months and come back to it later. OK?

BSA2.1.7 (AL = Alan, AG = Agata)

AG So, what you're saying is you won't be able to give me a pay rise now, but I'll get an increase in a few months' time?

AL Not exactly. I'm saying that we can discuss your situation again, providing you continue to perform well in the next six months.

AG So, would you be prepared to talk again at the end of the year?

AL Sure, I can't promise you that you'll get a salary increase, although we can certainly discuss it again.

AG Do you think you'll introduce performance-related pay in the future?

AL I'll suggest your proposal to management and we'll discuss it with you at the end of the year.

AG In the meantime, do you think I could have my own desk, Alan? Hot desking is really inconvenient ...

AL Well, as you know, the sales team are often out of the office, visiting clients. Hot desking is the company policy and most people don't mind it.

AG In that case, can I make a suggestion? I'd like to work from home one day a week. It's difficult to concentrate in the office and I could get my weekly reports done more quickly at home without distractions. Susie does it.

AL Well, Susie has small children ... I think that would be doable. Which day of the week?

AG Fridays.

AL We usually have meetings on Fridays.

AG Thursday then?

AL Fine. Starting next week. As long as you send the reports on time! Anything else?

AG Just one more thing. It would be really useful if I did some more sales training. The induction course you give us when we start is pretty basic. There's one on Negotiation techniques.

AL Yes, good idea.

AG So, to sum up, I'll work from home on Thursdays as from next week. I'll do the course next month. We'll talk about a possible pay increase and performance-related pay in six months' time.

AL That's right.

AG I'll put that in writing for us both.

AL Good idea. I'll confirm what we've agreed.

AG Thanks for your time Alan.

2.2 TELECONFERENCES

BSA2.2.8 (FK = Frances King, DG = Dave Green, LD = Luc Delacour, GA = Godfrey Allardyce)

FK Good afternoon. This is Frances here. I'm leading the call from the UK office in Hemel Hempstead. Luc, are you on the call?

LD Hello, Frances. Yes, I'm here.

FK Oh, good. How are things in Geneva?

LD Just fine, but we need to keep this quite quick, I'm afraid. I have a meeting in half an hour from now.

FK No problem. Godfrey, are you there?

GA Hello, everyone. Yes, I am. Though I must say it's awfully early for a conference call. It's only 8.00 a.m. here in the US.

FK Sorry about that Godfrey, but it was hard to find a time to suit everyone. If you will insist on going off to conferences ...

GA OK, point taken, Frances.

FK So, shall we get started? As you know, we have to fill the very important position of Head of Fundraising here in the UK and I would like your views on the two candidates as we need to decide soon. Dave, who holds this position now, will be retiring in five weeks from now. Our two choices are Annabel Maitland, who is currently Dave's Deputy, or Julian Huntley, who was suggested by a headhunter and who currently works as the Head of Fundraising for the British branch of the water charity Aqua Help.

GA/LD: Well, I think ... In my view ...

LD Go ahead, Godfrey.

GA No, that's OK, Luc. After you.

LD Thank you. Well, in my view, we need somebody with a lot of experience of fundraising. For a fundraiser, the field the charity operates in is not as important as that person's ability to attract substantial donations. It seems that Julian Huntley has an excellent record in that sense and so my vote goes to him.

FK Thank you, Luc. Godfrey, what do you think?

GA Well, I tend to agree with Luc. Annabel's very talented and a good learner, but she's rather young and inexperienced, so ...

DG I disagree completely. Annabel is thirty-two and she's been with us for seven years, so she's hardly inexperienced and ...

LD Excuse me, who is that speaking? Is there somebody else on this call?

FK Sorry, Luc. Dave, our current Head of Fundraising, just came into the room and would like to join the discussion.

GA/LD: Quite right. Why not? That seems a little ...

GA Sorry, Luc.

LD No problem, Godfrey. Do go on.

GA Yes, I was saying we should let Dave speak. He knows the job better than anyone else. Hello, Dave. Still hanging around the office?

DG I'm still employed, you know, Godfrey. Five weeks to go! Or are you trying to get rid of me early?

GA Certainly not. I say, Dave, you'd love the golf course here in ...

FK I'm sorry, but we've got limited time. Can we come back to the discussion about the two candidates, please, as ...

FK OK, so let me summarise the agreement. Our first choice is that Julian Huntley will be offered a six-month trial contract. Annabel will be moved sideways and become the Head of the Public Relations division. If Julian doesn't accept that idea, Annabel will be offered the position as Head of Fundraising. Do we all agree?

LD Yes, absolutely.

GA Fine with me, too.

DG I still don't think it's fair to Annabel, but OK.

FK Very well, then. I shall send you all a memo summarising our agreement and speak to the two candidates. Thank you all for participating.

LD My pleasure. Goodbye.

GA Bye. See you next week.

DG Bye everyone.

3.1 PRESENTATIONS

BSA3.1.9 (P = Presenter)

P You know, the writer Mark Twain once said there are only two types of speaker in the world. Can you guess what the two types are? Those who are nervous and those who are liars. OK, I know, it's a bit extreme, but it does make the point nicely that most of us feel nervous when giving presentations. One way to look and feel more confident is to be aware of the impact your body language can have on you and your audience.

BSA3.1.10 (P = Presenter)

P Let's take a look at this photo here. Yes, this poor woman is saying one thing with her words and her body language is sending us a completely different message. If she had practised her presentation in front of a mirror, she might have seen that. When people hear one thing and see that your body language, or hear that your tone of voice is not consistent with your verbal message, then they know something is not right and they'll trust the non-verbal message.

This brings me to Professor Albert Mehrabian's communications model. You may have seen this pie chart, or you might have heard the statistic that only seven per cent of the impact of our message comes from what we say. Really? Have you ever stopped to think about that? Can it possibly be true? Well, obviously, the answer is no. This is a myth which is repeated time and again. Let me put the record straight. Firstly, Mehrabian's findings were not related to *all* communication, but only when we talk about our attitudes and feelings. Secondly, his point was that if your verbal message is inconsistent with your tone of voice and your facial expression – for instance, if you say you are happy, but your voice and face don't reflect that message – then other people will trust the non-verbal clues more than the words you use. It's simply not true to suggest that the words we use in a presentation are a minor part of the message. In fact, they are and will always be the most important part.

So, as you can see on this next slide, there are many aspects of body language to think about – the way you stand, move your head, your facial expressions, how much eye contact you make with your audience, how you move your hands. Good hand gestures can help emphasise your points. I'd like to add just one more point and that's 'whole body movement'. We know we can use head motion and hand gesture to emphasise points, but you know you can also use body movement for good impact too. One neat technique is to move to a different position in the room when you want to introduce a new point. Did you notice that I just did that? This helps to signal the transition and keep the audience's attention. However, if you stand completely rigid and stare at one spot in the room, you'll be like a rabbit caught in headlights. If you move around a lot like this, you'll look like an animal in a cage. Both these types of body language are very distracting for any audience. Moving on to my final point for today. You know, using confident body language doesn't just make you look more confident, it actually has an effect on the chemicals in your brain so that it makes you feel more confident, too. This was demonstrated by American psychologist Amy Cuddy, whose experiments found that simply standing in a posture of confidence, with legs apart and hands on hips, can affect testosterone and cortisol levels in the brain. I'm not suggesting you adopt this posture actually during the presentation, but if you spend a few minutes in this 'power pose' before a presentation, you might notice the difference in your confidence next time. Try it and see.

3.2 MEETINGS

BSA3.2.11 (A = Amita)

A Hi everyone, let's get started. I hope you've all had a chance to read the agenda. Our aim today is to brainstorm ideas for a 40-second advert for High Flyers, our newest client. First, I'll ask Vijay to run us through the service and its target market. I'm sure that'll start to stimulate some of our creativity! Next, Sara's going to talk us through the budget and the filming schedule. After that, all we need to do is dream up a wonderful storyline for this advert and choose the filming location. We've got three hours for this meeting.

BSA3.2.12 (A = Amita, V = Vijay, S = Sara, I = Isabella)

A Right, I'll hand over to Vijay to tell us about the service. Vijay.

V Thank you, Amita. Well our client is a Swiss consultancy with a 15-year reputation in running management seminars and workshops ...

I Mmm. I'm not sure that's going to fuel our creativity. It's a pity it couldn't have been a more inspiring industry like travel, or something.

A Isabella, if you let Vijay finish, you might find that this client's service is a little bit more interesting than it sounds.

V Yes, actually, Isabella, you might be interested to know that their particular area of expertise is in setting up exotic team-building workshops for newly recruited executive teams. You know, those events where you have to abseil down Mt Kilimanjaro tied to one of your global counterparts before canoeing the length of Lake Tanganyika with them. The consultancy has become well established in Northern Europe, but its management now feel ready to go global. In fact, their goal is pretty ambitious – to be the number one management training consultancy in the world in five years' time. No prizes for guessing who the target market is ... senior executives, their HR departments, not to mention potential training consultants. Well, that's my bit done. I hope I managed to inspire you!

A Isabella, any comment?

I Yes, well done Vijay. That's great! This project sounds a lot more exciting now. Let's hope the budget doesn't change that.

A I don't think it will. Over to you Sara.

S Thanks Amita. Well, I don't think you'll be disappointed, Isabella. The filming budget is a whopping £1 million. I envisage up to four weeks for the shoot and we can schedule it any time over the next eight months. The client is very keen for us to get it right. They want to give us plenty of time to find the right location in the right season. The world is our oyster!

A Thank you Sara. So, let's get brainstorming. They're a pretty exciting client, aren't they? At this stage we want all your ideas, however crazy they are! Isabella, could you write them all up on the whiteboard as we go along?

BSA3.2.13 (A = Amita)

A Those were some of the best ideas I've heard for a long time. I think three storylines should be enough. So, we've now got a week to write outline briefs and prepare our pitches for the client. Vijay, if you could work on the Saharan storyline, Sara take the Mongolian one and Isabella the Amazonian one. Let's schedule a meeting for Tuesday to do a first run-through of them. Could you all send me your written briefs by Monday lunchtime? Good work everybody!

4.1 INTERVIEWS

BSA4.1.14 (N = Narrator, I = Interviewer, S1/2/3/4/5 = Speaker 1/2/3/4/5)

N 1

I What did you enjoy most about your last job?

S1 Oh ... Well, I've never really thought about that before ... Um ... I suppose the best thing about my old company was the restaurant?

N 2

I Why do you want this particular job?

S2 I'd absolutely love to work for this company! It has such a great reputation! I mean, there are so many other companies out there doing the same thing as you, but I just think this place is the best!

N 3

I Tell me about your present job.

S3 I've been out of work for six months, but in that time, I've taken some courses online to update my skills and I think I'm in a stronger position now than I was at the beginning of the year.

N 4

I Why did you leave your last job?

S4 I didn't really like my old job, so I decided to leave.

N 5

I Tell me about your current job.

S5 Well, I haven't worked for the last two years. It's been a tough time. Of course I want to work. But it's been hard.

BSA4.1.15 (N = Narrator, I = Interviewer, C1/2 = Candidate 1/2)

N 1

I Why should I hire you and not the other applicants?

C1 I know I can learn easily and I'll be good at this job.

I The standard of applicants has been very high this year.

C1 I have top grades in my studies – I think that says it all.

I So, let's look at your university record.

N 2

I Do you think you're overqualified for this position?

C2 I think I have the skills and experience that you need to do a great job and hopefully make a real difference to this company, reducing costs and increasing profitability.

I What about the salary though?

C2 These are tough economic times and we're all having to learn to live on less. So, yes, I was fully aware of the salary when I applied.

BSA4.1.16 (N = Narrator, I = Interviewer, C = Candidate)

I So, do you have any questions you wanted to ask us?

C Yes, I do actually. I wanted to ask what do you enjoy most about working for this company?

I Well, I've been here for four years and in that time, I've never had a dull day. The job is constantly changing and there's been a lot of support from the company to take my career forward.

4.2 PRESENTATIONS

BSA4.2.17 (P = Presenter)

P As you all know, we are one of the country's leading retailers of bicycles and cycling products. You may not know that our company faces an uphill climb today. I'd like to draw your attention to this chart.
As you can see, our full year pre-tax profit was just over £25.9 million in the twelve months to 31st March. That's down by 22% on last year. Last year's drop in profits was down by more than 27% on the previous year.
What's more, as you can see in this graph, in ten of the last twelve quarters we have had falling sales. There's no doubt that this performance is worrying, but it's also a challenge to gear up and get moving.
Today, I'd like to outline a three-point turnaround plan. My proposal is to raise annual sales from £312 million to a target of half a billion pounds within the next four years. How? By investing in three key areas of business: our stores, our staff and our IT systems. This will come at a cost to shareholders in the short term. We will need to cut the dividend for the next three years. However, long term, the benefits will be much greater. Let me explain ...

BSA4.2.18 and BSA4.2.19 (shown in bold)
(P = Presenter)

P As you all know, we are one of the country's leading retailers of bicycles and cycling products. What you may not know is that our company faces an uphill climb today. I'd like to draw your attention to this chart.
As you can see, our full year pre-tax profit was just over £25.9 million in the twelve months to 31st March. That's down by 22% on last year. Last year's drop in profits was down by more than 27% on the previous year.
What's more, as you can see in this graph, in ten of the last twelve quarters we've had falling sales. There's no doubt that this performance is worrying, but it's also a challenge to gear up and get moving.
Today, I'd like to outline a three-point turnaround plan. My proposal is to raise annual sales from £312 million to a target of half a billion pounds within the next four years. How? By investing in three key areas of business: our stores, our staff and our IT systems. This will come at a cost to shareholders in the short term. We will need to cut the dividend for the next three years. However, long term, the benefits will be much greater. Let me explain ...
Let's start by looking at our stores. Over the past six months my team and I have visited over one hundred stores nationwide. We've observed and we've talked to managers, staff and customers. Frankly, today our shops look worn out and poorly designed. In total, 150 of our stores need refurbishment to improve the shopping experience and the bicycle repair service. We calculate the store revamps will cost around £18 million in total over the next three to four years. A detailed breakdown of the investment is included in my report.
Turning now to our sales staff. Did you know that 22% of our new recruits leave the company within the first three months? Not only do we have that, but customers regularly complain about the lack of knowledge of our staff. Clearly, we need to invest in our people. I propose an initial two-month training programme for all new recruits on joining the company. Staff will then earn pay rises by completing further training. My target is to reduce staff turnover by half and create a friendly, expert sales and repair team. By investing a further £10 million in staff training, we will have a positive impact on staff morale, be able to expand the bicycle repair service and greatly improve our customer service and reputation. That brings me to my third point – our IT systems, in particular our website. Our biggest rivals today are online sellers, therefore we have to improve the company's website, supply chain and stock availability by investing £8 million in IT systems and infrastructure. We need to become an integrated multichannel business if we are going to stand any chance of competing in the future. Again, you'll find a detailed cost breakdown in my report.
To sum up, if we invest a total of £36 million in these three key areas, our stores, our staff and last, but not least, our IT systems, we will turn this company around in the next four years. Doing nothing is not an option. If we want to see big improvements in our performance, we need to invest in our business. As I mentioned in my introduction, we will need to cut the shareholder dividend by 35% for the next three years. Yes, I know the dividend is important to shareholders. I am also a shareholder and I will also lose out. However, if we do not address years of underinvestment, the company is highly likely to suffer even more and we will all lose out: staff, customers and you, our investors. I'd like to end by saying that our single most important objective is to drive profitable sales growth. Today, I'm asking for your patience and trust so that we can transform this company and achieve this objective. Thank you very much for your attention.

BSA4.2.20 (N = Narrator, P = Presenter)

N 1

P However, long term, the benefits will be much greater. Let me explain. Let's start by looking at our stores. Over the past six months my team and I have visited over one hundred stores nationwide.

N 2

P A detailed breakdown of the investment is included in my report. Turning now to our sales staff. Did you know that 22% of our new recruits leave the company within the first three months?

N 3

P By investing a further £10 million in staff training, we will have a positive impact on staff morale, be able to expand the bicycle repair service and greatly improve our customer service and reputation. That brings me to my third point – our IT systems, in particular our website.

N 4

P Again, you'll find a detailed cost breakdown in my report. To sum up, if we invest a total of £36 million in these three key areas, our stores, our staff and last, but not least, our IT systems, we will turn this company around in the next four years.

N 5

P However, if we do not address years of underinvestment, the company will suffer even more and we will all lose out! staff, customers and you, our investors. I'd like to end by saying that our single most important objective is to drive profitable sales growth.

1.2 E-mails

D WRITING

Dear Elio

Hope you are well.

Many thanks for your recent email and project update. It was good to hear that everything is currently on schedule. However, I share your concerns about the coming weeks with one project member leaving, and a busy time with local initiatives about to hit. These are likely to have a negative impact on the project and may put you behind schedule.

Thanks for your specific proposal to extend the project deadline by two months. It's a possibility, but it will be difficult to change deadlines agreed with our management board. We can certainly discuss this at the next team meeting. In advance, I would propose a 1:1 call just to go over the issues again, get more background information, and think through other solutions.

Shall we try to talk tomorrow morning around lunch in advance of the main meeting? After our 1:1 call I can then write an email to all the sub-project leads with a quick overview of project status, and give some suggestions on what are the priorities to discuss.

Best regards

Paul

2.1 Negotiations

B SPEAKING 2

Student A – Key Account Manager

- You are a Key Account Manager who has been working for the company Big Ideas for six months. You think you are good at your job, you enjoy the work, but would like a 10% salary rise. Otherwise, you will start looking for another job with better opportunities.
- Someone in your department with similar skills has been promoted recently but you haven't. In addition, your Sales Manager has free parking, free gym membership and a pension scheme but you don't.
- Other employees seem happy with the company benefits, e.g. flexible working hours, and the atmosphere at work, but this isn't enough for you. You hope to buy a flat next year.
- Aim high and establish what you want to achieve in the negotiation, e.g. a 10% pay rise, the chance of a future promotion and/or better working conditions. Your thinking is, '*If you don't ask, you don't get.*'

2.1 Negotiations

E LISTENING 2

Dear Alan

Many thanks for your feedback in my job [1]........... interview this morning. It was a very useful discussion. However, I understand that, for the [2]..........., the company is unable to offer me a salary [3]..........., or my own [4]........... .

I'd like to [5]........... what I understood from our conversation. Firstly, we agreed that I would work from home on [6]........... as from next [7]........... in order to be able to work more efficiently. Secondly, I would be interested in attending your [8]........... course on [9]........... techniques next month. I think this will really help me improve my performance. Thirdly, we said we would talk again about a possible [10]........... increase and/or performance- [11]........... pay in [12]........... months' time.

Finally, I'd like to take the opportunity to say that in the last six months, I've reached all my [13]........... targets, I've negotiated successfully with a key [14]..........., I have performed consistently and have outperformed many of my work [15]........... .

Please confirm that I've understood everything correctly. Thanks again for your time.

Best wishes

Agata Buchwald

2.1 Negotiations

B SPEAKING 2

Student B – Sales Manager

- You are the manager of a Key Account Manager who has been working for the company Big Ideas for six months. He or she is effective in the job and has managed the client well so far.
- Sales staff get a 5% commission. In addition, Big Ideas is a fun company that offers benefits that are not pay-related, e.g. flexi-time, sales training, unpaid leave and there's a positive atmosphere at work.
- You got a promotion after three years. Now, as Sales Manager, you're entitled to free parking, a pension scheme and free gym membership.
- Establish what you want to achieve in the negotiation, e.g. lower the employee's expectations, say 'no' politely, but leave the door open for a future discussion. In any case, there are lots of people with similar CVs. Your thinking is, '*You don't always get what you want.*'

4.1 Interviews

D SPEAKING 2

Student A

1. **You owned a sound and light engineering company which went out of business three months ago. You were your own boss for eight years. You have applied to join a television production company. Student B is interviewing you. Think about:**
   - the skills and qualities you have learnt from the experience
   - the reasons you went out of business
   - how to address the worries the interviewer might have (that you won't take instruction well, that you're not a team player, that you might not fit the corporate culture, etc.)
2. **You are going to interview Student B for a job as an engineer in an aerospace company. They have only ever worked in the military until now, and you are concerned that they might not fit in with your company culture. Ask them about their experience in the military to try and get more information.**

2.1 Negotiations

TASK

Group A

- You are a Key Account Manager at Big Ideas. You have been working for this dynamic company for 12 months. You are excellent at your job, you have completed further sales training and have outperformed many of your colleagues.
- You asked your previous Sales Manager, Alan, for a 10% salary rise six months' ago. You didn't get it but you agreed to discuss this again at the end of the year. You hope you will now get a salary increase and/or performance-related pay.
- Unfortunately, Alan has left the company and the Assistant Sales Manager has taken his place. He or she now has free parking, free gym membership and a pension scheme but you don't.
- Be realistic in your aims and establish what you want to achieve in the negotiation, e.g. a 10% pay rise, be promoted to Assistant Sales Manager, and/or better working conditions. Your thinking is, '*I need to play my cards right.*'

2.2 Teleconferences

TASK

International Public Relations Manager

You are the International Public Relations Manager of a successful educational technology company. You work at the company's head office in New York. The other participants are your colleagues.

You keep forgetting people's names.

Regional Marketing Manager

You are the Regional Marketing Manager of a successful educational technology company whose head office is in the US. You work in Germany. The other participants are your colleagues.

You have another conference call scheduled so are under pressure of time to reach an agreement.

Local Marketing Manager

You are the Local Marketing Manager of a successful educational technology company whose head office is in the US. You work in London. The other participants are your colleagues.

You have trouble with your connection and can't always hear properly.

Local Public Relations Manager

You are the Local Public Relations Manager of a successful educational technology company whose head office is in the US. You work in China. The other participants are your colleagues.

You can't always hear when other participants are speaking and you keep interrupting.

2.1 Negotiations

TASK

Group B

- You are the Manager of a Key Account Manager at Big Ideas. He or she is very good at the job and has managed the client well in the last 12 months. He or she is also one of the few team members that works from home one day a week.
- After Alan left the company you have been promoted because you're good at motivating your team. Now, as Sales Manager, you're entitled to free parking, free gym membership and a pension scheme.
- You need to take on an Assistant Sales Manager, although you're not sure if you can work with this Key Account Manager who sometimes seems unhappy and criticises other people on the team.
- Establish what you want to achieve in the negotiation, e.g. agree to promoting her with a salary increase, introduce performance-related pay for all sales staff, or say 'no' but leave the door open for future discussion. Your thinking is, '*I need someone I can work with.*'

4.2 Presentations

PRE-TASK

A According to market research in the UK, the sale of new cycles was worth £745 million last year. The value of this market has increased by a healthy 14% in the past five years. At the same time, many cyclists are also buying higher quality bikes. This boom in bike sales looks due to continue, with sales forecast for the next five years predicting a further 22% increase, bringing the total value to £909 million.

B The triumph of British cyclists in the Tour de France and other international events in recent years has driven interest in cycling throughout the UK. A growing number of competitive events and sponsored rides, such as the annual '100-mile Ride London' event have encouraged more people to get on their bikes or go out and buy new cycles. A recent survey shows that 10% of cyclists have participated in a sponsored ride and 8% have taken part in a competitive cycle ride.

C There is still a great deal of potential in the bike market as Britain trails behind countries with similar geography, climate and population density. According to the latest National Transport Survey, slightly over one in three (35%) Brits are cyclists. Almost half (49%) of 25–34 year olds cycle which makes this Britain's main cycling group. Men are nearly three times more likely to ride a bicycle than women. The gender difference is greatest amongst 11–21 year olds.

3.1 Presentations

D SPEAKING 2

Student A

1 **Make a statement (written in bold) about time management to your partner. Then listen and check if your partner gives the correct supporting details (in *italics*).**

- **You know, getting more things done is not about multi tasking.**
(*This was demonstrated by Professor Clifford Nass at Stanford University, whose experiments found high multi taskers consistently achieved less than low multi taskers.*)
- **It is essential to know what your job priorities really are.**
(In the words of General Dwight D. Eisenhower, '*What is important is seldom urgent and what is urgent is seldom important*').
- **Digital technologies are eroding our ability to concentrate at work today.**
(*On average American information workers now switch their attention every 59.5 seconds between email, social media and other digital distractions, according to a recent study from the University of California.*)
- **There are many useful time-management tools available.**
(*I would like to show you the Pomodoro Technique. You set a kitchen timer for 25 minutes of focused, uninterrupted work and gradually build up from there. Try it and see.*)

2 **Now your partner will make some statements about stress. Listen to the statements and for each one give the correct supporting details from 1–4 below.**

1 Well, this has been demonstrated by research showing that laughter reduces stress hormones.

2 As my family photo here shows, life-changing events like having a baby can be stressful, but these are ultimately good for you.

3 Notice how simply breathing deeply like this can help to calm your mind and body.

4 Research by the Mental Health Foundation indicates that 59% of British adults say their life is more stressful than it was five years ago.

4.2 Presentations

C SPEAKING 2

Student A

1 **You and your partner work for a supermarket chain called FoodCo. Read the business contexts, 1–3, and match them with proposals a–c.**

Business contexts

1 Our tinned goods sales are down by ten per cent on last year.

2 The government wants food retailers to respond to concerns about obesity.

3 We have started manufacturing our own brand ice-creams.

Proposals

a Redesign packaging to make nutritional labelling clearer.

b Have a new advertising campaign on TV.

c Offer three for two offers to boost sales.

2 **Present each business context and your suggested proposal to your partner using the following linking expressions.**

Let's start by looking at ...

Turning now to ...

That brings me to my third point.

3 **Listen to your partner's presentation and suggested proposals and make notes. What do you think about their business ideas? Do you have any questions?**

3.1 Presentations

D SPEAKING 2

Student B

1 **Your partner will make some statements about time management. Listen, and for each statement, give the correct supporting details from 1–4 below.**

1 I would like to show you the Pomodoro Technique. You set a kitchen timer for 25 minutes of focused, uninterrupted work and gradually build up from there. Try it and see.

2 This was demonstrated by Professor Clifford Nass at Stanford University, whose experiments found high multi taskers consistently achieved less than low multi taskers.

3 In the words of General Dwight D. Eisenhower, 'What is important is seldom urgent and what is urgent is seldom important.'

4 On average American information workers now switch their attention every 59.5 seconds between email, social media and other digital distractions, according to a recent study from the University of California.

2 **Now make a statement (written in bold) about stress to your partner. Then listen and check if your partner gives the correct supporting details (in *italics*).**

- **We often overlook simple and effective relaxation techniques in our hectic lives.**
  (Notice how simply breathing deeply like this can help to calm your mind and body.)
- **It is important to recognise the difference between good stress and bad stress.**
  (As my family photo here shows, life-changing events like having a baby can be stressful, but these are ultimately good for you.)
- **You may have heard the saying, 'laughter is the best medicine'.**
  (Well, this has been demonstrated by research showing that laughter reduces stress hormones.)
- **The economic situation is making work-life balance more difficult.**
  (Research by the Mental Health Foundation indicates that 59% of British adults say their life is more stressful than it was five years ago.)

4.2 Presentations

C SPEAKING 2

Student B

1 **You and your partner work for a supermarket chain called FoodCo. Read the business contexts, 1–3, and match them with proposals a–c.**

Business contexts

1 Parents complain about sweet treats placed by the checkout.

2 The government wants retailers to promote sustainability.

3 Ten per cent of customers abandon the company website before completing online shopping.

Proposals

a Put healthy snacks by the tills.

b Revamp the website to keep a record of customers' preferences and make it more user friendly.

c Charge five pence per plastic bag.

2 **Listen to your partner's presentation and suggested proposals and make notes. What do you think about their business ideas? Do you have any questions?**

3 **Present each business context and your suggested proposal to your partner using the following linking expressions.**

The first point I want to look at is ...

Moving on to ...

Last, but not least ...

3.1 Presentations

PRE-TASK Exercise 2

What are some of the things you can do to manage your time better?

'People get bogged down in tasks that are urgent but not important' and they never take the time out to think,' says Camilla Arnold, head of coaching at TXG, a leadership consultancy. This is a mistake. 'Forward planning and strategy allow you to decide what you are good at, what you will be judged on and what will move your career forward. They are very important – the trouble is, they are rarely urgent.'

Professional organiser Standolyn Robertson says that you should draw up a master list of things you want to do. 'In the evening, look at your list and decide what you need to accomplish the next day,' she says. 'Start the day with a plan in place – and let yourself do the things you enjoy once you've finished the things you have to do.'

How do I organise information?

Ms Robertson says you should not over-think this. 'Most people try and come up with a perfect system, but all you need is a way of retrieving information when you want it. It has to be good enough.' She adds that having one version of documents is best. 'Electronic files should mirror paper files. Do not be an electronic hoarder.'

'Treat your workspace as flexi-space, even if it is your own desk,' advises Francine Jay, author of *The Joy of Less*. 'Clear it at the end of the day. This has the effect of clearing your mental space too ... Go paperless, track things like expenses electronically and treat your laptop as your office. It is very freeing not to let stuff pile up.'

How do I deal with work that involves demands from others?

Ms Jay says that you need to be a bit hard. 'Learn to say no to people. Saying no to unimportant things means that you can say yes to important things.' She adds that you should also learn to ask what it is in it for you. 'You do not always have to benefit, but it will help you narrow things down.'

Ms Robertson cautions that you should be wary of the false sense of ease that comes with long deadlines. 'Don't agree to do things just because they are so far in the future that it's easy to say yes.'

How to streamline communications and social media

'Try and touch e-mail once and deal with it rather than letting it accumulate,' says Ms Jay. 'Set yourself limits and do not check it after a certain hour.' You should be selective about your social media. 'Stick to two or three outlets. Do not spread yourself too thin.'

Ms Robertson says a lot of electronic clutter is self-generated. 'Stop copying people in unnecessarily on e-mails and replying to all. You save other people's time and you do not generate replies. Use subject lines, too.'

SOURCE: Adapted from http://www.ft.com

4.1 Interviews

D SPEAKING 2

Student B

1 **You are going to interview Student A for a job as a sound and light engineer in a television company. They have run their own business for the last eight years and you're worried that they might be uncomfortable working for another person. Ask them about their experience of running their own company and to try and get more information.**

2 **You worked for the military before and this is the first non-military job you have applied for. You want to work as an engineer for an aerospace company. Student A is interviewing you. Think about:**

- the skills you have learnt from your experience in the military
- the qualities you have developed
- how to address the worries the interviewer might have (that you're unfamiliar with business culture, you lack communication skills suitable to an office environment, you won't know about commercial uses of engineering, etc.)

3.2 Meetings

TASK

Meeting leader

1 Use the expressions you have heard and practised in this unit to lead meetings.
2 Open the mini-meeting following the usual meetings procedure.
3 Introduce your product and ask the participants to brainstorm ideas for a storyline.
4 Ask one of the participants to take notes on what is said.
5 Make sure everybody has a chance to give their ideas.
6 At the end of the meeting, summarise the main points and try to reach agreement on the best storyline.
7 Close the meeting in a positive way.

Meeting leader

Name:	
Participating in the meeting	
Strengths	
One point to develop	
Phrases used for:	
1. Opening the meeting	
2. Leading the body of the meeting	
3. Summarising and closing the meeting	

Participant

Name:	
Participating in the meeting	
Strengths	
One point to develop	
Phrases used for:	
1. Giving detailed opinions	
2. Checking comprehension	
3. Showing understanding of the main points	

3.1 Presentations

PRE-TASK Exercise 2

The history of stress

Psychological stress is a twentieth-century invention. Its origins can be traced back to 1920s Montreal, where Hans Selye became convinced that there was a common denominator in all illnesses, which he attributed to the stress hormones released by the body when it was struggling to function properly.

It was not until the late 1950s, however, that John Mason expanded the concept, arguing that emotional states were also the cause of stress responses. The relatively late arrival of this psychological understanding is reflected in the fact that many people still dismiss the whole idea of stress, saying that it is a modern label for what used to be thought of as the ordinary pressures of living.

Fight or flight

Stress has all sorts of negative effects on us. We sense danger and our body goes into fight-or-flight mode, releasing stress hormones that affect our cardiovascular functioning and immune system, eventually for the worse. As a result, many think we should do all we can to banish stress from our lives.

Good and bad stress

However, the idea of 'good stress' – small doses of acute stress – can be helpful, enhancing learning, performance and immune function. American psychologist Kelly McGonigal, in her book *The Upside of Stress*, describes recent experiments in which telling people about the positive aspects of stress can even cause some to feel and function better. Whether stress is good or bad seems to hinge on how long it lasts, so warnings mainly apply if it is ongoing. It is the chronic version we need to avoid. In this case it is important to accept that emotional suffering is real and that there is no shame in seeking the help of others to diminish it.

Reducing stress

So do we need to reduce stress? It seems that in the short term we should learn to view what may appear to be threats as challenges and the reactions of our bodies as helpful rather than sinister. In the long term, however, it may help to re-evaluate situations that are giving rise to chronic stress. McGonigal says that when you do feel stress, do not make matters worse by stressing about that. Reframe the stress as 'excitement' and make it work for you.

We cannot get rid of stress, as it is so intimately connected with attaining purpose in life. However, we should be careful not to be misled into thinking that the stress of busyness automatically signals a life full of valuable pursuits. The most important question we need to ask ourselves regarding any stress-inducing situation we might be facing is how much we value it, or what we may gain from it. It is probably not worth trying to manage the stress caused by things we do not truly value if we could just let them go altogether.

SOURCE: Adapted from http://www.ft.com

4.1 Interviews

TASK, PRE-TASK

INSURE NOW

The position

The opportunity: We have an excellent opportunity for an experienced consultant with a passion for marketing. We're proud of our insurance products and our top-quality customer service. In fact, we think we have the potential to become the UK's number one insurer. We want to communicate that message with both new and loyal customers. Ultimately, our goal in marketing is to gain an in-depth and detailed view of our customers and their needs, and use that knowledge to expand the business.

Your role: Your role is to support the Marketing Manager in communications development, reviewing the performance of our different products against our objectives and initiating new strategies. Other responsibilities will be coordinating media bookings and schedules, and maximising opportunities to work with other media.

Our products: We offer a range of home, motor and pet insurance products.

The candidate will have excellent verbal and written communication skills with the ability to communicate to all stakeholders. He or she should also have experience of budget control and be able to work in a team.

Competitive salary benchmarked against our competitors, which will grow as you do. A range of other career benefits.

TASK, PART 1 Exercise 3

Candidate 1

You have 25 years of experience in media management and marketing. You spent the last 10 years working in the marketing department of a large international bank, but lost your position when the economy took a downturn. You have an excellent record of managing large advertising campaigns with budgets for television commercials and radio and print adverts. A specialist team in the marketing department dealt with media relations and customer data collection, but you used your redundancy money to take a university course to update yourself.

Interviewer

You are the head of Human Resources. You have two candidates applying for the job.

Candidate 1 has the ideal experience, but is much older and you have concerns that they may not have the media literacy skills needed for this position.

Candidate 2 has a strong background in media campaigns and data collection, but your target customers are in the 40–70 age range and this candidate only has experience working with very young customers.

Candidate 2

You have three years of experience and a degree in media communications. You have been working for the last three years in a small media start-up. The company has recently stopped trading, due to the arrival of a major new competitor. You are keen to work for a larger company because you want the opportunity to learn more and get promoted. Your customers for your previous company were in the 16–20 age group, and you have little experience working with older people.

Glossary

- **adjective** *(adj.)* Headwords for adjectives followed by information in square brackets, e.g. *[only before a noun]* and *[not before a noun]*, show any restrictions on where they can be used.
- **noun** *(n.)* The codes *[C]* and *[U]* show whether a noun, or a particular sense of a noun, is countable *(an agenda, two agendas)* or uncountable *(awareness, branding)*.
- **verb** (*v.*) The forms of irregular verbs are given after the headword. The codes *[I]* (intransitive) and *[T]* (transitive) show whether a verb, or a particular sense of a verb, has or does not have an object. Phrasal verbs *(phr.v.)* are shown after the verb they are related to.
- Some entries show information on words that are related to the headword. Adverbs *(adv.)* are often shown in this way after adjectives.
- **region labels** The codes *AmE* and *BrE* show whether a word or sense of a word is used only in American or British English.

account *n.* [C] an arrangement between a bank and a customer that allows the customer to pay in and take out money; **bank account**

accountable *adj.* [not before a noun] responsible for the effects of your actions and willing to explain or be criticised for them; **accountability** *n.* [U]

accounts *n.* [C] the department of a company that deals with its accounts

acquire *v.* [T] **1** to buy a company
2 to buy part of a company

acquisition *n.* [C, U] when one company buys another one, or part of another one

actuary *n.* [C] someone whose job is to calculate risks, in order to advise insurance companies or pension funds

admission of liability *n.* [C] when a person or organisation accepts legal liability for something

advertising campaign *n.* [C] an organisation's programme of advertising activities over a particular period of time with specific aims, for example to increase sales of a product

agenda *n.* [C] **1** a list of the subjects to be discussed at a meeting
2 someone's secret plan or aims, rather than the ones that they say they have

agent *n.* [C] a person or company that is paid by another person or company to represent them in business

appoint *v.* [T] to choose someone for a job or position

assess *v.* [I, T] to make a judgement about a person or situation after considering all the information

asset [1] *n.* [C] something or someone that is useful because they help you succeed or deal with problems

asset [2] *n.* [C] something belonging to an individual or a business that has value or the power to earn money

auction *n.* [C] a public meeting where land, buildings, paintings, etc. are sold to the person who offers the most money for them

audit *n.* [C] an official examination of a person's or organisation's accounts by an expert, to check that they are true and honest

award [1] *n.* [C] **1** an amount of money that is given to someone as a result of an official decision or judgement
2 something such as a prize or an amount of money given to a person or company to reward them for something they have done

award [2] *v.* [T] to officially give a prize or an amount of money to a person or company to reward them for what they have done

backer *n.* [C] someone who supports a plan, person or company, usually by giving money

bankrupt *adj.* not having enough money to pay your debts

bankruptcy *n.* [C, U] when someone is judged to be unable to pay their debts by a court of law, and their assets are shared among the people and businesses that they owe money to

benefit *n.* [C] something, especially money, that an employer gives to workers in addition to their normal pay, to encourage them to work harder or be satisfied where they work

benefits package *n.* [C] the total amount of pay and all the other advantages that an employee may receive, such as bonuses, health insurance, a company car, etc.

bid *n.* [C] an offer by one company to buy another, or the value of this offer

billboard *n.* [C] a large sign used for advertising

bond *n.* [C] an amount of money borrowed by a government or an organisation. The government or organisation produces a document promising that it will pay back the money that it has borrowed, usually with interest. The document, which can be bought and sold, is also called a *bond.*

bond market *n.* [C] the buying and selling of bonds

bondholder *n.* [C] a person or organisation that owns bonds

bonus *n.* [C] an extra amount of money added to an employee's wages, usually as a reward for doing difficult or good work

boost [1] *v.* [T] to increase something such as production, sales or prices

boost [2] *n.* [singular] something that helps to increase something such as production, sales or prices

brainstorming *n.* [U] a way of developing new ideas and solving problems by having a meeting where everyone makes suggestions and these are discussed

brand *n.* [C] a name given to a product by a company so that the product can easily be recognised by its name or its design

brand image *n.* [C] the collection of ideas and beliefs that people have about a brand

brand name *n.* [C] the name given to a product by a company so that the product can easily be recognised by its name or its design

budget [1] *n.* [C] a detailed plan made by an organisation or a government of how much it will receive as income over a particular period of time, and how much it will spend, what it will spend the money on, etc.

budget [2] *adj.* [only before noun] **1** very low in price – often used in advertisements
2 used for saying how much money has been spent on doing something, especially making a film

bureaucracy *n.* [C] all the complicated rules and processes of an official system, especially when they are confusing or responsible for causing a delay

bureaucratic *adj.* involving or having a lot of complicated and unnecessary official rules

business angel *n.* [C] a private investor who puts money into new business activities, especially ones based on advanced technical ideas

bust *adj.* If a business goes *bust*, it cannot continue to operate because it does not have enough money to pay its debts.

cashflow *n.* [U] the amounts of money coming into and going out of a company, and the timing of these

CEO *n.* [C] the manager with the most authority in the normal, everyday management of a company. The job of *CEO* (Chief Executive Officer) is sometimes combined with other jobs, such as that of president.

chair [1] *v.* [T] to be in charge of a meeting

chair [2] *n.* [singular] the chairman or chairwoman of a company or organisation, or the job of chairman or chairwoman

chairman *n.* [C] the person who is in charge of a large company or organisation, especially the most senior member of its board

client *n.* [C] someone who pays for services or advice from a professional person or organisation

collateral *n.* [U] assets promised by a borrower to a lender if the borrower cannot repay a loan

commission *n.* [C, U] **1** an amount of money paid to someone according to the value of goods, shares, bonds, etc. they have sold
2 an official organisation that ensures that the law is obeyed in a particular activity

commodity *n.* [C] a product that can be sold to make a profit, especially one in its basic form before it has been used or changed in an industrial process. Examples of commodities are farm products and metals.

compensation *n.* [U] an amount paid to someone because they have been hurt or harmed

compensation package *n.* [C] the total amount of pay and all the other advantages, such as stock options, that are offered to a company's important managers

competitive *adj.* **1** used to describe situations and behaviour in which businesses are trying very hard to be more successful than others, for example by selling their goods or services more cheaply than others
2 If a process is *competitive*, people have to compete with
each other, and those who do best will be successful.

competitive advantage *n.* [C] an advantage that makes a company more able to succeed in competing with others

conglomerate *n.* [C] a large business organisation consisting of several different companies that have joined together

consensual *adj.* [only before a noun] *Consensual* agreements, plans or actions are ones in which all the people involved agree with what is being done.

consensus *n.* [U, singular] agreement among a group of people

consumer *n.* [C] a person who buys goods, products and services for their own use, not for business use or to resell

consumer goods *n.* [plural] goods bought by people for their own use, rather than by businesses and organisations

contract *n.* [C] a formal written agreement between two or more people or groups which says what each must do for the other, or must not do

control [1] *n.* [C] **1** If someone has *control* of a company, they own more than half its shares, or enough shares to be able to decide how the company is managed.
2 an action taken to make sure that something does not increase too much

control [2] *v.* [T] to own more than half the shares of a company, or enough shares to decide how the company should be managed

convertible bond *n.* [C] a bond that can be repaid by a company in the form of shares in the company

corporate *adj.* [only before a noun] relating to a company, usually a large one, or business in general

credit *n.* [U] **1** an arrangement with a bank for a loan, or bank lending in general
2 an arrangement with a shop, supplier, etc. to buy something now and pay for it later

credit crunch *n.* [singular] when borrowing money becomes difficult because banks are forced to reduce the amount they lend

creditor *n.* [C] a person or business to whom another person or business owes money

damage [1] *n.* [U] a bad effect on something that makes it weaker or less successful

damage [2] *v.* [T] **1** to cause physical harm to something
2 to have a bad effect on something in a way that makes it weaker or less successful

damages *n.* [plural] money that a court orders someone to pay to someone else for harming them or their property, or causing them financial loss

deadline *n.* [C] a date or time by which you have to do or to complete something

debt *n.* [C] **1** the state of owing money
2 money that one person, organisation, country, etc. owes to another
3 capital borrowed by a business or government organisation on which it pays interest

debtor *n.* [C] a person, organisation or country that owes money

deceive *v.* [T] to make someone believe something that is not true in order to get what you want

decline [1] *v.* [I] If sales, profits, production, etc. *decline*, they become less.

decline [2] *n.* [C, U] when sales, profits, production, etc. become less

default *v.* [I] to fail to pay money that you owe at the right time

delivery *n.* [C, U] the act or process of bringing goods, letters, etc. to a particular place or person

demand *n.* [U] **1** the total amount of a type of goods or services that people or companies buy in a particular period of time
2 the total amount of a type of goods or services that people or companies would buy if they were available

deregulate *v.* [I, T] to remove or reduce the number of government controls on a particular business activity, done to make companies work more effectively and to increase competition

devolve *v.* [T] to give work, responsibility or power to someone at a lower or more local level

differentiate *v.* [T] When a company *differentiates* its products, it shows how they are different from each other and from competing products, for example in its advertising. This is done to show buyers the advantages of one product over another.

diligence *n.* [U] care that someone in a position of responsibility takes with their work

discount *n.* [C] a reduction in the cost of goods or services in relation to the normal cost

distribution *n.* [U] the actions involved in making goods available to customers after they have been produced, for example moving, storing and selling the goods

distributor *n.* [C] a person or business responsible for making goods available to customers after they have been produced, either one that sells directly to the public or one that sells to shops, etc.

diversify *v.* [I] **1** If a company or economy *diversifies*, it increases the range of goods or services it produces.
2 to start to put your money into different types of investments in addition to the investments you already have; **diversification** *n.* [C, U]

divest *v.* [T] If a company *divests* assets, it sells them, for example because it needs cash for another activity or to repay debts.

dividend *n.* [C] **1** a payment of a part of a company's profits to its shareholders
2 a part of the profits of a company for a particular period of time that is paid to shareholders for each share that they own

domestic market *n.* [C] the country you live in or where a company is based, seen as a place where goods or services can be sold

downturn *n.* [C, U] the part of the economic cycle when prices or the value of stocks, shares, etc. fall

draft *n.* [C] a document or piece of writing that has to be checked and possibly changed, and so is not yet in its finished form

earn *v.* [I, T] to be paid money for the work you do

earnings *n.* [plural] the profit that a company makes in a particular period of time, or the total profits that companies make in a particular industry or economy in a particular period of time

edge *n.* [singular] If a person, company or country has an *edge* over others, they are more successful, profitable, etc. because they have an advantage that the others do not have.

emerging *adj.* [only before a noun] **1** countries, especially those in Asia, Africa and South America that are just starting to have influence or power in trade, finance, etc.
2 in an early state of development

empower *v.* [T] to give a person or an organisation the power or the legal right to do something

empowerment *n.* [U] when workers in a company are given more responsibility by being allowed to organise their own work, make decisions without asking their managers, etc. For the company, this has the advantage of making their employees more involved and able to help clients more quickly.

entrepreneur *n.* [C] someone who starts a company, arranges business deals and takes risks in order to make a profit; **entrepreneurial** *adj.*

equity *n.* [U] the capital that a company has from shares rather than from loans

equity capital *n.* [U] capital in the form of shares, not debt

equity stake *n.* [C] when a company or organisation owns shares in a company

exceed *v.* [T] to go beyond an official or legal limit

exchange *n.* [C] the activity of buying and selling currencies

exchange rate *n.* [C] the price at which one currency can be bought with another

expand *v.* [I, T] **1** to become larger in size, amount or number, or to make something larger in size, amount or number
2 If an economy, industry or business activity *expands*, it gets bigger or more successful.

expansion *n.* [U] when an industry or company becomes bigger or more successful

fair trade *n.* [U] a system in which two countries which are trading partners agree not to charge import taxes on particular goods they buy from each other

flexible *adj.* **1** If arrangements for work are *flexible*, employers can ask workers to do different jobs, work part-time rather than full-time, give them contracts for short periods of time, etc. *Flexible* working also includes flexitime, job-sharing and teleworking.
2 A person, plan, etc. that is *flexible* can change or be changed easily to suit any new situation.

fluctuate *v.* [I] If prices, income, rates, etc. *fluctuate*, they change, increasing or falling often or regularly.

fringe benefit *n.* [C] an additional advantage or service given with a job besides wages. Pensions, company cars and loans at low rates of interest are examples of *fringe benefits*.

fund *n.* [C] **1** money that a person or organisation has available
2 a company whose activity is putting money from investors into a particular type of investment or a range of investments, or an amount of money invested in this way

fundraising *n.* [U] the activity of obtaining money for investment

globalisation *n.* [U] the tendency for the world economy to work as one unit, led by large international companies doing business all over the world. Some of the things that have led to *globalisation* are the ending of trade barriers, the free movement of capital, cheap transport and the increased use of electronic systems of communication such as the Internet.

glocalisation *n.* [U] the idea that companies should think globally, but use methods in each particular place that are suited to it

goodwill payment *n.* [C] a payment made to senior members of a business as a reward for hard work

growth *n.* [U] an increase in size, amount or degree

headhunt *v.* [T] to find a manager with the right skills and experience to do a particular job, often by persuading a suitable person to leave their present job; **headhunter** *n.* [C] **headhunting** *n.* [U]

headquarters *n.* [plural] the head office or main building of an organisation

hire [1] *v.* [T] **1** to agree to give someone a permanent job
2 to employ a person or an organisation for a short time to do a particular job for you

hire [2] *n.* [U] an arrangement by which someone borrows something for a period of time in exchange for money

holding *n.* [C] a quantity of shares held in a company by a particular shareholder

hospitality *n.* [U] services such as food and drink that an organisation provides for guests at a special event

hostile *adj.* A *hostile* bid or takeover is one in which a company tries to buy another company whose shareholders do not want to sell.

incentive *n.* [C] something which is used to encourage people to do something, especially to make them work harder, produce more or spend more money

income *n.* [C, U] **1** money that a company makes from its activities, after taking away some costs. Companies calculate their *income* in different ways according to the accounting system they use and the type of business they are in.
2 money that you earn from your job or that you receive from investments

income stream *n.* [C] regular amounts of money coming into a company or organisation from a particular activity or source, especially over a long period of time

instalment *n.* [C] one of a series of regular payments that are made until all of an agreed amount has been paid

interest *n.* [U] **1** an amount paid by a borrower to a lender, for example to a bank by someone borrowing money for a loan or by a bank to a depositor
2 shares that you own in a company, or a part of a company that a person or organisation owns

interest rate *n.* [C] the percentage rate used for calculating interest over a particular period of time, usually one year

invest *v.* [I, T] **1** to buy shares, bonds, property, etc. in order to make a profit
2 to spend money on things that will make a business more successful and profitable

investment *n.* [C, U] **1** when money is put into a business in order to make it more successful and profitable, or the money that is put into a business
2 an amount of money that you invest

investor *n.* [C] a person or organisation that invests money in order to make a profit

jeopardise *v.* [T] to risk losing or harming something

job loss *n.* [C, U] when people lose their jobs

joint venture *n.* [C] a business activity in which two or more companies have invested together

launch[1] *v.* [I, T] to show or make a new product available for sale for the first time

launch[2] *n.* [C] an occasion at which a new product is shown or made available for sale or use for the first time

lease *v.* [T] If you *lease* something from someone, you pay them to let you use it for a particular period of time.

ledger *n.* [C, usually plural] one of the books or computer records showing the totals of items shown separately in the books of first entry or day books

liability *n.* [C, usually plural] **1** an amount of money owed by a business to a supplier, lender, etc.
2 the responsibility that a person or organisation has for loss, damage or injury caused to others, or for payment of debts

liquidation *n.* [C, U] when a company stops operating because it is in financial difficulty and its assets are sold to pay its debts

liquidity *n.* [U] the ability of a company to make payments to employees and suppliers, interest payments to banks, etc.

loan *n.* [C] money borrowed from a bank, financial institution, person, etc. on which interest is usually paid to the lender until the loan is repaid

loan shark *n.* [C] someone who lends money at very high rates of interest

logo *n.* [C] a design or way of writing its name that a company or organisation uses as its official sign on its products, advertising, etc.

loss *n.* [C, U] an event that causes a person or organisation to make a claim on an insurance contract

loyal *adj.* If customers are *loyal* to a particular product, they continue to buy it and do not change to other products.

loyalty *n.* [U] the fact of being loyal to a particular product

management buyout *n.* [C] when a company's top managers buy the company they work for

manufacturer *v.* [T] to produce large quantities of goods to be sold, using machinery

market share *n.* [C, U] the percentage of sales in a market that a company or product has

merger *n.* [C] an occasion when two or more companies, organisations, etc. join together to form a larger company, etc.

minutes *n.* [plural] an official written record of what is said and decided at a meeting

mismanage *v.* [T] to manage a company, economy, etc. badly; **mismanagement** *n.* [U]

mortgage *n.* [C] a legal arrangement where you borrow money from a financial institution in order to buy land or a house, and you pay back the money over a period of years. If you do not make your regular payments, the lender normally has the right to take the property and sell it in order to get back their money.

negotiate *v.* [I, T] to discuss something in order to reach an agreement

nepotism *n.* [U] the practice of giving jobs to members of your family when you are in a position of power

networking *n.* [U] making use of meetings with other people involved in the same kind of work in order to share information, help each other, etc.

occupancy *n.* [U] used to talk about how many beds or rooms in a hotel, hospital, etc. are being used by guests, patients, etc.

outlet *n.* [C] a shop, company or organisation through which products are sold

outsource *v.* [T] If a company, organisation, etc. *outsources* its work, it employs another company to do it.
outsourcing *n.* [U]

overdraft *n.* [C] an arrangement between a bank and a customer, allowing them to take out more money from their current account than they had in it, or the amount involved

overtime *n.* [U] the money that you are paid for working more hours than usual

overwork *n.* [U] when someone works too much or too hard

partner *n.* [C] **1** someone who starts a new business with someone else by investing in it
2 a company that works with another company in a particular activity, or invests in the same activity

partnership *n.* [C] the situation of working together in business

pawnbroker *n.* [C] someone whose business is to lend people money in exchange for valuable objects

performance appraisal *n.* [C, U] a meeting between an employee and a manager to discuss the quality of the employee's work and areas for future progress

perk *n.* [C] something in addition to money that you get for doing your job, such as a car

pitch *v.* [T] to try to make a business agreement, or to sell something in a particular way

portfolio *n.* [C] all the products or services offered by a particular business

position *v.* [T] If a company *positions* a product in a particular way, it tries to get people to think about it in that way in relation to the company's other products and to competing products.

positioning *n.* [U] the way that people think about a product in relation to the company's other products and to competing products, or the way that the company would like them to think about it

premium [1] *n.* [C] an additional amount of money, above a standard amount or rate

premium [2] *adj.* [only before a noun] *Premium* products, goods, etc. are of higher quality than usual.

principal *n.* [singular] the original amount of a loan, not including any of the interest that is paid

production *n.* [U] the process of making or growing things to be sold as products, usually in large quantities

promote *v.* [T] **1** to help something develop, grow, become more successful, etc., or encourage something to happen
2 to try hard to sell a product or service by advertising it widely, reducing its price, etc.
3 to give someone a better paid, more responsible job in a company or organisation

promotion *n.* [C, U] an activity such as special advertisements or free gifts intended to sell a product or service; **promotional** *adj.* [only before a noun]

public offering *n.* [C, usually singular] an occasion when shares are offered to all interested investors, and the amount of shares involved

purchase [1] *n.* [U] **1** the act of buying something
2 something that has been bought

purchase [2] *v.* [T] to buy something, especially something big or expensive

rate [1] *n.* [C] **1** the speed at which something happens
2 the percentage charged for borrowing money, or a percentage you receive when you put money in a bank, make an investment, etc.
3 the number of examples of something or the number of times something happens, often expressed as a percentage

rate [2] *v.* [T] to think that someone or something has a particular quality, value or standard

rebrand *v.* [T] If a company *rebrands* a product or service, it tries to change the way that people think about it, often by changing its name or the way it is advertised. **rebranding** *n.* [singular, U]

recall *v.* [T] If a company *recalls* one of its products, it asks customers to return it because there may be something wrong with it. **recall** *n.* [C]

recession *n.* [C, U] a period of time when an economy or industry is doing badly, and business activity and employment decrease. Many economists consider that there is a *recession* when industrial production falls for six months in a row.

recipient *n.* [C] someone who receives something

recruitment *n.* [U] the process or the business of recruiting new people

reduce *v.* [T] to make something less or smaller in price, amount or size

redundancy *n.* [C, U] when someone loses their job in a company because the job is no longer needed

refund [1] *n.* [C] a sum of money that is given back to you

refund [2] *v.* [T] to give someone their money back, for example because they are not satisfied with the goods or services they have paid for

reinsurer *n.* [C] an insurance company that agrees to share a large insurance risk with another company and to pay part of any loss

reliable *adj.* Someone or something that is *reliable* can be trusted or depended on.

relocate *v.* [I, T] If a company or worker *relocates* or is *relocated*, they move to a different place.

rep *n.* [C] someone employed to sell a company's products or services by meeting customers or talking to them on the phone

repay *v.* [T] to pay back money that has been borrowed

replace *v.* [T] **1** to remove someone from their job, position, etc. and give the job to a different person
2 to give someone a product instead of one that they bought which was damaged or not perfect

retail *n.* [U] a shop, etc. that is open to members of the public

retailer *n.* [C] a business that sells goods to members of the public, rather than to shops, etc.

retain *v.* [T] **1** to keep something or to continue to have it
2 to continue to employ people after a company has changed ownership, reduced in size, etc.

return [1] *v.* [T] If you *return* a telephone call, you telephone someone because they have telephoned you.

return [2] *n.* [C, U] the amount of profit made from an investment

return [3] *adj.* a ticket, etc. that allows you to travel to a place and back again

returnable *adj.* Something that is *returnable* can or should be sent back to the place or person it came from.

revenue *n.* [U] money that a business or organisation receives over a period of time, especially from selling goods or services

savings account *n.* [C] a bank account for saving money over a long period of time, usually with higher interest than an ordinary deposit account

savings bond *n.* [C] a government bond sold to encourage people to save and invest small amounts of money

second *v.* [T] to arrange for an employee to work for another organisation for a period of time; **secondment** *n.* [C, U]

security *n.* [U] property or other assets that you promise to give someone if you cannot pay back the money that you owe them

segment [1] *n.* [C] **1** a group of customers that share similar characteristics, such as age, income, interests and social class
2 the products or services in a particular part of the market

segment [2] *v.* [T] to divide a large group of people into smaller groups of people of a similar age or with similar incomes, interests, etc., so that products that are most suitable for each group can be sold to it; **segmentation** *n.* [U]

service contract *n.* [C] an agreement between a company and one of its directors, stating what the director will do, how much they will be paid, etc.

sever *v.* [T] to end a business relationship or connection with someone because of a disagreement

severance *n.* [U] the act of officially ending an agreement or contract, especially between an employer and an employee

share *n.* [C] one of the parts into which ownership of a company is divided

shareholder *n.* [C] someone who owns shares in a company

slogan *n.* [C] a short phrase that is easy to remember and is used by an advertiser, organisation or other group

slowdown *n.* [C, usually singular] when something gets slower

sponsor [1] *v.* [T] to give money to pay for a television programme, a sports or arts event, training, etc. in exchange for advertising or to get public attention

sponsor [2] *n.* [C] a person or company that pays for a television programme, a sports or arts event, training, etc. in exchange for advertising or to get public attention

sponsorship *n.* [U] financial support given to pay for a sports or arts event, training, etc. in exchange for advertising or to get public attention

stake *n.* [C] money risked or invested in a business

standard *n.* [C, U] a level of quality, skill, ability or achievement by which someone or something is judged, and that is considered good enough to be acceptable

statement *n.* [C] **1** something you say or write publicly or officially to let people know your intentions or opinions, or to record facts
2 a list showing amounts of money paid, received, owing, etc. and their total

stock *n.* [C, U] **1** a supply of goods, kept for sale by a shop or other retailer
2 one of the shares into which ownership of a company is divided, or these shares considered together

stockbroker *n.* [C] a person or organisation whose job is to buy and sell shares, bonds, etc. for investors and sometimes for themselves

stockmarket *n.* [C] a place where companies' shares are bought and sold

strategic *adj.* done as part of a plan to gain an advantage or achieve a particular purpose

strategy *n.* [C] **1** a plan or series of plans for achieving an aim, especially success in business or the best way for an organisation to develop in the future
2 the process of skilful planning in general

subsidiary *n.* [C] a company that is at least half-owned by another company

supplier *n.* [C] a company that provides a particular type of product

supply [1] *n.* [C] an amount of something that is available to be sold, bought, used, etc.

supply [2] *v.* [T] to provide goods or services to customers, especially regularly and over a long period of time

supply chain *n.* [C] the series of organisations that are involved in passing products from manufacturers to the public

sustainable *adj.* strong enough to continue existing or happening for a long time

take over *phr.v.* [T] to take control of a company by buying more than 50 per cent of its shares

takeover *n.* [C] the act of getting control of a company by buying over 50 per cent of its shares

target [1] *n.* [C] **1** a limited group of people or area that a plan, idea, etc. is aimed at
2 a result such as a total, an amount or a time which you aim to achieve

target [2] *v.* [T] to aim products, programmes of work, etc. at a particular area or group of people

term *n.* [C] **1** one of the conditions of an agreement, contract or other legal document
2 a word or expression that has a particular meaning, especially in a technical or scientific subject

trade *n.* [U] the activity of buying, selling or exchanging goods within a country or between countries

turnover *n.* [singular, U] **1** the amount of business done in a particular period of time, measured by the amount of money obtained from customers for goods or services that have been sold
2 the rate at which workers leave an organisation and are replaced by others

venture *n.* [C] a new business activity or project that involves taking risks

venture capital *n.* [U] money lent to someone so that they can start a new business

viral *adj.* passed on to other people on the Internet or using mobile phones

voice mail *n.* [U] an electronic system on your telephone that lets you leave messages for people who phone you when you are not available, and lets them leave messages for you

wage *n.* [C] money that someone earns according to the number of hours, days or weeks that they work, especially money that is paid each week

wannabe *n.* [C] someone who tries to look or behave like someone famous or like a particular type of successful person, because they want to be like them (usually used to show disapproval)

webinar *n.* [C] a talk, lesson, etc. that is given on the Internet, in which all the people taking part look at the same information on their computer screens and can talk to each other, usually using their telephones

wholesaler *n.* [C] a person or company that sells goods in large quantities to businesses, rather than to the general public

withdraw *v.* [T] If a company *withdraws* a product or service, it stops making it available, either for a period of time or permanently.

work load *n.* [C] the amount of work that a person or organisation has to do

workforce *n.* [C] all the people who work in a particular country, industry or factory

work–life balance *n.* [U] a situation in which you are able to give the right amount of time and effort to your work and to your personal life outside work, for example to your family or to other interests

worth *adj.* If an item is *worth* something, it has a particular value in money.

Pearson Education Limited
Edinburgh Gate, Harlow, Essex, CM20 2JE, England
and Associated Companies throughout the world.

www.pearsonelt.com

First Edition first published 2000

Third Edition first published 2010

Third Edition Extra first published 2016

Third Edition Extra Premium Digital edition first published 2021

ISBN: 978-1-292-36114-7

Set in Meta OT 9.5/12pt

Printed in Slovakia by Neografia

Acknowledgements
The publishers would like to thank the following authors for writing the Business Skills lessons: Margaret O'Keefe, Clare Walsh, Iwona Dubicka, Lizzie Wright, Bob Dignan, Sara Helm and Fiona Scott-Barrett.

The authors would like to thank the following for their invaluable help during the project: Melanie Bryant, Peter Falvey, Sarah Falvey, Gisele Cotton, Mark Cotton, Jason Hewitt and Richard Falvey. Thanks also to Lewis Lansford for writing the Review units and John Rogers for the Glossary.

The authors and publishers are very grateful to the following people who agreed to be interviewed for the recorded material in this book: Madalyn Brooks, Dan Collins, Simon Davies, Alastair Dryburgh, Steve Fowler, Tom Hockaday, Professor Svend Hollensen, Darrell Kofkin, Professor Scott Moeller, Laurie Mullins, Philip Newman-Hall, Professor Craig Smith, Alison Ward.

Special thanks from the authors to Chris Hartley for his great help with the interviews.

The publishers and authors are very grateful to the following advisers and teachers who commented on earlier versions of this material and contributed to the initial research: Aukjen Bosma, Jonathan Clifton, Ian Duncan, Malgorzata Nowak, Nancy Pietragalla Dorfman, Dr Petra Pointner, Michael Thompson, Benjamin White, David Kadas, Hans Leijenaar, Sabine Prochel, Ulrich Schuh, Robert McLarty

Text
Extract on p.8 from 'A quiet word beats sending email' by Luke Johnson, *The Financial Times*, 23/06/2009, copyright © Luke Johnson; Extract on p.25 from 'You say 'guanxi', I say schmoozing' by Frederik Balfour, *Bloomberg Business Week*, 19/11/2007, by special permission, copyright © 2007 by Bloomberg L.P.; Extract on p.31 adapted from "how to declutter your life" by Rhymer Rigby, *The Financial Times*, 29/09/2013, copyright © Rhymer Rigby; Extract on p.39 from 'Profile: Carlos Slim' by James Quinn, *The Telegraph*, 22/01/2009, copyright © Telegraph Media Group Limited 2009; Extract on pp.47, 135 from 'The 100 Best companies to work for 2009 (KPMG and Marriott Hotels International)', *The Sunday Times*, 08/03/2009, copyright © The Times, 2009 www.nisyndication.com; Extract on p.69 adapted from "Anna Wintour, Behind The Shades" by Anna Wintour, produced by Ruth Streeter, 17/05/2009, copyright © CBS News Archives; Extract on p.77 from 'Recipes for teambuilding' by Rhymer Rigby, *The Financial Times*, 19/11/2007, copyright © Rhymer Rigby; Extract on p.99 from 'Customer service is changing the world' by Mike Betzer, *The Financial Times*, 07/11/2008, copyright © Mike Betzer; Extract on p.115 from 'Green targets from Corporate Knights' by Melissa Shin, *Corporate Knights 2008 Carbon 50 issue*, 2008. http://www.corporateknights.ca, copyright © Corporate Knights, Inc.; Extract on p.145 from 'Jim Buckmaster, CEO of Craigslist' by Carol Lewis and Julie Daniels, *The Daily Times*, 12/03/2008, copyright © The Times, 2008 www.nisyndication.com.

The Financial Times
Extract on p.16 from 'Diego Della Valle: Italian atmosphere is central to Tod's global expansion' by Vincent Boland, *The Financial Times*, 15/06/2009; Extract on p.31 adapted from "Should we stress about stress?" by Antonia Macaro and Julian Baggini, *The Financial Times*, 29/05/2015; Extract on p.85 from 'No more easy money' by Jonathan Moules, *The Financial Times*, 30/11/2009; Extract on p.107 adapted from 'How not to take care of a brand' by John Gapper, *The Financial Times*, 11/11/2009; Extract on p.107 from 'Expect the unexpected' by Morgan Witzel, *The Financial Times*, 19/08/2004, © The Financial Times Limited, 2004, 2009, 2015. All Rights Reserved.

Photos
The publisher would like to thank the following for their kind permission to reproduce their photographs:
(Key: b-bottom; c-centre; l-left; r-right; t-top)

123RF.com: Akiyoko A9b, Warren Goldswain A9c, Andrey Popov A7-A8, Wavebreak Media Ltd 11; **Alamy Images:** Cultura RM 57t, Damon Coulter 110b, Jochen Tack 111, Tony French 87c; **Corbis:** Adrian Weinbrecht / cultura 73cr, Amit Bhargava 99cr, D.Amon / photocuisine 77bl, Image Source 73cl, Michael S. Lewis 59br, Mirko Iannace 118t, Nik Wheeler 47t, Per Winbladh 51, Philip James Corwin 12t, Ryan Pyle 14t, Sanford / Agliolo 22t, Steve Giralt / Retna / Retna Ltd 71tr, Tim Pannell 77tr, Tim Shaffer 145; **Fotolia.com:** Giovanni Cardillo 89, Estherpoon 82, Monkey Business A9-A10, Tmc_photos A9cr; **FT.com:** 107tl; **Getty Images:** Brand New Images 41tl, Buena Vista Images 20b, Alberto Buzzola 6, Car Culture 16c, Chabruken 81cr, ColorBlind Images 80cr, Comstock 30, David Lees 81bl, DreamPictures 81tl, Jon Feingersh 121b, Frank van Groen 81cl, Friedemann Vogel - FIFA 66t, Giuseppe Bellini 42-43, Jamie Grill 19tl, Jetta Productions 81tr, Loungepark 27tl, 61tl, Loungepark 27tl, 61tl, Mel Yates 21r, Morsa Images A11bl, Nomadic Luxury 80cl, Pegasus / Visuals Unlimited, Inc. 58-59, Petrified Collection 96t, Reza Estakhrian 101tl, Sean Justice 81br, Siri Stafford 42bl, Stone 79, Wildestanimal 52t, Yukmin 25tl; **iStockphoto:** 13tr, 37tl, 73tr, 13tr, 37tl, 73tr, 13tr, 37tl, 73tr; **Lonely Planet Images:** Jon Davison 55tl; **Photolibrary.com:** Ann Brown 118-199t, Blend Images 60b, 61tr, 91, Blend Images 60b, 61tr, 91, Blend Images 60b, 61tr, 91, Brian Lawrence 72t, Caspar Benson 88t, GiorgioMesturini 28-29b, Hufton + Crow 40br, Imagesource 83tl, Jon Arnold 31cr, Mario Beauregard 109tr, Phillippe Body 44t, Roger Holden 50bl; **Plainpicture Ltd:** Oscar 49tl; **Press Association Images:** S.Vlasic / ABACA USA 69bc; **Reuters:** Henry Romero 39c, Joshua Lott 102-103; **Rex Shutterstock:** ABC Inc / Everett 85c, KPA / Zuma 104t; **Rob Palmer:** Rob Palmer 112t; **Shutterstock.com:** 115br, Bacho 9, Chantal de Bruijne 36, Caimacanul 12-13b, Germanskydiver 74, l i g h t p o e t 117tl, Monkey Business Images A1-A2, A11-A12, A15-A16, Monkey Business Images A1-A2, A11-A12, A15-A16, Myimagine A3-A4, Pressmaster A5-A6, StockLite A13-A14, Wavebreakmedia A12c

All other images © Pearson Education

Video Credits
© Pearson Education